NAVAL POWER
in the Conquest *of* Mexico

T0350036

NAVAL POWER
in the Conquest *of* Mexico

C. HARVEY GARDINER

AUSTIN : UNIVERSITY OF TEXAS PRESS : 1956

Requests for permission to reproduce material from this
work should be sent to:
  Permissions
  University of Texas Press
  P.O. Box 7819
  Austin, TX 78713-7819
  www.utexas.edu/utpress/about/bpermission.html

Library of Congress Catalog Number 55-008475
ISBN 978-0-292-74096-9, paperback

DEDICATED
TO THE MEMORY OF
G. R. G. CONWAY
(1873–1951)

Foreword

GENERATION AFTER GENERATION, the reading public of the United States has trudged through Mexico with Hernando Cortés and his followers. Quite possibly the conquest of Mexico has more persistently and more dramatically captured American attention than has any other one chapter of foreign history. The literary grace of the masterful William Hickling Prescott has transported millions through a memorable moment in sixteenth-century life. Countless youngsters have been wide-eyed witnesses of it all as cast in the stirring words of G. A. Henty. Some readers, interested in eye-witness reports of momentous matters, have turned to the writings of Captain-general Cortés or foot soldier Bernal Díaz. Others have glimpsed the action through the historical novels of Lew Wallace and Samuel Shellabarger.

From successive tellings of the conquest, whether sixteenth-century fact or the histories and fictions of later centuries, plus all the borderline interpretations, certain common denominators have emerged. There are always the heroics of supermen—daring and imaginative leaders, courageous and tireless followers, swashbuckling swordsmen, reckless horsemen. Ever present is the high drama of ships destroyed, odds faced, treachery averted, victories gloriously won. For reader and writer alike the conquest of Mexico has been a glimpse of the truth that is stranger than fiction. And from beginning to end this has always been a story of soldiers: infantrymen, cavalrymen, artillerymen, led by the greatest soldier of them all.

More fully stated, however, the early phase of the conquest of Mexico is even more dramatic, more fantastic, because hundreds of miles from the sea a prefabricated navy was built and climactic battle took place on waters that now scarcely exist. The present study relates the naval phase of a fighting story which previously has been peopled only by soldiers.

In addition to applying perspective to the relationship between navy and army combat operations, the pages that follow will also direct attention to such factors as the nautical backgrounds of the Spanish conquistadors, the unique geographic setting in which the climactic struggle of the spring and summer of 1521 occurred, the shipbuilding program which had to precede the actual combat operations, and the relationship of this episode to other significant naval actions.

In the pursuit of a study that has taken me to materials from archives and libraries of Mexico, Spain, Great Britain, and the United States, I have known assistance from many persons, to whom I take this occasion to direct my heartfelt appreciation: Arthur Scott Aiton, of the University of Michigan, as one primarily responsible for my continuing concern about the colonial period of Latin American history; Charles Gibson, of the State University of Iowa, France V. Scholes, of the University of New Mexico, and Edgar Anderson, of Washington University, for important leads to men and materials in Mexico. The co-operation of the following libraries in the United States has been most gratifying: the Library of Congress, Newberry Library, the libraries of Harvard University, University of Michigan, University of Illinois, University of California at Berkeley, University of Missouri, and the Latin American Collection of the University of Texas. The libraries and librarians of Cambridge University and the University of Aberdeen have been generously co-operative. In Mexico I would direct words of appreciation to the staffs of the Archivo del Museo Nacional, the Biblioteca Nacional, the Archivo General de la Nación, and the Sociedad Mexicana de Geografía y Estadística; and to Edward Heiliger, of the Benjamin Franklin Library, Pedro Sánchez, of the Instituto Panamericano de Geografía e Historia, and E. Hernández X., of Mexico City. In Spain appreciation is directed to the staff of the Archivo General de Indias.

Miss Ruth Harry, of the staff of Washington University Library, extended me innumerable kindnesses. To Miss Mary Ellen Henry I express sincerest appreciation of her cheerful and careful typographical work upon the manuscript in its earlier stages. My wife, Katie Mae Gardiner, in addition to doing routine things researchers seem to expect of their wives, has always radiated the kind of confidence that counts.

Special appreciation is tendered the American Philosophical Society, which generously made possible one of the three research-field trips to Mexico. Mrs. Anne E. Conway is warmly thanked in grateful remembrance of profitable hours spent in the library of her late husband. In rather oblique but nonetheless sincere fashion, thanks are due the United States Navy, for without that tour of duty in the 1940's I suspect I would never have reached back to the 1520's to do this study.

C. Harvey Gardiner

St. Louis, Missouri
September 16, 1955

Contents

Illustrations and Maps

Abbreviations

AC: Archivo de la Catedral, Mexico City.

AdeC: Mexico [City]. Cabildo (Ignacio Bejarano *et al.*, eds.), *Actas de cabildo de la ciudad de México*. 26 vols. México, 1889–1904.

AGI: Archivo General de Indias, Seville.

AGN: Archivo General de la Nación, Mexico City.

AU–CC, Martín López 1528–1574: Martín López, Conquistador— Documents, 1528–1574 (MS in Conway Collection), Aberdeen University.

BAGN: *Boletín del Archivo General de la Nación*, Mexico.

BDdelC: Bernal Díaz del Castillo (Joaquín Ramírez Cabañas, ed.). *Historia verdadera de la conquista de la Nueva España*. 3 vols. México, 1944.

BDdelC–M: Bernal Díaz del Castillo (Alfred Percival Maudslay, tr. and ed.). *The True History of the Conquest of New Spain*, in Vols. XXIII, XXIV, XXV, XXX, and XL of the Hakluyt Society, series II. 5 vols. London, 1908–1916.

BRAH: *Boletín de la Real Academia de Historia*, Spain.

BSMGE: *Boletín de la Sociedad Mexicana de Geografía y Estadística*, Mexico.

CDHM: Joaquín García Icazbalceta (ed.), *Colección de documentos para la historia de México*. 2 vols. México, 1858–1866.

CDIAO: J. F. Pacheco; F. Cárdenas *et al.* (eds.). *Colección de documentos inéditos relativos al descubrimiento, conquista y organización de las antiguas posesiones de América y Oceanía*. 42 vols. Madrid, 1864–1884.

CDIE: Martín Fernández de Navarrete *et al.* (eds.). *Colección de documentos inéditos para la historia de España*. 112 vols. Madrid, 1842–1895.

CDIHIA: Santiago Montoto *et al.* (eds.). *Colección de documentos inéditos para la historia de Ibero-América.* 14 vols. Madrid, 1927–1935.

CDIU: La Real Academia de la Historia (ed.). *Colección de documentos inéditos relativos al descubrimiento, conquista y organización de las antiguas posesiones españoles de Ultramar.* 25 vols. Madrid, 1885–1932.

DUHG: Lucas Alamán *et al.* (eds.). *Diccionario Universal de Historia y de Geografía.* 10 vols. México, 1853–1856.

ENE: Francisco del Paso y Troncoso (comp.). *Epistolario de Nueva España 1505–1818.* 16 vols. México, 1939–1942.

HAHR: *Hispanic American Historical Review.*

HC: Hernán Cortés. *Cartas de relación de la conquista de Méjico.* 2 vols. Madrid, 1942.

HC–MacN: Hernán Cortés (Francis Augustus MacNutt, tr. and ed.). *Fernando Cortes—His Five Letters of Relation to the Emperor Charles V.* 2 vols. New York and London, 1908.

IEPANM: A. Millares Carlo and J. I. Mantecón (eds.). *Indice y extractos de los Protocolos del Archivo de Notarías de México, D. F.* 2 vols. México, 1945–1946.

LC–CC, Martín López 1529–1550: Martín López, Conquistador—Documents, 1529–1550 (MS in Conway Collection), Library of Congress.

LC–CC, Martín López Osorio: Nobiliario of Martín López Osorio (MS in Conway Collection), Library of Congress.

MN–PyTT: Francisco del Paso y Troncoso Collection (MS), Museo Nacional, Mexico City.

MOyB, "Conquistadores": M. Orozco y Berra, "Los conquistadores de México," in Vol. IV of Bernardino de Sahagún, *Historia general de las cosas de Nueva España* (1938).

NCDHM: Joaquín García Icazbalceta (ed.). *Nueva colección de documentos para la historia de México.* 5 vols. México, 1886–1892.

RABM: *Revista de Archivos, Bibliotecas y Museos,* Spain.

UC–CC, Docs. Various Suits: Documents Relating to Various Suits (MS in Conway Collection), University of Cambridge.

UC–CC, Maldonado contra López: Francisco Maldonado contra Martín López, 1533–1539 (MS in Conway Collection), University of Cambridge.

UC–CC, Misc. Docs.: Miscellaneous Documents Relating to Martín López and Other Papers (MS in Conway Collection), University of Cambridge.

NAVAL POWER
in the Conquest *of* Mexico

CHAPTER I

Spanish Wake

THE SPANIARDS in the Caribbean world of 1519 were essentially landlubbers—who yet had known a variety of incidental experience with the sea that had conditioned in them an almost intuitive approach to maritime matters. No Spanish conquistadors had a more dramatic and significant opportunity to make use of that untapped reservoir of nautical intuition than those whom fate cast in the role of conquerors of Mexico.

The Leader

Hernando Cortés was typical of the landlubbers of 1519. Until his late teens, there is no indication that he had smelled the salt air of the sea, much less shipped aboard an ocean-going vessel. Bleak, wind-swept, pastoral Extremadura conditioned the Medellín youth completely in the ways of the landsman. Yet the very geography that on the one hand made the area one of the doubly landlocked regions of Spain could on the other have expedited the travel of rumors about the wider world beyond the plateaus, the mountains, and the meandering streams in the deep-set valleys. There was the Tagus River across north central Extremadura up which tales of the broad Atlantic and the welter of Portuguese activity thereon might have wended their way out of the west from that fountainhead of exploration, Lisbon. And out of the south, by way of the valley through which the fresh waters of the Guadiana carried the thin topsoil of southern Extremadura to the Gulf of Cádiz, it was possible that word had come to the home district of the schoolboy not only of the deeds of the great Discoverer who had sailed out of Palos but also of the fundamental challenge the new lands presented to adventure-seeking Spaniards.

Before Cortés got closer to the sea, he was to move farther from it. After fourteen years in and immediately around the tiny community of Medellín—years sufficiently uneventful to have remained in historical obscurity ever since—the youngster was sent northward to the University of Salamanca, where Columbus had enunciated his theories. There, though geographically remote from the ports where rode the sails that had known the winds of the New World, the impressionable young Spaniard must have found an intellectual setting surely agog with the implications and challenges of the discovery of new lands. After two years at the university, Cortés came back to Medellín and turned his attention to interests requiring little formal training, namely love-making and arms-bearing. The latter suggested a career in either Italy or the New World; the former hinted that Spain itself was not a bad place.

Twice the amorous adventurer missed his ship. In early 1502 a vessel of the Nicolás de Ovando expedition would have carried him to Española. But one night, using walls and roof tops as the romantic highroad to his ladylove, Cortés slipped on a decaying wall and noisily crashed to earth, truly an injured lover. While the teen-age Extremaduran was in bed recovering from his painful fall, Ovando's great fleet sailed from Sanlúcar.[1]

---

[1] A basic source for the outline of the first thirty-four years of the life of Cortés, down to the departure of his expedition to the mainland, is the *De Rebus Gestis Ferdinandi Cortesii* in *CDHM*, I, 310–324. For a recent historiographical analysis of this work, one which establishes it as the product of Francisco López de Gómara, see Ramón Iglesias, *Cronistas e Historiadores de la Conquista de México: el ciclo de Hernán Cortés*, 217–287. Little is known of the early years of Cortés, and those biographers who have expanded the record concerning them have done so out of speculation rather than research.

An additional, limited maritime experience was Cortés' as he and Diego de Orellano, on the heels of the expedition of 1517, were sent as *procuradores* to Santo Domingo. See I. A. Wright, *The Early History of Cuba, 1492–1586*, 74.

With no other early prospect of getting to the Indies, the would-be warrior hied himself to Valencia, seeking a chance to embark for Italy and service under the Great Captain, Gonsalvo de Córdoba. Illness caused him to miss his ship again. Fate seemed intent upon keeping the Extremaduran a landsman. Yet it is evident that the time he spent in coastal areas and port towns in his futile efforts to get abroad was not without future influence in his life. Though his physical and financial state took him inland once more to Medellín, the eighteen-year-old was now mentally prepared for foreign climes. The year at home that repaired his health probably whetted his desire for distant adventure.

In early 1504, hearing word that a small fleet was forming at Seville for an early crossing to the Indies, Cortés hurried to that city in time to take passage aboard the vessel of Alonso Quintero. In a few short weeks he came to know, ere reaching the Caribbean island of Española, more than a little about the sea, thanks to the experiences that came with a dishonest master, a dismasted ship, and that empty feeling that accompanies loss of course. However, he was essentially still a landlubber as he stepped ashore on Española in search of name and riches.

Early in the course of his seven-year stay in Española, Cortés had occasion to serve under the very man with whom he was to go to Cuba and in whose name he was later to lead his expedition onto the continent of North America. No brilliance was in evidence as Cortés' sword served royal interests in minor military roles on Española, but the association between Diego Velázquez and Hernando Cortés seemed to ripen into mutual respect, if not friendship, during the Española years. But despite a royal grant of land and a labor supply in the form of Indians held in *encomienda*,* despite the respect accorded a minor official, the social contacts that Spanish society afforded, and the occasional opportunities at arms —despite everything Cortés was restive. The limited nature of his achievements, for he had acquired neither a great name nor great

* For the meaning of this and all other italicized Spanish words and phrases, consult the glossary on pp. 221–222.

wealth on Española, may have contributed to this restlessness. And perhaps, too, it was the sea once more, exerting an irresistible inward tug; for though seven years had been spent landbound on one island, the salt air could have kept him ever conscious of the sea and its ships.

As men in Spain turned westward to the Indies, so those already in the Antilles were drawn still farther west. By 1511 Columbus' son Diego, as governor of Española, was busy fitting out an expedition destined for Cuba. The command was given to Velázquez, who asked his former colleague in arms Cortés to serve as his administrative assistant.

The Cuban experience was of limited but lasting significance in the maturing process of Cortés. No known incident points to a display of military genius on his part—in fact, the nature of the Cuban opposition, Cortés' role in the expedition, and all else hint the lack of it. Meanwhile Pánfilo de Narváez, later to appear so inept as the short-term rival of Cortés in New Spain, was possibly the leading field commander during the conquest of Cuba.[2] However, the Cuban experience surely contributed greatly to Cortés' capacity as an organizer and as an administrator of men. Then, following a speedy conquest, once more the commonplace set in, with the prosaic aspects of settlement and consolidation of Spanish power on Cuba. The next half-dozen years were a repetition for Cortés of the round of routine on Española; the new unknown turned inevitably into the known, leaving his restlessness still unsatisfied.

Then once more the sea became the avenue leading toward what he sought; again ships spelled the means to the end that might embrace prestige and power. With the passing of years, years of growing monotony for Cortés, Velázquez began to send expeditions westward, which succesively crossed what was to become known as the Channel of Yucatan and probed the giant thumb of land, Yucatan itself. In February, March, and April, 1517,

---

[2] In an account of the conquest of Cuba drawn from a mass of archival material, I. A. Wright never once mentioned Cortés as a military leader; see *ibid.*, 26–37.

Francisco Hernández de Córdoba led Cuban Spaniards to the mainland. In the spring of 1518 Juan de Grijalva was at the helm of the follow-up expedition. By mid-autumn of that same year, the third expedition westward was in the planning stage. As never before ships were to be significant to Cortés: he had been designated leader of that third undertaking. The three-ship venture of 1517 under courageous Córdoba and the four-ship expedition of 1518 under cautious Grijalva were not to be succeeded by a still bigger undertaking led by a man who was still a considerable question mark, Hernando Cortés.

From Spain to Española to Cuba to the American continent, westward lay the destiny of Cortés. From passenger to officer to commander in chief grew his experience with ships. Yet for all that incidental experience and the familiarity with the sea that island life encouraged, Cortés, as of the moment he gathered together his expedition, after a landlocked youth in Spain, seven settled years in Española, and almost eight years with both feet squarely on Cuban soil, was still essentially a landsman.

The Men

Though the measure of accidental and incidental concern with ships known by Cortés was on the whole characteristic of the average New World Spaniard, there were some who had a fuller acquaintance with salt water and sail, due to experience gained in the Hernández de Córdoba and/or Grijalva expeditions. Of the approximately 110 men in the three vessels of Córdoba, only about a third can be identified. Of the thirty who can be so named,[3] a list which includes perhaps 50 per cent of the survivors,

[3] In Henry R. Wagner, *The Discovery of Yucatan by Francisco Hernández de Córdoba*, 27, a total of thirty-one persons, several of whom Wagner himself questions, are named. Alonso de Ojeda, by virtue of the evidence presented by him in the statement of his merits and services, should be stricken from the list; see MN–PyTT, Leg. 96, Información de los méritos y servicios de Alonso de Ojeda (1553). The name of Alonso Ortíz de Zúñiga should also be deleted; see *ibid.*, Información de los méritos y servicios de Alonso Ortíz de Zúñiga (1553). The name of Juan Ruiz should be added to the list; see *ibid.*, Leg. 97, Información de los méritos y servicios de Martín Vázquez (1525).

a remarkably high percentage was associated with later expeditions to New Spain, for eleven of that number shipped with Cortés in 1519 and six others were in the flotilla commanded by Narváez in 1520. Given the hardship and the casualty rate suffered by the Córdoba contingent, it was remarkable that any man cared to undertake a second trip to the mainland. None of the eight accounts of the expedition employed by Wagner in his study directs more than passing attention to the shipping,[4] but it is plainly evident that old, unseaworthy craft made up the three-vessel fleet of two caravels and one brigantine. Men who sailed in such ships had to possess a full measure of seamanship as well as personal courage. Those who had departed from Cuba early in February, 1517, abandoned one vessel in continental waters and found it necessary to beach the other two as complete losses on their return to Cuba in late April.[5] For approximately two and one-half months Córdoba's men knew an almost unbroken nautical nightmare. Yet, unpleasant as the duty had been, such nearly continuous service at sea under conditions that taxed seamanship, ingenuity, and physical stamina meant much to the men destined to effect the conquest of New Spain.

In 1519 Cortés counted among his men shipping from Cuba the following veterans of the Córdoba expedition: pilot Antón de Alaminos, pilot Juan Álvarez, pilot Pedro Camacho, Benito de Bejar, the infantryman-chronicler Bernal Díaz del Castillo, Diego López, Francisco López, Martín Ramos, Juan Ruiz, Martín Vázquez, and Miguel Zaragoza. In addition to these eleven, who aided Cortés in the first nautical phase of his expedition, six more of Córdoba's men, coming to New Spain with Narváez in 1520, were available to Corés ere the second nautical problem had to be faced. These were Alonso de Benavides, Berrio, Benito de Cuenca, Pedro Hernández, Ginés Martín, and Diego de Porras. The Cortés and Narváez expeditions together were to draw 57 per cent of the

---

[4] Wagner, *Córdoba*, 19, 31, 33, 37, 40, 41, 44, 56. Of all the authors, Bernal Díaz demonstrated the least interest in Córdoba's ships.

[5] Bartolomé de Las Casas, *Historia de las Indias*, IV, 361–362.

known survivors among Córdoba's men back again to New Spain.[6] Meanwhile, through the Grijalva expedition, some of the above-named men and many other Spaniards resident on Cuba gained an increased acquaintance with ships and nautical skills that ultimately contributed to the success of Cortés' undertaking.

When the four-vessel fleet of Juan de Grijalva moved westward across the Channel of Yucatan to mainland America in the spring of 1518, since the shipping used by Córdoba was a complete loss, Grijalva had at least different, if not new, vessels.[7] In several respects more is known about the Grijalva fleet than about the later Cortés-led shipping. Because some of Grijalva's vessels were to see later service under the banner of Cortés and because the organization and operation of the expedition bore still other resemblances to that of the conqueror of New Spain, the fleet of 1518 merits attention.

The shipping initially included three caravels and a brigantine, but with the early loss of the latter a fourth caravel was added. Coasting along Cuba from settlement to settlement, Grijalva acquired his provisions and picked up the manpower which ultimately approximated two hundred. Proof that he too had old shipping which constantly required attention is seen in the careening of one ship at the end of the first month of the venture. The men on this longer and larger expedition—setting out in April and returning about November 1—encountered a variety of adversities: a

[6] Wagner, *Córdoba*, 27; MOyB, "Conquistadores," 362–423 *passim;* DUHG, I, 101; and MN–PyTT, Leg. 97, Información de los méritos y servicios de Martín Vázquez (1525). Diego de Porras is mistakenly listed among Cortés' original force by Orozco y Berra—see "Conquistadores," 382; proof he was with Narváez is in MN–PyTT, Leg. 96, Información de los méritos y servicios de Diego de Porras (1525).

[7] Bancroft declares that the two vessels of Hernández de Córdoba which had been beached on Cuban shores were refitted and used by Grijalva; see Hubert Howe Bancroft, *History of Mexico,* I, 16–17. If true, this eloquently bespeaks the shortage of shipping in Cuban waters. The picture is not at all clear concerning Cuban shipping and shipbuilding at this early date. However, a royal cedula permitting the residents of Cuba to construct and own ships had been issued on December 29, 1516; see *CDIU,* I, 69–70. One writer who, even in a brief statement of the Hernández de Córdoba and Grijalva expeditions, directs attention to the vessels is Cesáreo Fernández Duro, *Armada española desde la unión de Castilla y Aragón,* I, 170–172.

broken yard had to be repaired; tackle was broken when a number of vessels dragged their anchors and collided; the flagship was damaged heavily as it struck a shoal; a broken mainmast had to be replaced; and fifteen days were required to careen still another vessel. Some of the misfortunes that befell the fairly large ships as they attempted inshore surveys pointed up the usefulness of brigantines for duty in shallow waters. However, certain successes were also recorded. On one occasion a naval engagement occurred when fourteen or fifteen war canoes crowded with Indians attacked Grijalva's ships.[8] The Spaniards, turning their artillery and crossbows upon the Indians, killed and wounded so many of them that the courage of the remainder gave way to fear and, turning their canoes, they fled. Many of Grijalva's experiences mirrored coming events of concern to Cortés.

As was the case with the expedition of 1517, only a minority of the Grijalva personnel can be identified; yet from even that small group the relationship between the 1518 voyage and the effort directed by Cortés is clearly demonstrable. The survivors among sixty persons[9] who can be identified by name as members of Grijalva's expedition (and all but two did survive the experience) were to be found almost to a man in either the Cortés or Narváez groups. Forty-three[10] of the fifty-eight known survivors of the Gri-

---

[8] Henry R. Wagner, *The Discovery of New Spain in 1518, by Juan de Grijalva,* 26, 58, 75, 80–82, 84, 88–89, 96, 98–99, 124, 136–137, 139, 158. Wagner based his work upon eight sources but placed greatest credence and dependence upon Gonzalo Fernández de Oviedo y Valdés.

[9] Numerically the writer is in substantial agreement with Wagner (*ibid.,* 51–52), although name for name the lists of personnel vary. Dropping the second Juan de Saucedo listed by Wagner, the writer would add instead the name of Juan de Cuellar whose presence in the expedition is attested by his service record; see MN–PyTT, Leg. 93, Información de los méritos y servicios de Juan de Cuellar (1531). For documentary proof of the presence of Pedro Garao Valenciano in the Grijalva expedition, see *ibid.,* Leg. 94, Información de los méritos y servicios de Pedro Garao Valenciano (1548). Similarly the inclusion of Francisco de la Milla among the Grijalva men is supported by *ibid.,* Leg. 93, Información de los méritos y servicios de García de Aguilar (1533).

[10] With Juan de Saucedo listed twice, Wagner arrives at a total of thirty-eight. To this list, after dropping one Saucedo, the following should be added: Bartolomé de Astorga, Juan de Cuellar, Pedro Garao Valenciano, Gaspar de Garnica, Alonso

jalva venture took service under the standard of Cortés as he formed his expedition in Cuba,[11] among them pilot Antón de Alaminos; the trio Pedro de Alvarado, Alonso Dávila, and Francisco de Montejo, each of whom commanded a shipload of personnel for both Grijalva and Cortés; and Bernardino Vázquez de Tapia, who had served as Grijalva's chief ensign.[12] Ten more of Grijalva's men, returning to the American mainland with Narváez in 1520, were available to Cortés by the time the problem of building and manning a navy faced the conqueror of New Spain.[13] Among these ten

Guisado, and Francisco de Peñalosa. Astorga, whom Wagner fails to identify with any later expedition, should be assigned to Cortés, proof being presented in *ibid.*, *Información de los méritos y servicios de Bartolomé de Astorga* (1531). Cuellar and Garao Valenciano are to be included on the basis of the evidence cited in note 9 *supra*. Garnica and Guisado are mistakenly assigned to the Narváez group by Wagner, and Francisco de Peñalosa is listed as unrelated to any later expedition; for their association with Cortés' original group, see MOyB, "Conquistadores," 373–374, 381.

[11] Obviously the total number of Grijalva men with Cortés exceeds the figure stated. I. A. Wright, following Las Casas, states that "at Trinidad . . . a hundred of Grijalva's men joined him"; see *Cuba*, 85. Cervantes de Salazar asserts that Cortés gathered together about two hundred of the Grijalva personnel; see *Crónica de la Nueva España*, 103.

[12] Las Casas, *Historia*, IV, 421, and Cervantes de Salazar, *Crónica*, 62–63. Alonso Dávila and Alonso de Avila are one and the same person.

The following list represents the personnel that can be identified as having participated in both the Grijalva and Cortés expeditions: Antón de Alaminos, Melchor de Alabes, Jorge de Alvarado, Pedro de Alvarado, Juan Álvarez, Alonso de Arévalo, Bartolomé de Astorga, Alonso Dávila, Pedro de Balvas, Juan Bautista, Benito de Bejar, Tamborino Benito, Antonio Bravo, Pedro Camacho, Juan de Cervantes, Juan de Cuellar, Juan Díaz, Bernal Díaz del Castillo, García Alonso Galeote, Pedro Garao Valenciano, Gaspar de Garnica, Diego de Godoy, Alonso Guisado, Alonso Hernández Puertocarrero, Bernardino López, Francisco López, Francisco de Maldonado, Domingo Martín, Cristóbal Martín de Leyba, Cristóbal Martín de Millán de Gamboa, Francisco de Montejo, Alonso de Ojeda, Diego de Ordás, Bartolomé Pardo, Francisco de Peñalosa, Jacinto de Portillo, Pedro Rodríguez de Escobar, Juan de Saucedo, Pedro Sánchez Farfan, San Martín, Pedro Arnés de Sopuerta, Bernardino Vázquez de Tapia, and Miguel Zaragoza.

[13] These men included: García de Aguilar, Antonio de Amaya, Juan Bernal, Graviel Bosqui, Pedro Castellar, Benito de Cuenca, Pedro de Escobar, Alonso Ortíz de Zúñiga, Francisco Miguel de Salamanca, and Antonio de Villafaña. Wagner so identified all these men with the exception of Aguilar, whom he omits, and Villafaña, whom he spells Villasaña; see *Grijalva*, 51–52. For the inclusion of Aguilar, see MN–PyTT, Leg. 93, *Información de los méritos y servicios de García de Aguilar* (1533).

was Villafaña, the rebel whom Cortés ordered beheaded in Texcoco early in 1521 and who, accordingly, was not available for duty during the siege of Tenochtitlán. Of the remaining five identifiable survivors of the Grijalva contingent, three arrived in New Spain with minor groups, augmenting Cortés' force before the final siege of Tenochtitlán was inaugurated. One such person was Pedro Barba, a lieutenant of Velázquez, who initially captained a ship bearing dispatches for Narváez but who in the final instance won fame as a captain of crossbowmen and as a brigantine captain. He lost his life in the siege of Tenochtitlán. Another was Diego de Camargo, who captained a vessel belonging to Garay into Vera Cruz in 1520 with some sixty physically incapacitated men aboard. The third man to join Cortés in New Spain via an independent arrival upon the coast was Rodrigo de Nájara.[14] Only two of the identifiable survivors of the Grijalva expedition are without any clearly established relationship to the conquest of Mexico—Francisco de la Milla and Alonso Sánchez del Corral. The former may have figured in the conquest, since he was to be found in New Spain in mid-January, 1533.[15] In all, more than 98 per cent—fifty-six men —of the known survivors of Grijalva's venture served Cortés in the course of the conquest of Mexico between 1519 and 1521.

History has long recognized the inspirational relationship between the expeditions of 1517–1518 and the venture of Cortés; it but remains for justice to assign a considerable measure of the success enjoyed by Cortés to the mountain of experience brought to his undertaking by the hardened veterans of the voyages of previous years. Most prominent among the activities of those who had served Córdoba and Grijalva had been shipboard routine, for the two expeditions had involved a much greater emphasis upon nautical procedures than upon the problems that waited on the land. Little had been learned about the military might of the native masters of the heart of New Spain; much had been learned about

[14] *BDdelC*, II, 115–117, 122.

[15] MN–PyTT, Leg. 93, Información de los méritos y servicios de García de Aguilar (1533).

handling and repairing ships. Nautical mindedness and nautical skills had become part of the outlook of the veterans of 1517 and 1518. These men, though they represented a minority in the total force under Cortés' command and though they were admittedly above average in reference to their consciousness of the importance of shipping, brought to the conquest of Mexico knowledge and skills which supplemented magnificently the limited nautical experience of their leader, Hernando Cortés.

The Fleet

The third Cuban fleet to move toward mainland America differed markedly in numerous respects from either of its immediate predecessors. Whereas the Grijalva venture had been conceived and executed only after the completion of the voyage of Córdoba, the Cortés undertaking was far along in the planning and organizational stages before the Grijalva expedition returned. A certain amount of confusion surrounded the fate of the Grijalva group before its return. Grijalva, failing to maintain the unity of his fleet, allowed the vessel commanded by Pedro de Alvarado to turn back to Cuba before the month of June, 1518, had passed. Ere Grijalva's own belated return to Cuba, Velázquez had sent out a small vessel with a handful of men aboard under the command of Cristóbal de Olid to search for him. Though Olid was unsuccessful in the assignment and speedily returned to Cuba, the experience surely contributed to his nautical knowledge, preparing him for the day he would be called upon to co-operate with naval units in New Spain.[16]

For four months prior to Grijalva's return, the launching of an expedition of larger size and broader scope had been considered not only by Governor Velázquez and experienced men such as Pedro de Alvarado, but also by restive and adventuresome elements of the Cuban Spanish population at large. With Córdoba dead and Grijalva absent, the naming of a new leader was necessary—the more so because matters of temperament and other intangibles im-

[16] Bancroft, *Mexico,* I, 28–29, 31.

portant in the choice of a commander easily suggested that neither the quick nor the dead among past commanders would fit the challenge inherent in the new and widened opportunity. To Cortés went both honor and responsibility.

To this new undertaking Hernando Cortés brought a limited supply of money, an unlimited store of enthusiasm, and considerable though still uncharted ability. All of these personal assets were in evidence as he set about organizing the expedition. His funds went toward the purchase of shipping and supplies. His enthusiasm was ever present as he moved about the island recruiting personnel and directing organizational activities. His hitherto undisclosed abilities as a leader of men became clearly evident at an early moment. Though in time his funds were exhausted, his enthusiasm and abilities never knew equivalent limitation, despite the countless and varied challenges to be met in the years ahead.

The ships, which were so all-important to an expedition obliged to move by water before it could undertake anything in the land that was exciting the curiosity of the Spaniards, are cloaked in a veil of historical uncertainty—as to their number, their dimensions, their names, their pilots, their ownership. Activity got under way in the Santiago area, and soon on the waters of that beautiful land-locked bay[17] the sails increased rapidly in number. With his own funds Cortés bought several vessels; with funds supplied by men who joined the enterprise still other ships were acquired; and two or three vessels were promised by Velázquez. It was not long before Cortés had five ships at anchor in Santiago Bay.[18]

Like the story of the recruiting of the manpower, the assembling of the fleet cannot be told in relation to a single Cuban setting. For several reasons the work had to take on the complexion of a disjointed undertaking: no one shipping center on that recently con-

---

[17] A vivid word picture of this setting is found in Willis Fletcher Johnson, *The History of Cuba*, V, 89–90.

[18] *CDIAO*, XXVII, 308–309. This document, the questionnaire presented by Cortés in 1529 in reply to the *pesquisa secreta*, is not the treasure house of information on the vessels that one might hope. Its failure to treat them in detail stemmed from the fact that the pesquisa secreta also had neglected them.

quered island was able to supply the needs of this unusually large expedition; vessels had to be sent hither and thither to round up the men and supplies that likewise had to be acquired on a broad front; and some vessels were in such bad condition that they even had to be left behind temporarily for repairs.

About the time he had expanded his fleet to include as many as five ships at Santiago, Cortés dispatched one of the vessels, under the command of Pedro González de Trujillo, to Jamaica to buy meat and cassava bread for the expedition. Another of the Santiago ships, a caravel of some eighty tons' burden purchased from Alonso Caballo, had to be careened and so remained behind—it was some months before it rejoined the expedition on the coast of New Spain —as Cortés moved westward along the southern shore of Cuba with three ships to the port of Macaca where, in turn, he increased the store of foodstuffs for the forthcoming voyage.[19] These initial maritime movements by Cortés were the beginning of some three months of sporadic sea and land activity undertaken in the course of organizing the expedition before the ships were finally underway on the original assignment.

After the call at Macaca, Cortés ordered two of the three ships he had with him to proceed to the western tip of the island, the point of final rendezvous for the flotilla. This removal of certain fleet units to the distant, unsettled, and relatively inaccessible western tip of the island was not a foresighted preparation for an early crossing to the mainland. Rather, the action was defensive in nature. Cortés had learned, while at Macaca, of Grijalva's return to Cuban waters, and he feared that Velázquez might intensify already obvious efforts to block the departure of the new, third expedition. With the passing of time, Governor Velázquez had come to entertain doubts regarding the wisdom of his selection of Cortés to head the new undertaking. Increasingly Velázquez may have sensed that a man of Cortés' nature would prove restive as a

---

[19] *Ibid.*, 311–312, 315. The exact location of Macaca cannot be established. It is thought to have been located somewhere between Cape Cruz and Manzanillo; see Wright, *Cuba*, 85.

subordinate, that very likely Cortés would break from the authority of the Cuban governor, just as Velázquez years earlier had broken with the authority that had commissioned him to conquer Cuba. Not only had repeated demonstrations of the energy and ability of Cortés as he went about rounding up men and supplies seemed to disquiet the governor's mind, but also his doubts and fears were fed by comment falling from the lips of more than one wag who voiced opinions within earshot. The buffoon Cervantes el Loco, for instance, accompanying Velázquez to church one Sunday, asserted that Cortés, rebellious by nature, would run off with the fleet that was being put at his disposal. On another occasion Juan Millán told Velázquez that the sly Cortés would ruin him.[20]

Meanwhile, as the indecision and doubts of Velázquez grew, so grew the energy in action of the undaunted Cortés. He boarded the remaining ship and headed for the town of Trinidad,[21] where he purchased additional supplies and also bought a vessel owned by Alonso Guillén, a resident of that place. Learning in Trinidad that a ship belonging to another local resident, by name Juan Núñez Sedeño, was then en route from Habana to Trinidad, Cortés ordered Diego de Ordás to take the small ship *Alguecho* and intercept the approaching vessel. Stationing himself in the channel of the Archipelago of the Jardines de la Reina, Ordás intercepted and purchased both the vessel and its cargo of bread.[22] The seven vessels possessed by Cortés by this time had all been either purchased or otherwise directly acquired by him.

Leaving Trinidad, richer by shipping, supplies, and manpower—including the trio of captains of later fame, Pedro de Alvarado, Cristóbal de Olid, and Gonzalo de Sandoval—Cortés headed for

[20] *BDdelC*, I, 105, 112.

[21] This still populated community lies on the south coast of Cuba at approximately 80° west longitude.

[22] *CDIAO*, XXVII, 313. Lucas Alamán indicates this vessel belonged to Antonio Sedeño and was en route to Cuba from Jamaica; see his *Disertaciones sobre la historia de la República Megicana desde la época de la conquista que los españoles hicieron a fines del siglo XV y principios del XVI de las islas y continente americano hasta la independencia*, I, 53.

Habana Vieja[23] and then, rounding the western end of the island, sailed to Habana on the north coast to purchase still more supplies. While there he was joined by several prominent veterans of the Grijalva expedition, among them Francisco de Montejo and Alonso Dávila, who came thence in one of the ships Grijalva had used, the former flagship *San Sebastián*, which became one of the Velázquez contributions to the growing third Cuban fleet. Soon all the ships Cortés had on the north coast of the island, with a single exception, were ordered to the point of rendezvous, under the direction of pilot Francisco Gallego. As on the south coast, one vessel had to be careened on the northern shore of the island before it could be put to use.[24] The ship requiring this general overhaul is not further identified but it well might have been the *San Sebastián*, in view of its recent return from a strenuous six months of duty with Grijalva.

The blacksmith Hernán Martín, one of the artisan-conquistadors, related that in Habana he made "many nails and spikes and other necessary things" for the ships of the armada.[25] Repeatedly one learns that the components of the Cuban fleet assembled by Cortés were old and much in need of repair; never does one read of any newly launched shipping being put at his disposal. Yet even in this disadvantage, since it required the inclusion of artisans such as Hernán Martín in the expedition and the constant exercise of their professional skills, there was a hidden value. It guaranteed the presence of carpenters, blacksmiths, and related workers on later occasions when, in the midst of the conquest, shipbuilding was to be the urgent order of the day.

The confusion that has attended a specification of the total number of ships in Cortés' Cuban fleet stems from use of the original sources,[26] some of which give the number as eleven, others twelve,

---

[23] The first Habana was in the vicinity of the relatively insignificant present-day port of Batabano; see Wright, *Cuba*, 59. Batabano is due south of modern Habana.

[24] *CDIAO*, XXVII, 314–315.

[25] MN–PyTT, Leg. 95, Información de los méritos y servicios de Hernán Martín (1531).

[26] Bancroft quotes and summarizes a variety of sources in his *Mexico*, I, 57, note 4.

still others thirteen. Most writers reject the last mentioned figure, for which the leading authority seems to be Andrés de Tapia.[27] Those who say eleven and twelve are in substantial agreement, differing only regarding the moment at which the count is made. When Cortés finally assembled his ships near the westernmost tip of the island of Cuba and weighed anchor for the mainland, he had a total of eleven craft with him. One of the vessels that had required major overhauling, the same one he had been forced to leave behind much earlier as he had sailed from Santiago, was still not with the fleet. Before long, however Captain Francisco de Saucedo brought it, with some seventy men and between seven and nine horses, into port at Vera Cruz.[28] This larger than average twelfth ship—the great number of men and the high percentage of the expedition's total number of horses aboard attest its size—was a planned element of the undertaking and so should be included therein.

So little information is available concerning the sizes of Cortés' vessels that the subject scarcely admits of confusion or discussion. The same Tapia whose statement of the number of ships is not commonly accepted supplies some of the most detailed information available, namely that the largest approximated a hundred tons, three fell into the sixty–eight ton category, and all the rest were smaller still. This does not imply that all the smaller vessels were of uniform size—in fact the catch-as-catch-can basis upon which the shipping had been obtained would militate heavily against any prospect of uniformity. It merely seems evident, since Tapia classifies all vessels of less than sixty tons as small, that in his eyes such small ships were not significant enough to deserve individual consideration. With two thirds of the total fleet of such small dimensions as to resemble, if they actually were not, brigantines, many

[27] *Relación sobre la conquista de México,* in *CDHM,* II, 558. He is joined by Diego Velázquez (*CDIU,* I, 92) and Gonzalo Fernández de Oviedo y Valdés, *Historia general y natural de las Indias,* III, 258.

[28] *CDIAO,* XXVII, 315–316. In view of the phrasing of question 38, one wonders if the usual statements of the numbers of men and horses with Cortés included those on the tardy twelfth vessel.

of the conquistadors, during the time the ships moved in Cuban coastal waters, crossed to the mainland, and explored the coastal waters of New Spain, surely gained knowledge and experience closely paralleling that demanded of them in later brigantine duty during the siege of Tenochtitlán. If this assumption is justified, and logic would dictate that it is, the difficulties which had caused Cortés to resort to such small vessels served his expedition to advantage in at least two ways: the brigantines enabled safer and more thorough surveys of the coast on the mainland; and the prolonged duty aboard them prepared many men who were not seamen either psychologically or professionally for a later and unexpected chapter in the conquest.

While the paucity of such statistical information as the tonnage, length, beam, and other measurements of these vessels may well be viewed as proof of the lack of nautical-mindedness on the part of the men who wrote eyewitness accounts of the conquest of Mexico, it must be remembered that equivalent information is lacking for practically all early shipping in the Indies. One may reasonably conclude that during the periods of discovery and conquest the ends achieved received so much attention that shipping as a means to those ends was consistently taken for granted and therefore left virtually unmentioned in the historical record.

The three months' coasting along the shores of Cuba, a byproduct of the difficulties attending the organization of an expedition of the size of the one led by Cortés, may well have given Cortés more experience afloat than had all his previous career. If so (and one can only surmise concerning the percentage of his thought in that interval that was about ships and likewise the percentage of his time that was spent aboard ship) the possibly irking delay in Cuba actually served to prepare both him and his men more fully for nautical problems to be faced during the subsequent conquest.

In the second week of February, 1519, the fleet was making its last move in Cuban waters, as the ships gathered on the northern coast of Cape San Antonio at the western tip of Cuba. There the manpower was mustered and the naming of the captains and the

19

assignment of individuals to divisions took place. Eleven ships necessitated eleven commanders, the following serving in such capacity: Pedro de Alvarado, Alonso Dávila, Juan de Escalante, Escobar, Alonso Hernández Puertocarrero, Francisco de Montejo, Francisco de Morla, Diego de Ordás, Cristóbal de Olid, Juan Velázquez de León, and Hernando Cortés himself. Francisco de Saucedo tardily brought the twelfth ship to New Spain.

Antón de Alaminos, veteran of both the Córdoba and Grijalva expeditions, served as chief pilot, and each vessel had its own pilot. Among the pilots, some of whom can be identified but meagerly, were the following: Pedro Camacho, of Triana, on the vessel commanded by Pedro de Alvarado and who had served previously with both Córdoba and Grijalva; Ginés Nortes, on the smallest of all the ships of the expedition, a brigantine; Juan Álvarez (el Manquillo), of Huelva, a veteran of both the Córdoba and Grijalva expeditions; Gonzalo de Umbría, whose later demonstration of loyalty to Velázquez led successively to conspiracy against and punishment from Cortés; Juan Cermeño, a fellow conspirator, who paid with his life on the coast of New Spain; Cárdenas, of Triana; Sopuesta, of Moguer, another Grijalva man; Francisco Gallego, who had led a number of the vessels to the point of the Cuban rendezvous; and Galdín.[29] Except for the able Chief Pilot Alaminos, readily identified, relative obscurity attends even the names of most of the pilots and masters who on individual vessels were the maritime counterparts of the commanders named by Cortés. Were pilots and mariners, as well as ships, taken for granted? The fact that quite commonly the maritime aspects of the whole undertaking are stated so casually, or even ignored, suggests an affirmative answer. Even of the famed Antón Alaminos, a man whose services spanned most of the years of Spanish discovery and conquest in the New World, surprisingly little is known.

From February 18, 1519, the day of departure from Cuban

[29] Ramón Ezquerra, "Los compañeros de Hernán Cortés," in Instituto Gonzalo Fernández de Oviedo, *Estudios Cortesianos—recopilados con motivo del IV centenario de la muerte de Hernán Cortés (1547–1947)*, 41–44.

waters, until the final landing of the fleet in the vicinity of San Juan de Ulúa in Easter week, the expedition knew two distinct types of command. In nautical matters Chief Pilot Alaminos and the masters and pilots who carried out his will on the individual vessels had complete authority and gave maritime orders to the complement of seamen aboard each ship. Yet final and complete authority and responsibility for the well-being and performance of all the men aboard a given vessel, seamen and soldiers alike, rested with each shipboard commander appointed by Cortés. We find no disputes recorded by chroniclers between Alaminos and Cortés or between individual pilots and the shipboard commanders. The harmony marking such relations between landlubbers and professional seamen bespeaks the measure of dependence Cortés had to place upon the skill of the chief pilot, his subordinates, and the 109 seamen.

The End of the Beginning

Four months of planning gave way to operations as the tiny ships pointed their bows westward. The next half-dozen weeks saw the expedition on the open sea, then coasting the shore of the continent, where occasionally inlets and streams were probed and landings of limited duration were made. During that interval between Cuba and the mainland near San Juan de Ulúa, shipping was not only moving Cortés and his men toward their as yet unknown destination but was also contributing to the instruction of the Spaniards en route. Some of the small open vessels, used by Cortés out of sheer desperation rather than desire, now permitted the coasting and inspection of the shore line with a thoroughness unknown to both Córdoba and Grijalva. The ships pushed from westernmost Cuba across to the island of Cozumel on the east side of Yucatan and then doubled back to the north and Cape Catoche; rounding that northeast tip of Yucatan they probed westward along the north shore of the giant thumb separating the Gulf of Mexico and the Caribbean Sea. Then in clockwise fashion they skirted the west coast of Yucatan, slipped westward along modern Tabasco, and then began to head north again.

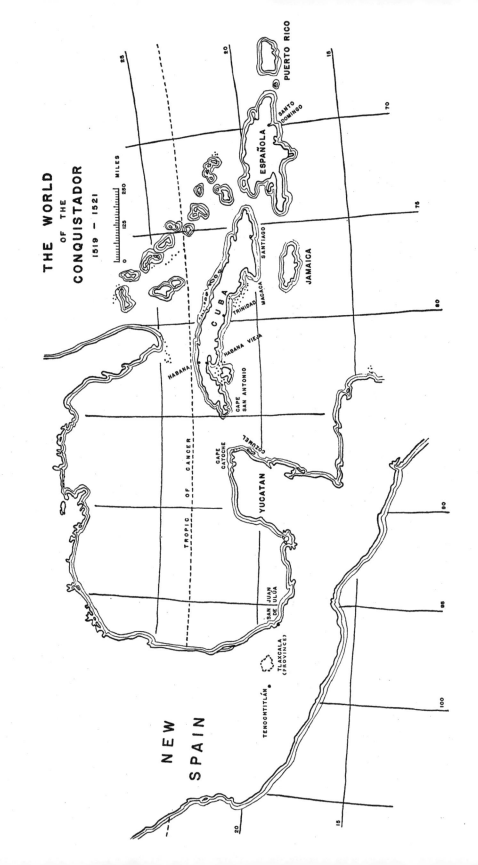

THE WORLD
OF THE
CONQUISTADOR
1519 — 1521

MILES

0   125   250

NEW
SPAIN

TENOCHTITLÁN

TLAXCALA
(PROVINCE)

SAN JUAN
DE ULÚA

TROPIC OF CANCER

YUCATAN

CAPE
CATOCHE

COZUMEL

CAPE
SAN ANTONIO

HABANA

HABANA VIEJA

C U B A

TRINIDAD

MACACA

SANTIAGO

JAMAICA

ESPAÑOLA

SANTO
DOMINGO

PUERTO RICO

25

20

15

70

75

80

90

95

100

15

20

After weeks of widening horizons—when interpreters Aguilar, a Spanish castaway churchman, and Marina, the Mexican maid who was to share both the confidence and the bed of Cortés, joined the ranks of the expedition; when the lengthening coast line presented such an enormous land mass as possibly to shake the view that Yucatan was an island; when natives were fought; and when the lure of the wealth of the interior set in—the seagoing expedition dropped anchor and established a temporary campsite. On Cuba almost four months had been required to assemble the fleet; on the mainland little time was needed for Cortés to conclude that the fleet had outlived its usefulness. Not long after his Easter season arrival in the vicinity of present-day Vera Cruz, Cortés' knowledge of the country, its people, and its wealth so widened as to foster within him an insatiable desire to penetrate the interior.

Speedily the presence of the strangers on the coast was made known to the emperor of the Mexicans, Montezuma II. Secure in Tenochtitlán, the capital city of his realm, that nestled hundreds of miles inland in the high Valley of Mexico, with several mountain ranges intervening between his seat of authority and the sandy coast the Spaniards knew, Montezuma was the most important native in all the land. Of average height and thin of figure, with shiny black hair that reached to his shoulders and dark eyes, he was the polished leader of a numerous and powerful people. Young and attractive, good-natured yet grave in a dignified royal fashion, proficient in military matters, and devoutly religious, Montezuma reciprocated the love and loyalty of his followers with a lively concern about the affairs of his domain. And the pictorial representations of the strangers supplied him by his clever artists on the coast now gave the Mexican leader reason to act in behalf of his people's interests.

Mexican tradition had it that Quetzalcoatl, one of the most powerful of their gods, would someday return in the guise of a white-skinned, bearded man. Possibly Quetzalcoatl, god of wind, was with those men whose giant ships were wind-propelled. Montezuma faced the possibility that a god had returned by sending a gift-bearing embassy to the Spaniards.

The first gifts the Mexican monarch bestowed upon Cortés consisted of food and such priestly ornaments as gold-studded headdresses of rich featherwork, masks, and tiger-head miters. The articles possessed unusual religious significance, something the Spaniards could not appreciate. They also constituted visible proof of the high level of the Mexican culture, something which probably prompted widespread speculation among the Spaniards.

Additional reports, including drawings of the Spaniards, their ships, horses, and guns, went over the mountains to Montezuma, and soon a second gift-laden embassy appeared before Cortés. Confusion attends our understanding of Montezuma's mind and purpose at this stage—and quite possibly our confusion is related to his own. Was the white-skinned leader really a god? Were the numerous white-skinned men mere mortal adventurers threatening the monarch's authority? Montezuma had to decide whether their entrance into the land was to be encouraged or whether their departure was to be hastened: in the first event, the Indian embassy carried gifts for the wanted god; in the second, the same articles were bribes to facilitate the withdrawal of unwanted interlopers.

The Spaniards preferred the presents brought by the second embassy. A disc of gold, said by Bernal Díaz to be as large as a cartwheel, had the sun engraved upon it. An equally big, thick wheel of silver bore the likeness of the moon. Other presents of gold and silver, as well as precious stones and featherwork and cotton, were given by the Mexican ambassadors. One glance at such proofs of the wealth of the Mexicans possibly sufficed to cause many of the Spaniards to conclude that the interior of that unknown land would bear further investigation.

Meanwhile Cortés and his men had come to realize that there was political dissent within Montezuma's realm which might be exploited. With the happy accident of their landing on a stretch of coast where the natives had but recently been subjugated by Montezuma's warriors, the intruders learned that restive Indian

24

elements, who resented paying the tribute imposed by the authorities in distant Tenochtitlán, might ally themselves with any Spanish attack against Mexican power.

If dreams of conquest and possible alliances flitted through the mind of Cortés, his thinking probably then turned to the related issue of the continued loyalty and unity of his own following, for loyalty and unity could not be taken for granted in early summer, 1519.[30] The loyalty of some of the men to Cortés had been tested and found wanting even before the expedition left Cuba. When Velázquez had tried unsuccessfully to relieve Cortés of his command, the elusive steps taken by Cortés had been inspired by a double need; while trying to keep the governor from getting control of the expedition, he had also to make certain that pro-Velázquez men were not given opportunity to desert the undertaking. Even as he sailed from Cuba, the young commander had a sizable task before him in regard to promoting a spirit of unity among his followers. Perhaps, as he reflected on the seeds of dissension within the ranks of his following at the outset of the undertaking, he had hoped that time, common experience, and distance from Velázquez would create an atmosphere of unity. However, in the six months following the departure from Cuba dissension had increased rather than diminished. Time was working no magic.

Implicit in Cortés' desire to conquer and settle the interior of the continent was a rejection of the legal foundation upon which his expedition had been formed. Thus, legal as well as personal factors were injected into the question of loyalty. No longer was it simply a question of Velázquez the man versus the man Cortés. Legality was always a potent factor in the motivation of Spanish actions; accordingly, Cortés did his best to perfect his position from the legal standpoint.

The days that had increased his desire to conquer and settle, pursuits not accorded him in the formal statement of his authority,

---

[30] *BDdelC*, I, 137–145; Bernardino de Sahagún, *Historia general de las cosas de Nueva España* (1938), IV, 37–40; Cervantes de Salazar, *Crónica*, 279–281; and Hernando Alvarado Tezozomoc, *Crónica mexicana*, 519–522.

had also widened dissension in his ranks. Taking this extralegal desire of the commander of the expedition as their cue, the Velázquez faction agitated for an early return to Cuba. Cortés, upset by this dissension and unalterably opposed to the early demise of the undertaking upon which he had staked his all, extemporized briefly. When the passing of time soon stamped as undesirable the mosquito-ridden temporary campsite on the barren, sandy shore, Cortés sent two ships northward to seek a more attractive setting for a permanent settlement. Most of the fifty men commanded by Montejo on that expedition were partisans of Velázquez. During those several weeks, for Cortés had reason to expect and was not disappointed in the speedy renewal of the clamor of the Velázquez men once they returned, Cortés probably matured certain plans that were soon put into effect.

After consulting with his stanchest following and making certain of their support, Cortés pretended to gamble with the destiny of the undertaking. Pretense it must be termed, because he had not only marked the deck but stacked the cards against the opposition. Having made certain of the loyalty of the majority, as he himself sold his viewpoint to the captains who then championed it within the ranks, he magnanimously entrusted the decision-making to the men. The showdown came when Cortés ordered the crier to proclaim that everybody should board ship, preparatory to setting sail for Cuba. Immediately his supporters rose in full-throated protest. In the ensuing atmosphere of crisis the order was revoked, the desire to colonize spread, and the indispensability of Cortés to the as yet vaguely stated project gained currency. But even a showdown between the Cortés and Velázquez factions in the realm of ideas still left two unsolved problems: how could the break with the authority of Velázquez be legalized; and how could the support of the pro-Velázquez following be guaranteed? Cortés faced the issues in just that order.

On the heels of the decision to stay on the continent came developments that cast a cloak of legality about all subsequent activities. Using the authority that devolved upon him as commander of the expedition, Cortés proceeded to appoint officials within the government of the first Spanish community in New Spain. From *alcaldes* to scrivener, Cortés filled the posts of the infant municipality of Villa Rica de la Vera Cruz. Since the erection of a municipal government did not in and of itself make legal the illegal position in which the rebellious Cortés had put himself, the commander paid careful attention to its personnel so that the municipal government would serve his purposes. Powerful, pro-Cortés men held most of the offices and authority. However, as he tried to legalize his break with authority, opportunity to appease and placate some of the Velázquez faction also presented itself. Because he was courting manpower and striving for the unity of his following at the same moment that he was concerned with casting the aura of legality over his defiance of instructions, Cortés used the founding of the municipality, with its attendant appointments, as the occasion to put certain pro-Velázquez men into places of prominence.

Once the municipality, with all the rights and responsibilities that Spanish law automatically bestowed upon it, had been brought into being, Cortés effected a legal rupture of the relations between his expedition and the Cuban authorities. Appearing before the *cabildo* of his own creation, Hernando Cortés surrendered his authority as commander of the Velázquez-inspired expedition. The cabildo accepted the commander's renunciation of authority, and for a short interval the direction of the leaderless body of men rested with that municipal organ. Then, loyal to the man who had appointed it, the cabildo, after a brief moment that produced a crescendo of pro-Cortés sentiment among the rank and file of the men, hastened to reappoint Cortés commander of the undertaking. This legal subterfuge whereby a commander created a municipality and then quickly surrendered and reassumed his role as leader resulted in a shift both of the source of authority and of the scope of the undertaking for Cortés. Now, with a show of legality that might prove eloquent even at Court some unforeseen day in the future, Cortés' authority devolved from pro-Cortés elements within his own expedition and his widened sphere of action embraced the very activities which formerly were not permitted. The legal tie to Velázquez had been severed; it but remained for Cortés to remove the physical tie, the fleet.[31]

No other episode in the total career of Hernando Cortés has received so much attention or has been the object of so much rhapsodic writing as the destruction of his Cuban fleet. Because of the show of courage inherent in an action which forced the expedition to go forward by making sure it could not turn back, Cortés has been represented as one whose heroism ranks with that of Achilles, Ulysses, Aeneas, Alexander, and Julius Caesar;[32] as one whose resolution knows but few parallels in all recorded history;[33] as one who, since he had fewer men with him, outstripped the feats of Agathocles and Timarchus.[34] Contradictions within the accounts of the destruction of the ships and desire to honor the commander who engineered it have combined to produce a mountain of literature on this favorite Cortésian theme.[35] Out of a welter of mixed uncertainties and forthright statements, some of which are downright contradictory, certain conclusions do emerge: (1) the heroics in the action have been much more apparent with the passing of the

[31] Bancroft, *Mexico*, I, 71–93, 116–139 *passim*.

[32] Gonzalo de Illescas, *Historia Pontifical*, in Joaquín Ramírez Cabañas (ed.), *Conquista de México*, 275–276.

[33] William H. Prescott, *History of the Conquest of Mexico*, I, 340–341. Prescott draws the closest parallel from Roman military history, citing the burning of a fleet of approximately 1,100 river craft in 363 A.D. by Emperor Julian as he launched an Alexander-like thrust eastward beyond the Tigris.

[34] Antonio de Solís y Rivadeneyra, *The History of the Conquest of Mexico by the Spaniards*, tr. Thomas Townsend, 171–173; and Fernando Soler Jardón, "Notas sobre la leyenda del incendio de las naves," in Instituto Gonzalo Fernández de Oviedo, *Estudios Cortesianos*, 541–542.

[35] Among the analytical treatments of the mass of evidence on this subject are the following: Bancroft, *Mexico*, I, 185–186, note 6; Cesáreo Fernández Duro, *Las joyas de Isabel la Católica, las naves de Cortés y el salto de Alvarado*, 27–45; Antonio L. Valverde, "Leyenda de América: Las Naves de Cortés," in *Contribuciones para el estudio de la Historia de América: homenaje al Doctor Emilio Ravignani*, 145–154; and Soler Jardón, "Notas . . . ," in Instituto Gonzalo Fernández de Oviedo, *Estudios Cortesianos*, 537–559.

centuries, and (2) at least three modes of destruction are reported to have been visited upon the ships.

Those writers who refuse to content themselves with vague generalization have indicated that, upon orders from Cortés, the Cuban fleet, owing to fire, beaching, or scuttling, became an almost one hundred per cent loss. Of these three forms of destruction, burning can most easily be discounted. No eyewitness account of the event states that the ships were fired. No account, until those of Juan Martínez and Suárez de Peralta[36] toward the end of the sixteenth century, so recorded the event. The present writer joins Valverde and Soler Jardón in the view that this account of the destruction of the fleet, a literary invention of the sixteenth century, was probably set forth to magnify the heroic proportions of Hernando Cortés. The tellers of a dramatic tale—and many who have treated Cortés must perforce be so classified—want a dramatic decision followed by equally dramatic action. In burning they obtain their end, though they serve history badly thereby.

A second explanation has the vessels scuttled off the coast of New Spain. Numerous authorities support this view, but chronologically the case for scuttling rests most heavily upon the *pesquisa secreta* of 1529, the writing of López de Gómara, and the account of the conquest by Aguilar.[37] The last-named source loses some of its value as an eyewitness account when it is realized that it was written long after that of López de Gómara. If, as there is reason to believe, Aguilar leaned upon the apologist of Cortés, we are left with but two versions and both of them the work of extremists. López de Gómara puts some stress on the worm-eaten condition of the vessels, thus absolving Cortés of having destroyed shipping of value. On the other hand, the enemies of Cortés who phrased the pesquisa secreta of 1529 included men who had lost property in the destruc-

[36] "Noticias," *BRAH*, Vol. X (1887), 337; and Juan Suárez de Peralta, *Noticias históricas de la Nueva España*, ed. Justo Zaragoza, 74–76.

[37] *CDIAO*, XXVII, 8; Francisco López de Gómara, *Historia de la conquista de México*, ed. Joaquín Ramírez Cabañas, I, 147; and Francisco de Aguilar, *Historia de la Nueva España*, ed. Alfonso Teja Zabre, 39.

tion of the ships. They give no emphasis to the worm-eaten state of the vessels and thus imply that scuttling amounted to willful destruction of serviceable, hence valuable, shipping. Accordingly both the friend and the enemy of Cortés, through choice of materials and varying emphasis, can employ the scuttling story to good account. With the passage of time this version gained many adherents.[38]

Beaching, however, seems the most probable of all the modes that have been suggested: it has the strongest support from the historical sources and it has on its side an inexorable logic in terms of the implications of the continuing conquest. In the letter of October 30, 1520, to his sovereign, Cortés declared that the vessels were beached;[39] and almost simultaneously the two commissioners sent to Spain ere the expedition plunged into the interior of the continent, Francisco de Montejo and Alonso Hernández Puertocarrero, made independent statements on the subject which supported the Cortés version.[40] Not long thereafter, in a suit between Cortés and Narváez, a representative of the latter, Fernando de Ceballos, also stated that the ships had been beached.[41] The much later written account of eyewitness Bernal Díaz del Castillo finds the foot soldier speaking of this maritime matter in his customarily vague fashion.[42] Logic is on the side of beaching, because that action insured maximum salvage from the vessels themselves. Too

---

[38] Representative statements are contained in the following: Las Casas, *Historia*, IV, 497; Motolinía, *Motolinía's History of the Indians of New Spain*, ed. and tr. Elizabeth Andros Foster, 38; Antonio de Herrera, *Historia general de los hechos de los castellanos en las islas y tierra firme del mar océano*, I, Pt. II, 133; Antonio de Solís y Rivadeneyra, *Historia de la Conquista de Méjico* (Vol. IV of *Colección de los mejores autores españoles*, ed. José de la Revilla), 123; Baltasar Dorantes de Carranza, *Sumaria relación de las cosas de la Nueva España*, 97; Francisco Javier Clavigero, *Historia antigua de México*, III, 49–50; Prescott, *Mexico*, I, 338; Alamán, *Disertaciones*, I, 72; *DUHG*, II, 573; Bancroft, *Mexico*, I, 184; and Marcos Jiménez de la Espada, "No fué tea, fué barreno," *BRAH*, Vol. XI (1887), 238.

[39] *HC*, I, 40.

[40] MN–PyTT, Leg. 1, Doc. 49 Bis, Ynformación recibida en la Coruña, fols. 162–162r, 166–166r (1520).

[41] Valverde, "Leyenda . . . ," in *Contribuciones*, 149 (quoting *Colección Muñoz*, LXXXVI, fol. 195).

[42] *BDdelC*, I, 221–223.

commonly the burning and scuttling versions leave the impression that the men took themselves, their arms, horses, and foodstuffs off the vessels and allowed everything else to disappear with the hulls.

As important as the fact that the vessels were destroyed, and much more important than the comparative quibbling over the precise form of that destruction, is the issue: what was salvaged from the vessels? Even as he knew that the destruction of the ships would cut the tie that bound his expedition to the past, Cortés, with enough nautical experience to realize that the salvage of certain things from the vessels was absolutely necessary against the prospect of an uncertain future that might require the rebuilding of ships on that selfsame coast, probably saw to it that a systematic and remarkably thorough salvage operation was pursued. With a show of responsible concern for the future characteristic of a thoughtful commander, Cortés surely had the sails, the tackle, the rigging, the cordage, the nails and, quite probably, other metal fittings removed from the ships. He could scarcely have foreseen, as he ordered the stowing and safeguarding of such things by the coastal garrison, that some part of these supplies, instead of being again employed on the high seas, would contribute to the military well-being of the Spaniards during their first venture into Tenochtitlán, and that another part of them would play a major role on inland waters in effecting the final conquest of Tenochtitlán in 1521.

For too long the interpretation of the action of July and August, 1519, on the coast of New Spain has been oversimplified. True it is that Cortés did break sharply with the past, that he did force the Velázquez men to continue with him, and that he did add the mariners to his ranks through action that called for bravery, tempered by necessity. But it is equally true that even as he was breaking with the past he served the present needs of the garrison on the coast and cast an eye to the future, when he saved the ships' gear. There is something overwhelmingly negative about destruction— something that smacks simply of brute force and the courage of blind desperation. On the other hand, the construction of positions

31

for the coastal garrison and the retention of the ships' supplies against an uncertain future that might call for the construction of other vessels suggest farsightedness and planning that could only spring from wisdom. Necessity, courage, wisdom—a number of factors combine in the destruction of the fleet, and history should record the event as the complex happening it actually was.

When Cortés began to push inland in late summer, possibly nothing was farther from his mind than things nautical and the idea that he would soon need shipping again. And as he moved westward over the coastal plain, mounted the foothills of the Sierra Madre Oriental, fought the Tlaxcalans in their mountain fastness, and turned near annihilation into sweeping victory at Cholula, a future that might call for the use of the salvaged ships' supplies must have been so remote as to be nonexistent. The concern of the present to a leader who found himself and his men thousands of feet above sea level and hundreds of miles deep in a region that was becoming increasingly hostile was movement on land. Yet time, and only the short interval from late August to mid-November at that, was to merge the past and the future; by mid-November, 1519, the pendulum of necessity that had seen a fleet destroyed but three months earlier was to demand that Cortés construct another fleet.

CHAPTER II

Seat of Power

GEOGRAPHICALLY a new phase of the conquest of Mexico opened when the Spanish conquistadors, pushing westward after their victory at Cholula, mounted the pass between the noble peaks of Popocatepetl and Ixtaccihuatl and looked down upon the Valley of Mexico. Behind them lay months of nearly constant movement, repeated land engagements, and shifting climactic patterns. Before them, in the immediate future, were months of comparative inaction, battle-free. In the lake country of the valley, the mobility of the cavalry and infantry upon which so much Spanish military success had been predicated would be so limited that the changed circumstances would harass the invaders and finally force their commander to the realization that new, bold strategy was needed. But on that morning in the first week of November, 1519, Cortés could not know the full significance of the geographic setting before him and his men.[1]

[1] This study, wherein geography is quite prominently a handmaid of history, has been facilitated by study of map collections at the Division of Maps of the Library of Congress, the William L. Clements Library of the University of Michigan, the Latin American Collection of the University of Texas, the library of the Sociedad Mexicana de Geografía y Estadística of Mexico City, and the Instituto Panamericano de Geografía e Historia of Mexico City. The following general catalogues and bibliographies were most helpful: Manuel Orozco y Berra, *Materiales para la cartografía mexicana*; Pedro Torres Lanzas, *Relación descriptiva de los mapas, planos, & de México y Floridas existentes en el Archivo General de las Indias*; Woodbury Lowery, *A Descriptive List of Maps of the Spanish Possessions within the present limits of the United States, 1502–1820*; Philip Lee Phillips, *A List of Maps of America in the*

In the brilliant visibility under the noonday sun, the Spaniards could look greater distances into their geographic future than they had been able to do since their landing on the coast of New Spain. From their vantage point two and one-half miles above sea level at the southeastern corner of the Valley of Mexico, they were able to gain some rough and general approximations of the terrain to the west, northwest, and north of them. Stretched out before them was more level terrain in one unbroken unit than they had yet encountered on the continent. The sunlight fell upon more water than they had seen since their departure from the coast. Before them lay evidence of denser population than they had met anywhere in the New World.

Here rimmed into essential unity by mountain ranges lay a valley which centered the political, economic, and military might of the principal native people of the region. Only the unadorned comments of Cortés and foot soldier Bernal Díaz record this moment.

"I mounted the pass between the two mountains of which I have spoken, and, descending it, we beheld one of the provinces, of the country of the said Montezuma," wrote Cortés as he tersely reported the occasion to his sovereign.[2] The foot soldier's version, even more prosaic, suggests it was merely another moment in the routine of a warrior in the field. "Early the next morning we began our march, and it was nearly midday when we arrived at the ridge of the mountain where we found the roads just as the people of Huexotzingo had said. There we rested a little and began to think about the Mexican squadrons on the intrenched hillside."[3]

Yet even in the face of this terseness of commander and common

---

Library of Congress—preceded by a list of works relating to cartography and A List of Geographical Atlases in the Library of Congress—with bibliographical notes; and A. Curtis Wilgus, Maps Relating to Latin America in Books and Periodicals. In addition, these works were of primary assistance: Manuel Orozco y Berra, "Memoria para la carta hidrográfica del Valle de México," BSMGE, Vol. IX (1862), 337–509; Manuel Toussaint, Federico Gómez de Orozco, and Justino Fernández, Planos de la Ciudad de México; Ola Apenes (comp. and ed.), Mapas Antiguos del Valle de México; and S. Linné, El Valle y la Ciudad de México en 1550.

[2] HC–MacN, I, 226.
[3] BDdelC–M, II, 29.

soldier, it is not difficult to imagine that the newcomers gazed on the surrounding peaks and on the gleaming lakes with a certain amount of emotion. Probably to none of them, not even to Cortés, occurred the significance of the essential unity of the land and water—much less the phrase "valley of decision"; yet given what they viewed and the arduous journey behind them, some slight sense of the valley's ultimate meaning to them must have been borne in as they stood poised for the descent.

The Causeways

Eagerly, yet also wearily and charily, the Spaniards and their Indian allies descended the western slope. As they moved across the valley, it was not long before they came to the first of the shallow lakes and its narrow, traversing causeway. Lake Chalco introduced them to the strange lacustrine world. On the thin ribbon of earth and stone which constituted a causeway—in breadth only equaling the length of a cavalryman's lance—the Spanish-Indian legion marched for two thirds of a league (the old Spanish measure of a league being 2.63 miles). Montezuma's messengers, accompanying Cortés on this final leg of the journey, urged the newcomers on from the city of Cuitlahuac on Lake Chalco to Iztapalapa on still larger Lake Texcoco. Like the entrance into Cuitlahuac, the departure therefrom was via causeway, this one extending more than one third the distance to Iztapalapa. The night of November 7 was spent on Iztapalapa Peninsula, between Lakes Xochimilco and Texcoco. The following day the invaders moved from Iztapalapa, by way of the causeway of the same name, toward the imperial city of Tenochtitlán.

For approximately a half league the strangers moved westward, via causeway, from Iztapalapa to Mexicaltzingo and then, not far beyond, they headed northward, still by causeway, for nearly two leagues across the waters separating Tenochtitlán from the mainland. The first and east-west segment of the causeway served not only as a part of the highroad to the Mexican capital from the south but also as a dam against Lakes Chalco and Xochimilco waters,

35

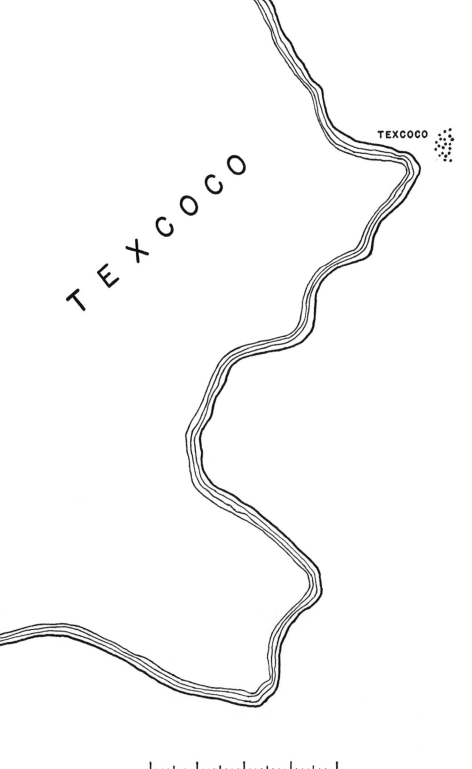

TEXCOCO

TEXCOCO

MILES
0 1 2 3 4 5 6 7 8

which, being higher than those of Lake Texcoco, frequently flowed northward into Lake Texcoco, menacing Tenochtitlán.

As the Spaniards rapidly widened their acquaintance with lakes and causeways, they also had opportunity to note the increased density of the native population. Iztapalapa contained more than twelve thousand families; nearby Mexicaltzingo some three thousand; within a stone's throw, additional communities sheltered still other thousands upon thousands of Indian families. The manpower potential of the enemy seemed to increase in direct proportion to the mounting difficulties the terrain presented for purposes of battle.[4] Markedly less information is available concerning the east-west stretch of the Iztapalapa causeway than for the longer portion on the north-south axis. One author states the former to have been 5,200 *varas* long and 11 *varas* wide.[5] It is probable that until the causeway turned abruptly northward toward Tenochtitlán somewhat west of Mexicaltzingo, its importance was not clear to the Spanish mind—it seemed just another causeway and hence received no special attention.

The main portion of the causeway, probably constructed about 1429, the Spaniards seem to have observed closely.[6] Cortés said its breadth equaled the length of two lances, sufficiently wide that eight horsemen might proceed abreast over it.[7] Infantryman Bernal Díaz, not given to thinking automatically in terms of horses, declared the causeway was eight paces wide.[8] Francisco de Aguilar is both conservative and confusing in his statement that three, four, or more horses could easily move abreast on it.[9] In the Cortés and Díaz statements one sees apparent agreement that the causeway was approximately twenty-five feet wide. In length the Iztapalapa

[4] *BDdelC*, I, 323–331; and *HC*, I, 69–74.

[5] A. P. Maudslay, "The Iztapalapa Causeway," in *BDdelC–M*, II, 307 (Appendix A), at which point Maudslay is quoting Cepeda and Carillo, authors who wrote more than a century after the conquest. No eyewitness account describes the Mexicaltzingo portion of the causeway in such detail.

[6] A description of the Iztapalapa causeway, summarized by Maudslay from the eyewitness accounts, is offered in *ibid.*, 307–317. Also see Linné, *El Valle*, 32.

[7] *HC*, I, 74.   [8] *BDdelC*, I, 332.

[9] Aguilar, *Historia de la Nueva España*, ed. Teja Zabre, 59.

causeway approximated two leagues: a half league between the cities of Iztapalapa and Mexicaltzingo, one league between Mexicaltzingo and the juncture of the Coyoacán spur at Acachinanco, and another half league between Acachinanco and the outskirts of Tenochtitlán.

If uneasiness accompanied the Spaniards in their step-by-step movement from mainland toward the center of the lake, further

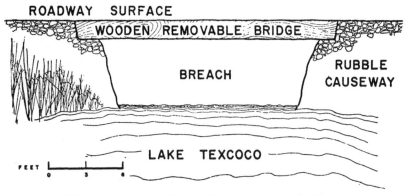

Conjectural Reconstruction of Aztec Causeway on Lake Texcoco

apprehension must have been roused by the sight of countless Indian canoes on the lake waters. With the enemy before and behind them, and with both flanks vulnerable to canoe-borne warriors, the invaders could scarcely take consolation even from the fact that they had a thin ribbon of terra firma underfoot, for on numerous occasions the rock and earth of the causeway yielded to wide, wooden, readily removable bridges. As Spaniards, Tlaxcalan allies, and Mexican escort trudged together northward from Mexicaltzingo, in time another causeway, this one out of the southwest, came into view. The point of union of this Coyoacán spur with the Iztapalapa causeway, approximately a half league to the south of Tenochtitlán, was strongly fortified with towers and walls. This point was named Acachinanco, and here a multitude of native chieftains awaited Cortés and his following; after a lengthy halt, the crowd of marchers, re-enforced now by the chieftains, surged

39

on toward the city proper. Near the northern limit of the man-made roadway, Montezuma himself came forward to greet the strangers and to escort them to living quarters in the center of his metropolis.[10]

One cannot help but wonder about the choice of causeways over which the Spaniards were escorted into Tenochtitlán. With the Iztapalapa causeway not only the longest but also the best-defended of the land routes in and out of the city, could it have been that the Indians chose that route for the Spaniards in the hope that appreciation of the unfavorable military position into which they were moving would deter the entrance of the invaders into the island-city? If the Mexicans were indulging in such a show of psychological warfare, they failed; but nonetheless the Spanish experience did point up dramatically and immediately the invaders' need of naval power.

In various accounts of Cortés' approach to the island-city, the causeway bridges have been mentioned innumerable times, but usually in a fashion that promoted inaccurate impressions of them. Too commonly they have been termed drawbridges. But the accepted use of the term drawbridge implies a degree of mechanization not present in the Mexican bridges. Further, a drawbridge after being raised can be restored to usefulness very simply by an operator—he merely crosses to the side on which it pivots and lowers the bridge again; had such a simple solution been available at the time of the Spanish retreat of 1520 from Tenochtitlán, it is clear that the withdrawal would not have been the military debacle it became. The Mexican causeway bridges which were to cause the Spaniards so much trouble were a series of removable beams. Once the heavy beams had been floated away, the resultant breach was a permanent obstacle to traffic on foot or horse.

When finally at the close of that eighth day of November the weary Spaniards lay down to rest in the Palace of Axayacatl, probably many of them were disturbed by the realization that the waking hours of that day had been spent in a lacustrine setting

[10] HC, I, 75–77; and BDdelC, I, 332–336.

which made impossible the kind of warfare to which they were accustomed. In the days to follow, they were to gain fuller knowledge of their untenable position, and uneasiness would swiftly turn into the fear that dictated the creation of naval power.

On succeeding days the visitors moved about the city, gathering further knowledge of the metropolis and its lake setting. On the fifth day after their entry, they had an outstanding opportunity to add to their knowledge when they mounted the principal pyramid-shaped temple. They looked down on the general pattern of the city and all three of the causeways which linked the island-capital to the mainland. They saw the aqueduct upon which the city population had to depend for drinking water.[11] And to the west they saw the Tacuba causeway, the shortest roadway to the mainland—and hence the one they employed when finally the fury of their hosts produced their expulsion from the island-city.

This was the causeway written indelibly into history by the events of the Sad Night. Linné probably was thinking of the Sad Night when he wrote, "To the west the city was joined to the shore by the most important of the causeways, that of Tlacopan [Tacuba]."[12] In the light of the significance attached to the Iztapalapa causeway in the siege operation of 1521 (discussed in Chapter VI), the present writer believes that Linné's judgment can be challenged. Yet one point of uniqueness and significance of the Tacuba causeway mentioned by Linné is valid: its relationship to the aforementioned aqueduct which supplied the city with potable water. Certainly no other causeway has so appealed to writers. No other causeway has been the subject of such a study as Artemio de Valle-Arizpe's *Por la vieja calzada de Tlacopan*. As a subject it has had a continuing popularity, possibly both because of the ease with which its location has been fixed by later students and because of the fact that many names related to it and to events upon it have been retained in modern Mexico City. Such popularity might easily be considered synonymous with importance.

More renowned for its breaches than for its width or length, the

---

[11] *Ibid.*, 355–356.   [12] Linné, *El Valle*, 32.

Tacuba causeway counted four breaches in the open lake area and a fifth one where it joined the island. The principal street that stretched westward from the most important plaza of the city and merged with the causeway at the edge of the island was traversed by three more watercourses.[13] Nowhere else in the whole conquest of New Spain—one might broaden the area to include all the New World—were so many Spaniards to be lost in such a short time as at the breaches of the Tacuba causeway.

The Tepeyac causeway, which stretched from the island-city northward to the mainland, was the least important, by far, of the three earthen links between capital and mainland. In length it fell between the Tacuba and Iztapalapa causeways, the southern one being approximately seven miles long, the northern one three miles in length, and the western one about two miles long.[14] The eyewitness accounts of this phase of the conquest, through utter omission of references to the Tepeyac causeway, lead us to believe that the Spaniards did not bestow much attention upon the northern roadway. Several circumstances may have accounted for this lack of attention: the Tepeyac causeway was of third-rate importance to the natives themselves, quite probably because the communities on the northern shore of the lake were neither so numerous nor so populous as those to the west and the south of the city; and between the heart of Tenochtitlán, base for the Spanish garrison, and the Tepeyac causeway there possibly lay an abnormally wide watercourse which cut through the city, dividing it into a northern district (Tlatelolco) and a southern sector (Tenochtitlán proper), and making the causeway at least an inconvenient road, if not a dangerous one, for the Spaniards. Structurally the northern causeway resembled the others in that it was intersected by a number of watercourses over which wooden bridges were suspended. For all

---

[13] Ignacio Alcocer, *Apuntes sobre la antigua México-Tenochtitlán*, 14–15. Alcocer's statement that the water-filled breaches in the causeway varied between two and four meters in width (p. 106) is seemingly without historical support; see Maudslay, "The Tacuba (Tlacopan) Causeway," in *BDdelC–M*, II, 318–319 (Appendix B); and *HC*, I, 137–138.

[14] F. A. MacNutt, "Mexico-Tenochtitlan," in *HC–MacN*, I, 330 (Appendix II).

of the causeways, such water breaches served at least three purposes: they permitted the ebb and flow of waters which otherwise would have damaged the causeways; they permitted the freer movement of cargo-carrying canoes throughout all parts of the lake; and they became pivotal points in the defense of the city against any army attempting to storm it via the causeways.

Dispute and confusion are rampant among writers on the subject of causeways between the island-city and the mainland other than the forementioned southern (Iztapalapa), western (Tacuba), and northern (Tepeyac) routes. Some writers, among them Cortés,[15] list four altogether by counting as a distinct unit the spur linking Coyoacán with the Iztapalapa causeway. Other authors create sundry additional causeways out of thin air, Robertson, for example, insisting that one stretched eastward from Tenochtitlán to Texcoco.[16] If a fourth separate and distinct causeway actually existed—the Coyoacán spur being but an adjunct of the Iztapalapa causeway—the weight of authority would suggest that it stretched from Tlatelolco, the northern part of the island-capital, to Nonoalco, which lay somewhat to the north of Tacuba on the west shore of the lake. But the literature is sufficiently confusing that the existence of this causeway cannot be asserted with the assurance that attends the previously mentioned trio. Alcocer, however, strongly supports the reality of the Nonoalco causeway, stating that Pedro de Alvarado's division made its principal thrusts against the city over that route rather than via Tacuba. Schottelius, a close student of the Nuremberg (Cortés) map of 1524 on which six causeways are indicated, is another who supports this viewpoint.[17] The present writer inclines toward the view that but three serviceable causeways existed, not merely because he is in good company with such authorities as Bernal Díaz, the Anonymous Conqueror,

---

[15] HC, I, 98. Also listing four, but failing to identify them, is Fernán Pérez de Oliva, *Algunas cosas de Hernán Cortés y México*, in *Conquista de Mexico*, ed. Joaquín Ramírez Cabañas, 344.

[16] This view, expressed in the earliest edition, was later corrected; see William Robertson, *History of America*, II, 51, note Y.

[17] Alcocer, *Apuntes*, 109; and Linné, *El Valle*, 32.

and Motolinía,[18] but also because at a later date Cortés, blockading and besieging the island-fortress, was able to control every land route to the beleaguered city with three land divisions.

Whether or not there were more than three land routes for traffic in and out of the city, it is certain that the population of Tenochtitlán was dependent upon a single aqueduct for potable water to be conducted from Chapultepec to the metropolis. This very considerable engineering achievement, said to have been completed in 1466,[19] paralleled the Tacuba causeway for much of the distance across the lake. In one brief paragraph Cortés penned this unusually complete description:

Along one of the causeways which lead to the city, there are two conduits of masonry each two paces broad, and five feet deep, through one of which a volume of very good fresh water, the bulk of a man's body, flows into the heart of the city, from which all supply themselves, and drink. The other which is empty brings the water, when they wish to clean the first conduit, for, while one is being cleaned, the water flows through the other. Conduits as large round as an ox's body bring the fresh water across the bridges, thus avoiding the channels by which the salt-water flows, and in this manner the whole city is supplied, and everybody has water to drink.[20]

The City

Much of the Spaniards' early interest in causeways—aside from their aspect as avenues of possible escape from as well as entry into the city—stemmed from increased knowledge of Tenochtitlán itself, the largest and most unique native city in the Western Hemisphere. Though variation attends the estimates of the conquistadors, it is generally held that the city was composed of some sixty thousand houses, with a population that must have approximated three hundred thousand. After summarizing the statements in the primary sources, Prescott suggested that the population might have been even higher because many of the

[18] BDdelC, I, 355; El Conquistador Anónimo, Relación de algunas cosas de la Nueva España y de la gran ciudad de Temestitan Mexico, in CDHM, I, 391; and Motolinía, Motolinía's History, ed. and tr. Foster, 214.

[19] Linné, El Valle, 34.   [20] HC–MacN, I, 262–263.

houses surely contained more than a single family. Cortés, refrain-
ing from a numerical statement, declared that Tenochtitlán was the
size of Seville or Córdoba.[21] Founded in 1325, the almost two-
century-old city beheld by the conquistadors rested primarily upon
two narrowly separated islands. Originally each seems to have been
the seat of an independent community, but in bloody warfare of the
1470's, some four decades prior to the coming of the Spaniards, the
southern part, Tenochtitlán, was victor over Tlatelolco, the northern portion. From that time on there was but a single city, though
the natural dividing line between the two sections and the presence
of duplicating broad plazas, markets, important religious shrines,
and noteworthy public buildings still suggested the bifurcated
nature of the metropolis at the time of the conquest.[22] The area of
the rather circular-shaped island-community was approximately
twenty square miles.

Tenochtitlán of 1519 had a structural pattern that has prevailed
until very recent years in almost all Latin America: the plazas, the
most important buildings (among them a shrine to Tlaloc, god of
the rains and the waters), and the substantial housing that belonged to the better classes of society composed the heart of the
community; the farther one moved from the center of the city
toward its periphery, the lower the economic level of the population and the more fragile the housing. The houses and other buildings in the heart of the city were of solid construction, being chiefly
adobe and the volcanic rock tezontle. Many of the buildings were

---

[21] Maudslay, "The Valley of Mexico," in *BDdelC–M*, II, 49; and Prescott, *Mexico*,
II, 104. The most recent study of the population of Tenochtitlán as of 1519 is in
Sherburne F. Cook and Lesley Byrd Simpson, *The Population of Central Mexico in
the Sixteenth Century*, 30–34.

[22] Despite the inclusive use of the name Tenochtitlán to embrace Tlatelolco as
well, the old northern sector of the native city has drawn considerable scholarly
attention in and of itself. See, for example, Fidel de J. Chauvet, *Tlatelolco, interesante recopilación histórica*; R. H. Barlow (ed.), "Resumen analítico de 'Unos
Annales Históricos de la Nación Mexicana,'" and Heinrich Berlin and R. H. Barlow
(eds.,), "Códice de Tlatelolco," in *Fuentes para la historia de México*, ed. Salvador
Toscano, II; and various authors and articles under the general heading, "Tlatelolco
a través de los tiempos," *Memorias de la Academia Mexicana de la Historia*, Vols.
III–V (1944–1946) *passim*.

quite new at the time of the conquest, having been constructed after the disastrous flood of 1499. In size, basic pattern, and magnificence, Tenochtitlán reminded many of the conquistadors of the major cities of Spain as well as the fabulous cities-of-gold of Spanish writers.[23]

Everyday living in Tenochtitlán, as one would expect in a city of such size, was a combination of the simple and the complex, both within the family and in relation to the state. In the absence of pack animals and wheeled vehicles, many thousands of persons were reduced to the role of bearers of burdens. Antlike they moved about the capital city, over the causeways, throughout the Valley of Mexico, and off to the limits of the realm. Yet even these burden-ridden Indians possessed remarkable dignity in their deportment, and lives made drab by repetitive labors were enlivened by love of colors and flowers and music.

Housing and furnishings varied with the social level of the family, but it was generally customary, in Tenochtitlán, for the living quarters to flank a patio. In the rooms that were meant for rest and sleeping, mats and cushions bespoke repose. In the corner of at least one room would be found the arms of the able-bodied males of the family—wooden clubs edged with blades of obsidian, javelins, bows and arrows, wooden helmets, and shields. In the kitchen area rich pepper-laden sauces would be made, and the rhythmic patting of the tortilla makers must have been a common sound. Mothers and grandmothers worked skillfully with the spindle, young daughters watching and hoping to duplicate their mastery; and the little boys learned the use of tools and weapons from fathers and uncles. Lighthearted joy ruled at the fiestas of birthday celebrations, when the rich sauces were served and musi-

[23] MacNutt, "Mexico-Tenochtitlan," in *HC–MacN*, I, 330 (Appendix II); Maudslay, "The Valley of Mexico," in *BDdelC–M*, II, 49–50; El Conquistador Anónimo, *Relación*, in *CDHM*, I, 390; Ignacio León de la Barra, "Geografía histórica: Tenochtitlán y Tlaltelolco," *BSMGE*, Vol. XLVII (1937), 74; George C. Vaillant, *Aztecs of Mexico*, 225; Linné, *El Valle*, 26; Norman S. Hayner, "Mexico City: Its Growth and Configuration," *The American Journal of Sociology*, Vol. L (1945), 295; Jesús Galindo y Villa, "México, la ciudad capital," *BSMGE*, Vol. XLIII (1934), 398; and Cook and Simpson, *Population*, 32–33.

cians played their wood drums and reed flutes—instruments that might also accompany an army into battle.

Outside the home, as the Mexicans took their places in the work-aday world and in the armies of their ruler, they were almost constantly aware of their religion. Long-gowned priests moved through the streets, walking reminders of the numerous gods the worship embraced. And at the base of the sacred pyramid there were always worshipping throngs, drawn by the smoke of burning incense curling from the top around the ritual of human sacrifice. Dignified in their social life, obedient to their political and military and religious obligations, the citizens of Tenochtitlán were highly disciplined, highly civilized. Full of life and yet prepared for death, they were supremely submissive.

Their joys and their sorrows, their work and their play, their religion and their government constituted a way of life for the inhabitants of Tenochtitlán that was mirrored in Tacuba on the west shore of the lake, in Iztapalapa on the south shore, in Texcoco to the east—in fact it was the way of life of more than a million and a half Indians in the Valley of Mexico alone. And beyond the mountains rimming the valley the way of life was basically the same for scores of miles in almost every direction. Local variations here and there testified to the recency of Mexican mastery of certain districts, yet even the newly-won regions rapidly became like the rest as they made their regular tribute payments to the authorities in the island-capital.[24]

Traffic in Tenochtitlán moved both by land and by water, drawing the comment from writers that the city was an American Venice. Many of the streets were wide and picturesque, a few of the most prominent being built of earth and stone; but the average thoroughfare consisted of an earthen lane plus a canal parallel and immediately adjacent to it. Narrow canoes hollowed from single tree trunks moved easily, naturally, and in great numbers through-

[24] Prescott, *Mexico*, II, 70–144 *passim;* Vaillant, *Aztecs, passim;* Henry R. Wagner, *The Rise of Fernando Cortés*, 212–241; and Cook and Simpson, *Population*, 18–36.

47

out the city. With considerable regularity, the streets adhered to a rectangular pattern; in the later Spanish reconstruction of the city it was therefore comparatively easy to follow the general outline of the native metropolis.[25] The pattern of the leading arteries that pivoted from the central plaza of old Tenochtitlán can today be fairly well traced from the center of modern Mexico City.

As the population of the island-capital grew, the original islands no longer offered sufficient terrain. The natives demonstrated considerable skill in creating new land and new canals. Tiny new islands, or *chinampas*, were constructed by lifting wet muck from the shallow bottom of the lake and placing it upon wickerwork. (The present residents of the Xochimilco district have a very similar practice.) At first the little islands would actually be "floating gardens," but in time, with the repetition of the process as the first wet earth dried out to a degree and packed down, the chinampas served as planting areas. It was not long before the thickness of the earthen rafts permitted the planting of larger and still larger crops. Meanwhile, aquatic plants would have reached down to the lake bottom to anchor the chinampas, hastening the process by which they became real island additions to the peripheral area of the city. Farming and residing on them, the poorer laboring elements, repeating this process indefinitely, added to the area of Tenochtitlán, gradually reduced the expanse of water which served as a moatlike defense between the city and the mainland, and contributed, with the countless small canals among the chinampas, to the Venetian aspect of the city. Even more important than physical expansion for the capital was the increased food supply made possible by the new land, especially when Tenochtitlán became later a beleaguered city.[26] To the foundations of earth and stone usual to

[25] The Anonymous Conqueror, *Narrative of Some Things of New Spain and of the Great City of Temestitan*, ed. and tr. Marshall H. Saville, 63; El Conquistador Anónimo, *Relación*, in *CDHM*, I, 391–392; and Linné, *El Valle*, 33. A journalistic treatment of twentieth-century life in the Valley of Mexico keeps the Venetian aspect of the setting before modern readers; see Walter Hough, "The Venice of Mexico," *National Geographic Magazine*, Vol. XXX (July, 1916), 69–88.

[26] This unusual aspect of life in the lake country has attracted considerable attention. Representative accounts are to be found in Robert C. West and Pedro Armillas,

most cities, Tenochtitlán's situation had added a third and basic one—water. And the citizens were of necessity nautical-minded; their military security depended on the lake, their economic security on the canals.

The Lakes

The causeways and the canals of Tenochtitlán can be understood only in terms of Lake Texcoco, and that body of water, in turn, cannot be comprehended aside from its relationship to the over-all lake system of which it was the pivotal portion. The Valley of Mexico counted a total of six lakes, of which Lake Texcoco was the political, economic, military, and hydrographic center. The two smaller lakes to the south, Xochimilco directly south and Chalco east of Xochimilco, were connected to each other and Xochimilco opened into Texcoco. This interconnection had special importance in terms of the fact that Chalco was higher than Xochimilco, which in turn was higher than Texcoco.[27] Out of the south repeatedly had come the danger of flood for the island-capital, and, accordingly protective measures had been taken. It is thought that, prior to the reign of Montezuma Ilhuicamina in the late fifteenth century, there was but one lake south of Texcoco and that the division of the waters which produced the two lakes had been effected by the construction of a causeway-dike that not only helped regulate the water level but also served to facilitate land transportation in the area. It was over this causeway that the invaders moved northward to Iztapalapa on their initial entry into Tenochtitlán. Near the point

---

"Las chinampas de México—poesía y realidad de los 'Jardines Flotantes,'" *Cuadernos Americanos*, Vol. L (1950), 165–182; Vaillant, *Aztecs*, 225–226; Herbert J. Spinden, *Ancient Civilizations of Mexico and Central America*, 183; and Linné, *El Valle*, 26.

[27] One of the finest treatments of this aspect of the topography of the valley is by an eminent Mexican who repeatedly directed his attention to the nineteenth-century hydrographic problems faced by Mexico City; see Manuel Orozco y Berra, "Memoria para la carta hidrográfica del Valle de México," *BSMGE*, Vol. IX (1862), 337–509 *passim*. A by-product of efforts to drain the valley and to improve the drainage system of ever-expanding Mexico City has been, across the centuries, a mass of literature, scientific, pseudoscientific, and popular, relating to the historical geography of the Valley of Mexico.

where the waters of Lake Xochimilco joined those of Lake Texcoco by flowing through the Strait of Mexicaltzingo, a portion of the Iztapalapa causeway constituted still another man-made effort to control the lake waters and reduce the prospects of flooding for the capital. Lake Chalco, with its clear, clean, fresh water, was the scene of considerable fishing—and remained so for centuries—hence along its shores were a series of small communities.[28] Both of the southern lakes contained more aquatic vegetation than did Lake Texcoco, a condition which contributed to their greater wealth of marine life. Chalco was further to be distinguished by several small islands, the largest and most beautiful bearing the name Xico. Lake Xochimilco, more than any other body of water in the entire valley, was characterized by the number of fresh-water springs feeding it.

To the northeast of Lake Texcoco lay three more lakes, San Cristóbal, Xaltocan, and Zumpango. Their successively higher levels and connecting channels meant that on occasion the waters of the northeast also plagued the residents of Tenochtitlán. The southernmost of the trio, San Cristóbal, the smallest in the entire lake system, was salty by nature. Its hinterland supported very limited population. Immediately to the north of San Cristóbal lay larger Lake Xaltocan, its reddish and salty water interrupted by two islands, one of which gave its name to the lake. Population was scant in the Xaltocan district also. Still farther north was Lake Zumpango, largest of all the lakes. In comparison with its two neighbors Zumpango almost passed as a body of fresh water, owing in part to the volume of water poured into it via the Cuautitlán River, and its mud-caked shores were conducive to agriculture.

Though in general the northeastern lakes had little importance for the island-capital, they contributed to the threat of periodic inundation, and the inhabitants of Tenochtitlán had therefore been obliged to reckon with them and seek a means of controlling them as well as the southern waters. For years a series of damaging floods had visited such tribulation upon Tenochtitlán that when still an-

---

[28] *Ibid.*, 485–486.

other long-sustained deluge came upon the city in the mid-1440's the citizens resolved upon a project that might safeguard the metropolis for all future time. A huge dike was planned which would bisect Lake Texcoco on a north-south axis. Though the project was of but secondary importance to all the other lacustrine communities, Tenochtitlán was able to enlist the co-operation of many people from the shore communities. So considerable was the contribution of Nezahualcoyotl, the then ruler of Texcoco, the region to the east of the lake of the same name, that the resultant dike, stretching sixteen kilometers from Iztapalapa on the south to Atzacoalco on the northern shore of Lake Texcoco, has generally been referred to as Nezahualcoyotl's Dike. To an undertaking which required the driving of parallel rows of a great amount of piling and the filling in of the intervening space with earth and rock, some thousands of workmen must have dedicated themselves for a considerable time. Nezahualcoyotl, poet-philosopher-engineer king of Texcoco, cousin of the flood-plagued Montezuma I of Tenochtitlán, and the only man who emerges in truly human dimensions from the shadow of the pre-Hispanic era,[29] personally directed the efforts of 20,000 of his subjects on the great project. Azcapotzalco, Coyoacán, Xochimilco, Tenayocan, and Iztapalapa were among the lake-front communities that contributed workmen and materials to the gigantic undertaking.

Like the causeways that connected Tenochtitlán with the mainland, this dike was broken by occasional sluices through which canoe traffic could freely move.[30] They were open, of course, at all times except when the threat of the eastern waters made necessary their being closed by gates or portable barriers, of which no full description has come down to us. It is quite probable, and here again precise information is lacking, that the dike did not serve as a

[29] Linné, El Valle, 182. For an interesting, interpretive study, see Frances Gillmor, Flute of the Smoking Mirror—A Portrait of Nezahualcoyotl Poet-King of the Aztecs.

[30] Clavigero, Historia antigua de México, I, 321–322; Linné, El Valle, 182; Gillmor, Flute of the Smoking Mirror, 120; and Maudslay, "The Valley of Mexico," in BDdelC–M, II, 47–48.

roadway, given the relative unimportance of the communities at its terminal points, and in that case the surface of the dike would not have been so smoothly finished as that of the causeways and the sluiceways probably not bridged. Yet the potential of the dike as a roadway cannot be ignored when it is recalled that its width was reported as more than eight varas, which approximates the widths of the causeways leading to Tenochtitlán.

In time the two-part nature of Lake Texcoco was further emphasized by the presence of the dike: gradually the western waters, fed as they were by fresh-water streams and the fresh-water lakes of Chalco and Xochimilco, lost a great deal of their saline content, and the salty nature of the eastern waters, fed as they were by brackish Xaltocan and San Cristóbal, was intensified. In the course of the seventy years between the completion of Nezahualcoyotl's Dike[31] and the coming of the conquistadors, the sweetening of the waters around Tenochtitlán increased their capacity for sustaining plant and human life, thereby quite possibly contributing to the rapid population growth of the island-city. There are some writers who take the bifurcation of the waters by the dike so seriously that they refer to the portion of the lake to the west of it, that surrounding Tenochtitlán, as the Lake of Mexico and term only the portion east of the dike by the old name, Lake Texcoco. This assignment of terminology is viewed by the present writer as highly artificial and will not be adhered to in the following discussion of Lake Texcoco, a body of water that knew essential unity in its broadest extent in the days of the conquest as well as in the pre-Hispanic period.

In the form of a giant ellipse with its greater extent on a north-south axis, Lake Texcoco, as already indicated, was a strange com-

---

[31] The heavy precipitation that made the construction of the dike necessary is depicted as an event of 1447 in E. T. Hamy (ed.), *Codex Telleriano-Remensis*, plate 32. Juan de Torquemada states the dike was completed in 1449; see his *Monarquia Indiana*, I, 157–159. There is no reason to believe, as stated in "The Drainage of the Valley of Mexico," *The Scottish Geographical Magazine*, Vol. XII (1896), 155, that Cortés destroyed this dike during the siege of 1521.

bination of fresh and salt waters, and the pattern of those waters seemingly was not without effect upon the distribution of its lake-front population. While its shores in general played host to more communities and more people than did all the other lake districts of the valley, it is interesting that an overwhelming concentration of those communities lay to the west of the Nezahualcoyotl Dike, in the region of the sweeter waters. An almost unbroken ring of sizable communities, in the shape of an enormous half-moon, popu- lated the shore-front areas to the north, the west, and the south of Tenochtitlán. On the other hand, on all of the considerable shore- line to the east of the dike there was only one seat of significant population—Texcoco, the city on the eastern shore which had given its name to the lake and which was second in importance only to Tenochtitlán.[32] Home of the Texcocan dynasty, which in league with the rulers of Tenochtitlán and Tacuba had known victories and extensions of authority in years past, Texcoco even surpassed the island-metropolis in some respects. Recent research suggests a probable population of 400,000 in 1519. Not without reason was it denoted the Athens of the Valley of Mexico, and out of its strength, its pride, its sense of superiority, and its strategic location could well come an opposition that might embarrass Tenochtitlán in the extreme, should Texcoco be forced to a loyalty choice between the inhabitants of island-capital and the conquistadors.[33]

Today Lake Texcoco has been practically eliminated by the steady shrinkage that set in soon after the conquest. But in 1519 its size and the great number of communities that rimmed it led Cortés to consider it an inland sea. Its small fish, many varieties of aquatic animals, and range of plant life, mostly frowned upon by the Span- iards as food, not only played a significant role in the native diet at

[32] Cortés stated that Texcoco lay six leagues distant from Tenochtitlán by canoe and ten leagues by land; see *HC*, I, 90, 180.

[33] Juan Bautista Pomar, *Relación de Tezcoco*, in *NCDHM*, III, 3; Motolinía, *Motolinía's History*, ed. and tr. Foster, 209; Guillermo Hay, "Apuntes geográficos, estadísticos e históricos del distrito de Texcoco," *BSMGE*, 2ª época, Vol. II (1870), 541–548, 554; Vaillant, *Aztecs*, 256; and Cook and Simpson, *Population*, 34–36.

the time of the conquest but continued to supplement the dietary needs of the Indian population centuries thereafter.[34] Like some of the other lakes, Texcoco contained a number of small islands. None of these was important as a seat of population or from a strategic standpoint, though one was to serve as a signal station for the de-fenders at the beginning of the siege of 1521. Previously that same Peñón of Tepepolco served Montezuma II as a recreational site; and in taking him there aboard one of the first Spanish-built vessels on those inland waters, the Spaniards were able to reconnoiter the waters of that section of the lake at the same time as they tested their recently completed shipping.[35]

The populous shore line, the protective dike of Nezahualcoyotl, the causeways, the aqueduct, the chinampas, the canals—all of these features of Lake Texcoco were to be significant in days of battle. All added up to a most unique setting for the decisive test at arms between the defending natives and the invading conquista-dors.

One of the best indices to the importance of Lake Texcoco—and at the same time the factor of final integration for a lake district—is the nature of the native shipping that moved thereon. With adequate shipping, the chinampas and shore districts could supply the needs of the island population; without it, a blockade that could reduce the proud capital to starvation and surrender might well be imposed. If attackers mustered shipping, the native units had to meet them in combat as well. In peace and in war the canoes of Lake Texcoco were pivotal to the life of Tenochtitlán. Cervantes de Salazar stated there were more than 100,000 canoes and other small, one-piece craft on the lake. An earlier writer put the number at 200,000.[36]

In nautical matters the eyewitness accounts of the conquest are

[34] Orozco y Berra, "Memoria . . . del Valle de México," *BSMGE*, Vol. IX (1862), 474–478, discusses at length the animal life present in Lake Texcoco as late as the second half of the nineteenth century.

[35] *BDdelC*, I, 389–390; and Linné, *El Valle*, 136.

[36] Cervantes de Salazar, *Crónica*, 302; and López de Gómara, *Historia*, ed. Ramírez Cabañas, I, 235.

at least consistent: they fail to give anything like a full description of the vessels of the natives, just as they failed concerning those of the conquistadors. Cortés, for example, in all the instances in which he refers to Indian canoes between November, 1519, and July, 1520, never offers any details on the carrying capacity of the craft in terms of either men or goods; and never does he mention numbers of canoes. Vague generality pervades his statements on the subject.[37] Out of the fragments of written information, however, one can glean the following: the native canoes varied in size from those that one man could operate up to those capable of efficiently carrying from six to ten warriors; some few craft of unusually large dimensions carried as many as sixty persons; all seem to have been propelled only by paddles; the total number of canoes available in the Lake Texcoco area mounted into the tens of thousands; the canoes saw almost constant use for moving foodstuffs and other goods, for fishing, transportation of passengers, and military operations. Generally flat-bottomed, without keel, and a bit narrower at the bow than at the stern, the canoe was hollowed out from the trunk of a single tree by a process which is not exactly known.[38]

The paucity of Spanish reporting on the canoes cannot be interpreted as a sign of limited contact with them. In the course of the campaigning in the valley the Spaniards had so many clashes with canoe-borne enemies—and had suffered sufficiently at native hands —that one is surprised that growing respect for the vessels did not lead to fuller statements about them. Instead, the writers repeatedly express themselves in brief phrases such as: "their spies . . . came, some in canoes by water";[39] "we had a skirmish with some powerful Mexican squadrons which had come in more than a thousand canoes . . . [and] although the Mexicans fought like brave men, we made them take to their canoes"; "more than two thousand canoes carrying over twenty thousand Mexicans had come to Chal-

---

[37] *HC,* I, 71, 128.

[38] *Ibid.,* 215, 217; *BDdelC,* II, 155, 185, 205–207, 208–209, 213; *CDIAO,* XXVII, 385; Motolinía, *Motolinía's History,* ed. and tr. Foster, 204, 215; Clavigero, *Historia antigua de México,* II, 287; Hubert Howe Bancroft, *The Native Races,* II, 397–399; and Linné, *El Valle,* 127. [39] *HC–MacN,* I, 228.

co"; "we heard a sound of many canoes being paddled, although they approached with muffled paddles";[40] "all the salt lake was covered with canoes filled with warriors"; and "we saw an infinite number of canoes on the water with countless warriors in them."[41]

Understanding of the Indian canoes comes best from study of certain of the early maps and the numerous codices which offer pictorial representations of the craft. In his fine analysis of this subject as it relates to a mid-sixteenth-century map of the Lake Texcoco area, Linné writes:

> Of a total of twenty canoes that are being used, seven carry crews of two men and the rest one each. With prow and poop curved upward they have a sufficiently singular design that it is doubtless original. They coincide with the representations of canoes in the codices.[42]

Such pictorial sources as the Códice en Cruz,[43] Codex Florentino,[44] Codex Mendoza, Codex Boturini, Codex Vaticanus No. 3738, Codex Dresden,[45] and the Lienzo de Tlaxcala[46] do much to augment our knowledge of the Indian canoes. It is evident that they were long, narrow, shallow, and in almost all instances made from single tree trunks. The paddling was performed in a standing position. The remarkable similarity of lines for the vessels in the various pictorial representations suggests that there was no considerable variation in design at any one time, nor was there much

[40] BDdelC–M, IV, 16, 52, 76.

[41] HC–MacN, II, 19, 54.

[42] Linné, El Valle, 127. A particularly full treatment of Indian canoes in general is to be found in Georg Friederici, Die Schiffart der Indianer. Mexican craft receive special attention in A. Núñez Ortega, "Los navegantes indígenas en la época de la Conquista," BSMGE, 3ª época, Vol. IV (1878), 47–57. Meanwhile such a reputable scholar as Spinden, Ancient Civilizations, makes no reference to Mexican canoes.

[43] Charles E. Dibble (ed.), Códice en Cruz, 120.

[44] Codex Florentino, in Bernardino de Sahagún, Historia de las cosas de Nueva España, ed. Francisco del Paso y Troncoso, IV, Lám. CL, Núms. 91, 92; Lám. CLIII, Núms. 116, 117, 118; Lám. CLIV, Núms. 119, 120, 121, 122; Lám. CLV, Núm. 134; Lám. CLVI, Núms. 138, 140; and Lám. CLVII, Núms. 147, 148, 149, 150.

[45] Lord E. K. Kingsborough, Antiquities of Mexico, I, Pt. 1, plates 4, 17; Pt. 2, plates 61, 64, 65; Pt. 3, plates 1, 6; II, Pt. 1, plates 104, 128, 137; and III, Pt. 2, plates 43, 65.

[46] Alfredo Chavero (ed.), Lienzo de Tlaxcala, láminas 41 and 47 in Homenaje a Cristóbal Colón: Antigüedades Mexicanas, ed. Junta Colombina de México.

modification thereof with the passing of generations.[47] The wide range of uses to which the canoes were put is graphically depicted in the codices, making clear that the craft were of the highest importance to the native way of life. Further reflection of that importance is found in the harsh treatment provided by law for those caught stealing canoes.[48]

The lake country had robbed the Spaniards of the advantage of cavalry, usually so effective in land campaigns; the multitudinous, mobile canoes of the natives doubled the disadvantage for the invaders. Obviously the Spaniards needed a navy, because the object of their desire, Tenochtitlán, did not stand in isolation; its relationship to the lake within which it lay made control of that lake a necessary preliminary to the control of the capital city. Nor did the concentric circles of geographical interdependence stop with city and lake. Beyond them and intimately related to them was the rest of the Valley of Mexico.

The Hinterland

The Valley of Mexico, sometimes called the Plain of Anáhuac,[49] is an oval-shaped basin with an area of approximately 2,050 square miles situated some 7,800 feet above sea level. It is possessed of features which have led some people to conclude that it is the enormous crater of an ancient volcano.[50] The plain is possibly

[47] The passengers aboard a four-engine commercial plane which made a forced landing in the shallow waters of the much reduced present-day Lake Texcoco in the summer of 1951 were evacuated from the damaged plane by natives in canoes remarkably reminiscent of those pictured in sixteenth-century records; see *New York Times*, September 2, 1951.

[48] Marshall H. Saville, *The Wood-Carver's Art in Ancient Mexico*, 19.

[49] For an interesting discussion of this and other significant native terms, see Eufemio Mendoza, "Anáhuac-México-Tenochtitlán," *BSMGE*, 2ª época, Vol. IV (1872), 263–273, wherein the author concludes that the island-capital should be termed Tenochtitlán-México.

[50] Among those entertaining this view are Antonio García y Cubas, *Atlas geográfico, estadístico é histórico de la República Mexicana*, unnumbered page of text accompanying map XVII (Valle de México); and Manuel Orozco y Berra in *DUHG*, V, 602. On the other hand, the eminent geographer Pedro C. Sánchez, in conversation with the writer on September 12, 1951, repudiated that interpretation of the geological structure of the Valley of Mexico.

57

seventy leagues in circumference, with the north-south extension about fifty per cent greater than the distance across it from east to west. The unbroken rim of forest-clad mountains that border it tower majestically over the almost level floor of the valley, making of it a watershed for which there is no natural outlet to the sea. On the east is the Sierra Nevada, so named because it embraces the eternally snow-capped Ixtaccihuatl and Popocatepetl, the peaks between which Cortés initially moved into the valley; on the south the Ajusco Range; on the west the range of Las Cruces; and on the north the Pachuca Range. Numerous short, torrential streams carried waters from these slopes into the valley, feeding the sizable lake system that stretched at the time of the conquest from Zumpango on the north at the base of the Pachuca Range to Xochimilco and Chalco on the south close by Ajusco.

Certain weather data pertaining to the Valley of Mexico derived over long periods of time in the nineteenth century, and hence illustrative of averages, might profitably be borne in mind by the student of sixteenth-century Mexico. The rainfall pattern was marked by cyclical variations, with 603 mm. the average annual precipitation; with 355 mm. the minimum and 924 mm. the maximum in the twenty-year period 1855–1875. A study of wind patterns indicated the following order of frequency: (1) northwest, (2) east, (3) southeast, (4) northeast, (5) north, (6) southwest, (7) south, and (8) west. The winds were most vigorous in February, March, and April and least so in November and December. The daily wind pattern was as follows: between 1 A.M. and 6 A.M., light and diminishing; between 6 A.M. and 9 A.M., light but increasing; between 9 A.M. and 4 P.M., heavier and increasing; between 4 P.M. and 1 A.M., heavy but diminishing. Minimum velocity was at 6 A.M., maximum at 4 P.M. Generally the strongest winds were out of the north and northeast. Such information permits at least partial reconstruction of the timetable, intensity, and efficiency of movement of sailing vessels on Lake Texcoco. The hottest month of the year was April and the wettest one was August; January and February were the driest months.

Discussion of the lake system has already suggested that the valley was divided into three zones; a low one in the area of Lake Texcoco and two slightly higher ones, that to the northeast embracing the region of Lakes San Cristóbal, Xaltocan, and Zumpango, and that to the south including the area of Lakes Xochimilco and Chalco. At the time of the conquest roughly 20 per cent, possibly 442 square miles, of the valley area was covered by the waters of the six lakes.[51] Though the lakes dominated the whole region, the 80 per cent of the total area of the valley that was land constituted a sizable and important hinterland. It was from the foodstuff production of the valley that Tenochtitlán, in all probability, drew most of its supplies. It was out of the land as well as the nearby waters that such seats of authority as Texcoco and Tacuba derived much of their wealth and power. It was off the land as well as out of the waters of the valley that such communities as Chalco, Xochi-

[51] Vincente Reyes, "La ley de la periodicidad de la lluvia en el valle de México," *BSMGE*, 3ª época, Vol. IV (1878), 314–319 and "El régimen de los vientos en la ciudad de México y sus relaciones con la higiene," *BSMGE*, 3ª época, IV (1878), 553–561; Jesús Galindo y Villa, *Reseña histórico-descriptiva de la ciudad de México,* 3–5; *DUHG,* V, 601–602, 604, 984–985; Alfonso Hernández Varela, "Los peligros a que ha estado expuesto el Valle de México debido a su situación orohidrográfica y las diferentes obras de defensa construídas para salvaguardar las vidas y los intereses de sus habitantes," *BSMGE,* Vol. LVII (1942), 363–365; "The Drainage of the Valley of Mexico," *The Scottish Geographical Magazine,* Vol. XII (1896), 155; Juan Mateos, *Apunte histórico y descriptivo sobre el Valle de México y breve descripción de la obra de su desagüe y del saneamiento de la capital,* 3; and Jesús Galindo y Villa, *Geografía sumaria de la República Mexicana,* 85–86, 287; and *BDdelC–M,* II, 45. Cortés, with his knowledge of the valley still limited as he wrote his second letter to Emperor Charles V, declared that the two lakes, Texcoco and Chalco, occupied almost all of the valley; see *HC,* I, 97–98. Needless to say, the elimination of certain of the lakes completely and the sizable reduction of the areas of others make current resolution of this problem impossible.

A particularly significant source used in studying the Valley of Mexico has been the remarkable scale model in the Instituto Panamericano de Geografía e Historia in Mexico City. The construction of this representation of the valley, on scales of 1:50 on the horizontal and 1:20 on the vertical, occupied Ing. Pedro C. Sánchez for ten years. Close study of the model has permitted a unified comprehension of the valley, which admirably supplements and integrates information acquired firsthand by flights over and drives and walks through it. Brief mention of the model and its builder is found in *Tiempo,* Vol. XIX, Núm. 479 (July 6, 1951), 13. A not very serviceable photographic reproduction of the model can be seen in Jorge A. Vivo, *Geografía de México,* 305.

milco, Mizquic, Cuitlahuac, Iztapalapa, Cuauhtitlán, Culuacan, Azcapotzalco, Xaltocan, Mexicaltzingo, Huitzilopochco, Coyoacán, Coatlichan, Huexotla, Chiauhtla, Acolman, Teotihuacán, Citlaltepec, Ecatepec, Tequixquiac, and others derived their daily sustenance.[52]

The valley, with its foodstuffs, its manpower, and its vast array of supplies, had a potential that might be placed at the disposal of either the defenders or the invaders. To say the least, it behooved the commander of the invading army to learn in detail the nature of this strange setting in which he was to do climactic battle. Cortés came to the rim of that valley with one thing in mind—mastery of the seat of power of the people whose evidences of wealth and high level of civilization had lured him into the interior of the continent. In the narrowest sense, Tenochtitlán was that seat of power. But in the course of a seven months' stay in Tenochtitlán in 1519–1520 the conquistadors came to appreciate the indelible relationship between city and lake, between land and water. They, accordingly, took steps in that interval to dominate the water, as the realistic road leading to control of the city they desired. Initially Cortés failed to gain control of the lake, and the cost, in terms of the losses sustained on the Sad Night, was catastrophic. Ere he returned to the valley, the Spanish commander had time to ponder and comprehend many of the geographic implications of that powerful seat of enemy strength. When he planned accordingly, realizing that to take the city he must first dominate the lake and prior even to that he must control the land mass in the valley, then, and only then, was Cortés to know victory.

[52] M. Orozco y Berra, *Historia antigua y de la Conquista de México*, II, 197–198. At the time of the conquest, the lake district probably contained more than fifty communities; see López de Gómara, *Historia*, ed. Ramírez Cabañas, I, 235.

CHAPTER III

Trial by Water: Failure

The First Ships: 4 Brigantines and 1 Caravel*

As Cortés entered the Mexican capital in early November, 1519, among his mixed emotions was the gnawing fear that his military position therein would be an untenable one. Even the most courageous and least professional military man among the invaders must have realized that a Spanish force of fewer than five hundred men, hundreds of miles within the interior of a hostile and strange land, literally had entered a lion's den as it marched into the populous island-city of Tenochtitlán via the narrow and ever so vulnerable causeway that stretched some seven miles between it and the mainland. The captain-general's courage and curiosity took him into Tenochtitlán, without hesitation; but his military mind and his sense of responsibility for the welfare of his men led him almost at once to seek a means whereby the Spaniards could dominate the waters of Lake Texcoco and the lacustrine communities, including Tenochtitlán itself. It was clear that only after the Spaniards had become masters of the adjacent countryside—in this instance the waters and shores of a lake—could they know that inner satisfaction and quiet confidence that comes from a sense of physical security. Only when they had established their mastery over the lake area could it be said that the initiative so important

---

* A slightly modified version of the opening section of this chapter appeared in *The Americas*, X (April, 1954), 409–419.

to continuance of the conquest rested in their hands. With his infantry, his cavalry, and his artillery momentarily stalled in the insular setting in which they found themselves, Cortés needed to create a new military factor which, when thrown into the balance, would tip the scales once again in favor of the Spaniards.

Naval power was needed. Accordingly, the leader who a few months earlier, in August, had achieved unity among his followers by destroying a fleet on the coast must now create a navy, if he wanted to maintain the mobility and morale without which his force, in all likelihood, would face ultimate defeat. The invading Spanish army had entered Tenochtitlán via the Iztapalapa causeway on November 8, 1519. In his second letter to Charles V, Cortés gave this word picture of the dilemma faced by the Spaniards:

> Perceiving that, if the inhabitants wished to practise any treachery against us, they had plenty of opportunity because the said city being built as I have described, they might, by raising the bridges at the exits and entrances, starve us without our being able to reach land, as soon as I entered the city, I made great haste to build four brigantines, which I had completed in a short time, capable whenever we might wish, of taking three hundred men and the horses to land.[1]

In his self-proclaimed haste to gain control of the waters surrounding Tenochtitlán, Cortés was beset by at least two difficult questions: to whom could he turn to have the vessels constructed; and how could he so camouflage their construction as to belie to the Indians the fear that actually motivated the project? Since, up to this moment, Cortés had had no reason to canvass his following on the subject of shipbuilding talents, he wisely took the problem to his men. One man in the ranks, Martín López, stated bluntly at a later date that Cortés, troubled and prevented from continuing the conquest, begged him (Martín López) to design four brigantines. Bernardino Vázquez de Tapia, another conquistador, declared that Cortés, worried, spoke to him on the subject of the in-

---

[1] *HC–MacN*, I, 257. For evidence of the uneasiness the lake-country setting inspired in Cortés, see Bernardino Vázquez de Tapia, *Relación del conquistador Bernardino Vázquez de Tapia*, ed. Manuel Romero de Terreros, 35–36.

sular position in which they found themselves, the vulnerability of the causeways, and the absence of men who understood carpentering. Vázquez de Tapia adds that when the issue was put before the soldiers, Martín López was proposed as being capable of supervising ship construction, all the more so because he had with him two servants who were skilled carpenters, and that accordingly Cortés summoned Martín López and requested that he and his men construct four brigantines.

Still other conquistadors expressed themselves concerning the emergence of Martín López as the shipbuilder of the conquest of Mexico. Antonio Bravo, another of the small band with Cortés, testified in 1540 that when Cortés consulted with his men concerning the difficulty before them, it was agreed that the conquest must continue by water; but no one volunteered to undertake the construction of ships until Martín López stepped forward with his servants. Andrés de Tapia, justly renowned for his own short account of the early phase of the conquest,[2] speaks bluntly of the affair in such a manner as to magnify further the impression that Martín López, suddenly catapulted into prominence from previous obscurity, was soon considered indispensable. Tapia said that Cortés turned to Martín López when he was unable to push the conquest further and asked him what means should be adopted. When López suggested that four brigantines be built, Cortés asked him to submit plans for the project, after which the captain-general asked him to supervise the undertaking.[3]

Stripped of conflicting statements on matters of detail, the foregoing eyewitness accounts clearly indicate that Cortés, by mid-November, 1519, had discovered the heretofore unknown talents of Martín López and had put him in charge of the shipbuilding program without which Spanish capacity to continue the conquest would have been a matter of grave doubt.

Many of the men constituting the crew of workmen at López'

[2] *Relación sobre la conquista de México*, in *CDHM*, II, 554–594.

[3] LC–CC, Martín López 1529–1550, pp. 118–119, 126, 141, 149 (interrogatory and testimony, 1540).

disposal can be identified. His previously mentioned servants were two brothers, Pedro and Miguel de Mafla, carpenters who contributed their talents not only on this occasion but later as well. A cousin of Martín López, Juan Martínez Narices, seems, in the light of subsequent association, also to have assisted, though this is not quite certain.[4] The blacksmith Hernán Martín, according to his own affirmation, was present throughout the project, being charged with the making of the necessary tools for the workmen. Given the scarcity of tools one would expect among such a gathering of military adventurers, his forge must have been exceedingly busy those closing weeks of 1519. Antón de Rodas, mentioning his role in the brigantine construction as he served as a witness in behalf of Martín López in the course of litigation between López and Cortés in 1528, indicated that he assisted the shipwright upon orders from Cortés. This leads one to speculate concerning Cortés' method of designating such a work force—was it a simple matter of assignment of a man who happened to catch the eye of the captain-general at a given moment, or did Cortés continue to canvass his manpower systematically in search of hidden talents? One cannot speak with assurance upon this point. Still another blacksmith, Pedro Hernández by name, testified that he had worked diligently upon the vessels and could vouch that they were well made. Despite the fact that Juan Gómez de Herrera offered no details concerning the specific kind of contribution he made toward the completion of the brigantines,[5] the later information that he was one of the two men who calked the thirteen brigantines completed in 1521[6] suggests he might have worked upon the first four vessels in a similar capacity. The sawyer Diego Hernández, instituting a suit against Cortés in 1529, claimed that he deserved at

---

[4] AGI, Patronato 57–1–1, fols. 19–19r, 37r, 42r, 45, 47r (interrogatory and testimony, 1534); translation in AU–CC, Martín López 1528–1574, pp. 60, 112–113, 126, 133, 140. None of these three workmen survived the final conquest of Tenochtitlán.

[5] AGI, Patronato 57–1–1, fols. 5, 9, 16r, 17r (testimony, 1528); translation in AU–CC, Martín López 1528–1574, pp. 14, 27, 51, 54.

[6] AGI, Patronato 57–1–1, fol. 27r (testimony, 1534); translation in AU–CC, Martín López 1528–1574, p. 84.

least 200 gold pesos for services rendered in connection with the brigantines, because he personally had sawed and prepared all of the timber used in the construction of the four ships. Such an obviously extravagant claim of work performed was deflated by one of Hernández' own witnesses, sawyer Sebastián Rodríguez. The latter, while asserting that Diego Hernández had helped, upon orders from Cortés, to saw all the timber, insisted that he, Rodríguez, was in charge of the sawing of the timber for all four vessels and, in fact, had taught the previously unskilled Diego Hernández how to perform that labor.[7] Andrés Núñez, carpenter, is still another of the identifiable craftsmen who worked on the four small ships.[8] The total number of Spanish workmen who assisted the master shipwright cannot be established.

The garrulous old infantryman Bernal Díaz throws considerably more light upon the construction of these earliest vessels than does Captain-general Cortés. He is, however, distinctly in error when he asserts that only two brigantines were constructed.[9] He it is who informs us that Cortés, following the death of Juan de Escalante, sent Alonso de Grado to the coastal garrison at Villa Rica de Vera Cruz with instructions to forward to Tenochtitlán at once two heavy chains which two blacksmiths who had remained at Vera Cruz had been commissioned to make from the anchors and ironwork of the vessels that had been destroyed on the Gulf coast.

[7] UC–CC, Documents Relating to Various Suits, 86, 93 (interrogatory and testimony, 1530). Documents connected with Diego Hernández' suit serve to clarify a confusion of names resulting from Martín López' action of 1528 against Cortés. In the 1528 document two men bearing the name Pero [Pedro] Hernández appear as witnesses, the one a carpenter, the other a blacksmith. The legal action by carpenter Diego Hernández serves to indicate that in the written record of 1528 his name was stated incorrectly. In all instances, accordingly, the writer refers to the carpenter as Diego Hernández.

[8] BDdelC, I, 386. At times he is referred to as Alonso Núñez.

[9] Ibid., 381, 386. The comparative fullness of Bernal Díaz' reference to the first brigantines has led later writers to lean heavily upon him, e.g., Prescott, Mexico, II, 166, 171; Orozco y Berra, Historia antigua, IV, 328; and Bartolomé Juan Leonardo de Argensola, Primera Parte de los Anales de Aragón que prosigue los del Secretario Gerónimo Curita desde el año MDXVI, del Nacimento de Nº. Redentor, in Conquista de México, ed. Joaquín Ramírez Cabañas, 191. All mistakenly state that only two brigantines were built.

When Alonso de Grado failed to comply with the orders Cortés had given him, Gonzalo de Sandoval was dispatched to the port area with instructions that he immediately send to the island-capital not only the desired chains but also sails, tackle, pitch, tow, a mariner's compass, and everything else that would assist in the project of the brigantine construction.[10] (The smallness of Lake Texcoco precluded the prospect of any navigational problems that would dictate the need of a compass. However, because of his own half-knowledge of nautical matters at this time and his burning desire to get everything that might be useful at his fingertips, plus his early ignorance of the real extent of these inland waters, Cortés may well be excused for including the compass in the list of supplies. It is possible, too, that he might have intended using the compass in connection with land operations, as he did in established fact do several years later during the overland trip to Honduras.)[11] In addition, two blacksmiths, quite possibly the above-mentioned Hernán Martín and Pedro Hernández, with their tools, bellows, and some of the miscellaneous iron salvaged from the Cuban ships, were to join Cortés in Tenochtitlán and assist in the building of the brigantines. Cortés did not ask for the total supply of any of these materials, but seemingly just enough to meet his immediate needs at Tenochtitlán. Villa Rica de la Vera Cruz, continuing as the repository of salvaged nautical equipment, was an important point of supply for subsequent shipbuilding as well.

Sandoval complied with the orders, and before long Indian bearers brought the desired supplies into Tenochtitlán. Only when Cortés had those building materials on hand did he, according to Bernal Díaz, tell Montezuma that he wished to build some ships and ask for the help of native carpenters. The logic of this statement by Bernal Díaz is open to question—why wait until the nautical supplies arrived before even beginning to cut the timbers? Given the urgent need of shipping, plus the fact that none of the coastal supplies were required in the earliest stages of construction, one suspects that the earlier work on timbers had actually occurred

---

[10] *BDdelC*, I, 378–381.   [11] *HC*, II, 146, 159.

while the salvaged supplies were still en route. The pattern of subsequent shipbuilding supports this line of reasoning.

Montezuma was asked to send his native carpenters, along with Martín López and Andrés Núñez, to cut the required wood. Four leagues distant a suitable stand of oak was found and exploited. Such a distance would indicate that the stand of timber was in the Valley of Mexico, probably on one of the mountain slopes that edged the valley. Although the precise location of the exploited timber cannot be ascertained, Mora inclines toward the belief that the cedars of Tacuba and the harder timbers on the slopes of Ixtaccihuatl and Telapón were used. The then plentiful supply of oak to the east of Texcoco might also have been used.[12] Within a very brief interval, timbers were being transported into the city for the necessary sawing, shaping, and assembling operations. The division of labor between the natives and the Spanish carpenters is open to speculation. It is probable, again in the light of the subsequent construction of the thirteen brigantines, that the Indians felled the trees and did the preliminary dressing of the timbers, readying them for transportation by Indian bearers, and that the Spanish carpenters performed the more skilled operations—the measuring, sawing, fitting, and fastening of the timbers.

In the course of an interrogatory connected with his suit of 1528 against Cortés, Martín López asserted that these first four brigantines were constructed at his own expense. None of the sixteen witnesses called by López in support of his contention disputed that statement and several gave it warm and specific support. The shipwright added that his expenses had totaled 2,000 gold pesos. Workers and nonworkers alike testified that the shipwright deserved such a sum, though whether the payment was considered as simple reimbursement or as remuneration well deserved for services rendered is not clear. Diego Ramírez, a carpenter who, though not employed on the first four brigantines, worked on the thirteen vessels of 1520–1521, asserted that López deserved to be paid be-

---

[12] Ignacio de Mora y Villamil, "Elementos para la marina," *BSMGE*, 1ª época, Vol. IX (1862), 301; and Pomar, *Relación de Tezcoco*, in *NCDHM*, III, 60.

cause, owing to the brigantines, the Indians did not dare to rebel. One cannot help but wonder how generally such appreciation of the military and psychological significance of the completed ships prevailed among the men of Cortés, for Ramírez was not alone in giving expression to such sentiments.[13]

Even as he stated that the vessels were built at his own expense, Martín López informed the court that each one measured between twenty-five and twenty-six cubits in length, which specifications were corroborated by workman Gómez de Herrera.[14] With the cubit reckoned at eighteen inches, each vessel measured between thirty-seven and one-half and thirty-nine feet in length. It is curious that such precise information should turn up concerning four little-known vessels, whereas in more than four centuries of relatively persistent research equivalent information has never been disclosed for the trio of ships made famous by Columbus' discovery of America.[15] With this the only measurement available, it is impossible to establish the general over-all dimensions, but certain additional information does help us sharpen the image of the vessels as cast up in the mind's eye.

In Cortés' report to the Crown on the subject, it was recorded that the four ships were capable of transporting three hundred men and all the horses. If all ships were the same size each would presumably transport seventy-five men and three or four horses. Bernal Díaz adds that four bronze cannon were mounted in the vessels,[16] presumably one in the prow of each brigantine. The ships quite probably were broad of beam: they were propelled by oars

[13] AGI, Patronato 57–1–1, fols. 3, 4, 6r, 7r, 8 (interrogatory and testimony, 1528); translation in AU–CC, Martín López 1528–1574, pp. 6–7, 10, 19, 23, 25.

[14] AGI, Patronato 57–1–1, fols. 3, 17r (interrogatory and testimony, 1528); translation in AU–CC, Martín López 1528–1574, pp. 6–7, 54. Incidentally, the phrasing of the document does not make clear whether this measurement is for the keel or the over-all length.

[15] Samuel Eliot Morison, *Admiral of the Ocean Sea—a Life of Christopher Columbus*, I, xliv, note 8, and 151–152. Morison's techniques, as he tries to reconstruct the tonnage of Columbian craft, would be even less admissible in reference to these brigantines, which were designed to operate under unusual rather than normal circumstances.

[16] *BDdelC*, I, 389.

as well as by sail; the waters for which they had been designed were extremely shallow; and the aforementioned loads they might be called upon to carry called for width.

The time spent in construction, according to the master shipwright himself, was upwards of five months. Most of the witnesses who expressed themselves on the subject in the course of López' legal action of 1528 against Cortés felt the time consumed was somewhat less than five months. Alvar López, another carpenter who seemingly witnessed the shipbuilding but did not assist in it, asserted that the project consumed approximately four months, and Melchor de Alabes and Juan Ramos de Lares, co-workers on the brigantines, joined him in that estimate.[17] The shorter time seems closer to the truth, because it must be remembered that during the seven and one-half months between initial entry into Tenochtitlán on November 8, 1519, and expulsion on June 30, 1520, Martín López, in addition to building the four brigantines at Tenochtitlán, was ordered to build a caravel on the Gulf coast, on which a large percentage of the work had been completed before operations were suspended when shipping was acquired with the arrival and defeat of Narváez.

The second problem thrust upon Cortés by the brigantine project, namely, the camouflaging of the real motivation behind their construction, was handled adroitly. The Aztec ruler knew of the large ships in which the Spaniards had landed upon the coast; and he entertained, in addition, certain beliefs concerning the return of the god Quetzalcoatl. All of this could well have established a consuming interest on his part in the ships of the white men. Capitalizing upon the combination of knowledge and superstition feeding the curiosity of Montezuma, the pattern of pretense to be followed easily unraveled itself for use by the Spaniards. Cortés informed Montezuma that the projected vessels were intended for pleasure trips on the lake, and indeed they were put to that use as soon as they were finished. Construction proceeded; the vessels

---

[17] AGI, Patronato 57–1–1, fols. 3, 4r, 6r, 8 (interrogatory and testimony, 1528); translation in AU–CC, Martín López 1528–1574, pp. 6, 12, 19, 25.

were built and calked, rigging was set up, sails were cut, cannons mounted, and oars fashioned. Banners were fixed to the mastheads, and sailors were trained to maneuver the vessels. Tests indicated the vessels operated efficiently under oars, under sails, and under the combination of oars and sails. Cortés was well pleased.[18]

Earlier, however, Cortés had been displeased. Not long after the Spaniards and their native allies—chiefly Tlaxcalans—had entered Tenochtitlán, extreme uneasiness had beset the mind of the Spanish commander. Fearful that his small force, engulfed as it was by three hundred thousand people in Tenochtitlán, might not be able to extricate itself if relations between hosts and guests deteriorated, Cortés had gained a measure of security for himself and his followers by a most daring course of action. One day Cortés and a small group went to Montezuma's palace and quietly kidnaped their host. The Spaniards let it be known he would not be harmed but that he could not have freedom of movement and positively could not leave them. Thus the ruler of millions of people was held hostage by a bare handful of men whom he had invited into his capital, men whose lives depended upon his good will. Until his death months later, Montezuma remained the prisoner of the Spaniards, a circumstance which guaranteed two things: Mexican hostility, yet Spanish survival in spite of it.

On occasion Montezuma and certain of his courtiers had opportunity to see the brigantines in action. Given permission by his jailer, Cortés, to cross the lake toward the southeast to engage in some hunting on a royal preserve on the Peñón de Tepepolco,

---

[18] BDdelC, I, 389. Francisco Flores, who prior to coming to New Spain had successively engaged in the conquests of Puerto Rico, Jamaica, and Cuba, asserted that he was in charge of the first two brigantines that were built. Oddly enough Flores knew no subsequent identification with brigantines, either in construction or operation, for he served in the Pedro de Alvarado division based at Tacuba during the final siege of the island-city; see MN–PyTT, Leg. 94, Información de los méritos y servicios de Francisco Flores (1526).

Bancroft, apparently leaning on Martyr, refers to "tiers of oars," thereby conjuring up a vessel reminiscent of either the naval units of Greece and Rome or the galleys of sixteenth-century Europe; see Mexico, I, 326.

Montezuma was able to note the superiority of the brigantines over the swiftest canoes of his finest warriors. Several of the principal Spaniards, including Pedro de Alvarado and Cristóbal de Olid, and a company of some two hundred soldiers accompanied Montezuma and his retinue on the brigantines. Gunners Mesa and Arvenga further impressed the Indians by discharging the cannons as the vessels sped over the surface of the lake. Closing his coverage of this matter, Bernal Díaz states that Montezuma was charmed by the Spaniards' clever combination of sail and oar.[19] Charmed seems scarcely the word for it, since the size, speed, maneuverability, and fire power demonstrated by the brigantines must have struck unquenchable fears into the mind of any thinking Indian.

The brigantines ranged over the waters of the lake for several months during the spring of 1520. No details are available concerning the exact duties they were assigned. But it seems logical to assume that the vessels made reconnaissances of the entire lake area, gleaning information that was invaluable in later siege operations against the island-city, and thus preparing security for the future. It goes without saying that the ships gave the Spaniards a feeling of immediate security.

Meanwhile, earlier in 1520, during the same months that saw Martín López and his men laboring hard to complete the four brigantines which were intended to make the Spanish military position secure, the Mexicans had begun to contract the show of hospitality with which they had initially ushered the warrior strangers into the city. And as the powerless position of Montezuma in his role of hostage-puppet in the hands of the Spaniards became more and more apparent even to the man in the street, hospitality gave way entirely before the Indians' fears and rising hatred.

Finally the captive Montezuma reported to Cortés the increasingly ugly temper of the populace, informing him that the Indians wanted to rise and expel the Spaniards from the country. Thanking his royal captive for the information, Cortés indicated he was

[19] *BDdelC*, I, 371–378, 382–387, 389–390.

troubled by the fact that he and his men could not sail back toward the rising sun because they had no ships at their disposal on the Gulf coast. Hinting thus that with more shipping the Spaniards could be expected to effect a withdrawal from the Aztec domain, Cortés hurried to put two requests to Montezuma—he wanted order maintained in Tenochtitlán, and he wanted shipping on the Gulf coast. To achieve both ends he needed the continued co-operation of Montezuma.[20]

In the absence of precise statements by Cortés, one can only surmise what his intentions were at this time. Did he want Montezuma, through the priests and chieftains, to snuff out the flame of restlessness within the native population so that, in time, pessimism and docility might set in and enable the Spaniards to control the nation all the more easily and completely? If this was in his mind, Cortés certainly did not intend to withdraw from the country but hoped, with time as an ally, to become undisputed master of it. Under such circumstances Cortés' interest in ship construction must be judged subterfuge pure and simple. Such a ruse could not be maintained for long, because Montezuma, having observed the rapidity with which Martín López and his workmen had built the four brigantines, knew well that ships could be readied in a relatively short time. The very meagerness of the number of ships projected on the coast inclines one all the more to stamp this program as planned deceit.

Bernal Díaz, who was not a party to this construction but had an opportunity to get close to it and possibly hear about it while accompanying Cortés on the expedition eastward to meet Narváez and his men, stated that three ships were to be built.[21] However,

---

[20] Ibid., 421–422. Cortés, in his letters to his sovereign, fails to mention the inauguration of this new shipbuilding venture.

[21] Ibid., 422. On this point Orozco y Berra follows Bernal Díaz; see Historia antigua, IV, 351. Bancroft, in Mexico, I, 356, is another who accepts three as the number. López de Gómara, without stating a number, indicated that ships were needed; see Historia, I, 274. Herrera, relying on the account of Cortés' chaplain at this point, is likewise vague; see Historia general, I, Part II, 223–224. Such early

most available information indicates that only one vessel, a caravel, was projected. In a document executed August 20, 1520, in Tepeaca, no fewer than nine men testified that a single ship had been ordered built.[22] In a second document executed shortly thereafter, on September 4, 1520, in the town of Segura de la Frontera, the interrogatory itself, as well as a number of the statements of testimony, emphasized that but one vessel had been ordered by Cortés.[23] Later still, in the course of Martín López' litigation with Cortés over the matter of services rendered during the conquest, additional evidence appeared to support the contention that just one ship had been ordered built on the Gulf coast.[24] At the time this vessel was ordered, Cortés' original expeditionary force had not known as yet any serious depletion of its ranks. Accordingly, the captain-general, whose manpower had required a dozen vessels between Cuba and the mainland, scarcely could have entertained the idea of evacuating his force from New Spain in a single ship. Reaching such a conclusion, however, does not remove every question.

---

writers as Sahagún and Cervantes de Salazar make no mention of this shipbuilding episode.

[22] G. R. G. Conway (ed.), *La Noche Triste: Documentos: Segura de la Frontera en Nueva España, año de MDXX*, 15, 20, 23, 25, 27, 29, 31, 32, 34. Those who so testified were: Bernardino Vázquez de Tapia, Gonzalo Alvarado, Cristóbal Corral, Fray Bartolomé de Olmedo, Gerónimo de Aguilar, Juan Rodríguez de Villafuerte, Diego de Ordás, Alonso Dávila, and Juan Díaz.

[23] *Ibid.*, 47, 54, 57, 60, 63, 66, 69. Of six witnesses so testifying, four (Alonso de Benavides, Juan Ochoa de Lexalde, Pedro Sánchez Farfan, and Cristóbal de Olid) were not among the witnesses of August 20, while the other two, Diego de Ordás and Gerónimo de Aguilar, were repeating themselves, already having so replied on the earlier occasion.

[24] AGI, Patronato 57–1–1, fols. 3–3r, 4, 5r, 6, 6r, 7r–8, 9, 9r, 13, 14, 15, 15r–16, 16r, 17r (interrogatory and testimony, 1528), 18–19, 20r–22, 24, 25–25r, 27–28r, 30, 31–31r, 33–34r, 36–37r, 39–40, 43r–45, 46r–47r (interrogatory and testimony, 1534); translation in AU–CC, Martín López 1528–1574, pp. 7–8, 10–11, 15, 17, 19–20, 23–24, 27–28, 29, 40–41, 43, 46, 49, 51–52, 54–55, 57, 59, 60, 65–66, 67–68, 69, 74–75, 77–78, 83–84, 86, 87, 92–93, 94, 95, 101, 103, 104, 109, 111–112, 117, 118–120, 129–130, 131, 132, 136–137, 139; and LC–CC, Martín López 1529–1550, pp. 118–119, 125–126, 134–135, 141, 148–149, 155, 162 (interrogatory and testimony, 1540).

Was the construction of the vessel mere subterfuge to satisfy the not-too-nautical-minded Montezuma? Or did the single ship actually have a purpose for being? In the late summer of 1520, as the Spanish commander garnered witnesses and testimony to buttress his contention that he had been diligent in his concern about the royal treasure, the planned use for which the one caravel had been designed was made apparent. Cortés had not sent the treasure to the Crown earlier because he was without any vessels; the ship put on the ways near Vera Cruz was to transport the royal treasure across the Atlantic.[25]

Whatever the motives behind the ship's construction, Cortés, even as he asked Montezuma for Indian assistance, turned for a second time to shipwright Martín López. The master craftsman discloses that following the completion of the four brigantines he was ordered to depart with his tools for the forests of Orizaba. It is presumed the forests of Orizaba were on the slopes of the majestic mountain of the same name, and logic would have dictated the exploitation of the eastern slope because of its nearness to the Gulf coast. There he was to cut the required timber for a caravel, the length of which was scheduled to be forty-two feet (twenty-eight cubits). This ocean-going ship was to be but a trifle longer than the newly completed Lake Texcoco brigantines. Once the framework had been shaped and the planks sawed, all the ship's timbers were to be transported to the coast, for final assembly in the vicinity of Vera Cruz.

In contrast to the just completed brigantines, the caravel seems to have had surprisingly few Spaniards identified with it as workmen. Numerous explanations may be advanced: possibly the assisting Indian labor could contribute more of the skilled work because of the experience gained on the four brigantines; possibly the shipwright had been instructed to turn to the coastal garrison for his labor supply; possibly the assignment of a small number of Spaniards to the project was deliberate, to assure construction delays

[25] Conway (ed.), *La Noche Triste*, 9, 15, 20, 23, 25, 27, 29, 31–34, 54, 57, 60, 63, 66, 69.

which Cortés could use as an excuse for the failure of the conquistadors to withdraw speedily from the mainland; and possibly the
whole matter may be due to the continued obscurity of pertinent
records. We also are not told how many Indians accompanied
López, nor do we know whether they were from the Aztec Confederation or from Tlaxcala.

The herculean nature of the undertaking before shipwright
López is apparent when we take stock of the problems facing him.
Complete responsibility was thrust upon him, with Cortés and his
captains remaining in Tenochtitlán. No military patrol or guard
accompanied the handful of workmen; the consequent feeling of
insecurity and aloneness in native-dominated areas could scarcely
have contributed to their peace of mind, and without the compul-
sion that Spanish military power, even in a small unit, represented
to the natives the entire problem of daily procurement of foodstuffs
must have been greatly complicated. The new vessel was to be of
seagoing proportions and larger than any of the four brigantines.
The magnitude of the task of transporting the ship's materials from
forest to coast would in itself have taxed the capacity of even the
most thoroughly demonstrated leader of men. One can only conclude that the four brigantines had pleased Cortés so completely
that he now counted on López not only as an ingenious artisan but
as a leader who could surmount all obstacles.

Following orders, Martín López proceeded to the designated
forest area, cut the timbers, and sawed them up into the necessary
framework and planking for the projected caravel. Once those
operations were completed, Indian bearers transported the materials down to a point on the coast, which López designated as the
site for his shipyard. Statements of several conquistadors, that they
had seen some of the timbers intended for the caravel afloat in the
Cempoala River, hint that at least some of the arduous movement
of the timber from mountain slope forest to coastal shipbuilding site
might have been by water. Next the fitting of the pieces was undertaken. As this stage of the work got underway, it is evident that
additional Spaniards helped the shipwright; Rodrigo de Nájara, for

instance, stated that he had helped Martín López to set up the stern post and the bow of the vessel. Work on the caravel continued until suspended upon Cortés' own order.[26]

In the spring of 1520, while Hernando Cortés and hundreds of his men were in Tenochtitlán and Martín López and a handful of men were trying to complete a caravel on the coast, a new and decisive chapter of the conquest was in process. The first person in Tenochtitlán to learn that still more strangers had landed on the coast was Montezuma. As previously, the oral reports brought back to him by his messengers were supplemented by drawings of the ships. Passing this word on to Cortés, Montezuma indicated that with these ships the Spaniards could easily make their promised withdrawal from his land. Cortés' uncertainty about what was happening a couple of hundred miles to the east quickly dissolved when a Spanish messenger reached him with word that Pánfilo de Narváez, heading an expedition of eighteen ships and more than a thousand men, had landed near San Juan de Ulúa.

The Narváez expedition, with orders from Velázquez to seize the rebellious Cortés and then continue the conquest, had been conceived in the autumn of 1519. When Cortés had designated Puertocarrero and Montejo as the agents to present his case to the Crown and assigned them a ship for the trip to Spain just before he destroyed his Cuban fleet, he had ordered them to go direct to Spain. However, for a combination of reasons, the two men saw fit to violate his instructions by stopping briefly on Cuba en route to the home country. That brief disobedience served to acquaint Velázquez with two facts: Mexico was rich, and Cortés was rebellious. At once the irate sponsor of the Cortés venture set to forming a still larger expedition to chasten Cortés and keep the conquest of Mexico under Cuban control. Command of this fourth Velázquez-inspired expedition to the mainland was vested in tall, ruddy-

---

[26] AGI, Patronato 57–1–1, fols. 3, 4, 5r, 7r–8 (interrogatory and testimony, 1528); translation in AU–CC, Martín López 1528–1574, pp. 7, 10, 15, 23.

complexioned Pánfilo de Narváez, a man whose military talents had been demonstrated amply in the conquest of Cuba itself. Sailing from Cuba with his massive flotilla in March, 1520, Narváez reached the vicinity of San Juan de Ulúa—and Cortés' coastal garrison—in late April. Then it was that words and pictures told Montezuma and Cortés of the arrival of more Spaniards.

Once again Montezuma sent presents eastward to the bearded strangers on his coast. Simultaneously Cortés' very able garrison commander on the coast, Sandoval, sent still more information to the captain-general. With early May came a series of events which greatly affected the future. Narváez sent agents to Sandoval demanding the surrender of his garrison force. Sandoval replied by seizing the Narváez agents—one was a churchman—and speedily transporting them to Tenochtitlán. Firsthand, Cortés learned much about Narváez and his men. Adroitly he won at least some of the prisoners over with kind words, promises of wealth, and the like, and having done so he released them. Their return to Narváez' camp was the first wave of Cortés' propaganda campaign, augmented by Fray Olmedo, whom Cortés sent from his Tenochtitlán force to talk with Narváez. Though failing to win the leader over, Fray Olmedo did gain support among numerous of Narváez' captains. Another blow was thus dealt the unity of Narváez' force.

By mid-May Cortés had decided it was absolutely necessary to proceed to the coast to deal with the threat posed by Narváez. The decision to go could not have been an easy or a happy one—it was surely a lesser of evils proposition at best. If Cortés did not go to the coast, he might well expect Narváez to defeat whatever small forces were stationed other than in Tenochtitlán, after which Narváez would surely proceed toward the capital. The ultimate contest between them, merely postponed, would then likely draw the embittered Mexicans into the fray and all would be lost for Cortés and his men. Better by far the idea that Cortés take the offensive and meet Narváez on the coast at once. Yet the thought of leaving Tenochtitlán and taking some of the limited Spanish manpower with him was a disturbing one. Already the Indians were increasingly restive. What would happen in Cortés' absence, while a smaller Spanish force tried to remain secure in Montezuma's capital? No one knew, but Cortés had to make a decision. And with the decision to face Narváez immediately, came the collateral decision to leave Pedro de Alvarado in command in Tenochtitlán, with considerably fewer than two hundred Spaniards.

Accompanied by even fewer men than he left with Alvarado, Cortés set out for the coast. After the coastal garrison manpower led by Sandoval was added to the force, as well as other Spanish elements here and there in the countryside, the expedition still totaled no more than two hundred and sixty men. It was at this moment, in dire need of every additional fighter he could muster, that Cortés ordered the suspension of the caravel project. Why bother about one ship anyway, now that eighteen ships were on the coast! So Martín López and his crew laid aside their tools and, seizing their weapons, joined Cortés' small army.[27]

The never-to-be-completed caravel on which the shipbuilders were turning their backs might seem to be utterly meaningless in the historical record; yet it was actually a precedent-making preliminary to the significant shipbuilding venture inaugurated later the same year. The affair of the caravel presented many features which were to be duplicated in the subsequent building of the thirteen brigantines. Martín López had demonstrated not only his capacity for doing a complex job without supervision but also his own supervisory ability. Precedent was established for a work force of a small number of Spaniards, aided by an indefinite number of natives, to sustain themselves and satisfy all their wants during a lengthy undertaking in the field apart from the main body of Spanish soldiers. Precedent was established, too, for the long, tedious operation involved in the overland transportation of ship's timbers.

The caravel of 1520 is in itself unimportant. But since the Spanish

[27] BDdelC, II, 9–37; HC, I, 111–120; Bancroft, Mexico, I, 357–381; and Wagner, Cortés, 266–273.

force was soon to lose the temporary naval power represented by the four brigantines on the lake and then suffer tremendous personnel losses in the withdrawal from Tenochtitlán, it would become increasingly evident that definitive victory inevitably would demand the creation of greater Spanish naval power on the inland waters. It is in the light of that handwriting on the wall presaging events of 1520–1521 that the caravel construction is brought into proper perspective, for without the backlog of experience this episode represented for Martín López and his fellow-workmen, overwhelming uncertainty might have attended Spanish military prospects in New Spain.

With native auxiliaries, the Spaniards from Tenochtitlán, the garrison force, and shipbuilders from the coast, Cortés was ready to proceed against Narváez. Once more diplomacy came to the fore as the two Spanish commanders consumed some days in moving delegations and demands between the two camps. The magnet of the gold Cortés and his followers knew about, plus the captain-general's threat that untold hordes of natives were soon to join forces with him, increasingly stole the loyalty of Narváez' men from their leader. Finally Cortés decided upon a quick nighttime showdown battle. Shortly after midnight on May 28, Cortés attacked and quickly demoralized the camp of the enemy. The early erroneous hue and cry, "Narváez is dead," did much to speed the surrender of the larger force. With the dawn of May 28, 1520, Cortés, victorious, had effected the union of the two armies.[28]

Scarcely had the complexion of things improved for Cortés on the coast when word came down from Tenochtitlán that all was not well with the Spaniards there. In a difficult position, and something less than the leader Cortés was, Alvarado had been a party to the rapid deterioration in Indian-Spanish relationships which set in soon after Cortés departed. When the handful of Spaniards in Tenochtitlán had seen fit to interfere, with armed might, in the

---

[28] *BDdelC*, II, 37–63; *HC*, I, 120–126; Bancroft, *Mexico*, I, 382–398; and Wagner, *Cortés*, 273–277.

conduct of certain Aztec religious festival activities, bitter fighting ensued. The angry Indians cut off the flow of provisions to Alvarado and his men. Under such circumstances it was imperative that Cortés be notified. Amid the gloomy news the messenger brought to Cortés was word that the Mexicans had destroyed the four brigantines. Cortés recorded the situation in a letter to his monarch in these words: "Our people had been in much trouble and danger. . . . In the fight, the Indians had captured a great part of the provisions I had left them, and had burned my four brigantines."[29]

Leaving the defeated Narváez a prisoner in the Vera Cruz garrison, Cortés combined the late opposing armies and headed west for trouble-torn Tenochtitlán. At midday on June 24 the capital of the Aztecs was re-entered. Even though Cortés returned to Tenochtitlán with a force that more than doubled his original army in the city, it could not have been a lighthearted entry, for the conquistadors no longer dominated the lake. With the reduced food supplies rapidly dwindling, with his force subjected to siege by the Indians, Cortés knew that he and his army—now that they were without the brigantines—were like so many rats in a trap.

Out of tactical realism and physical desperation the Spaniards tried to rehabilitate some of the shipping. In the few days between the return of Cortés to Tenochtitlán and the disastrous withdrawal of the night of June 30—days of increasing pressure from the maddened Mexicans—an abortive effort was made to resurrect the lost naval power. Francisco Rodríguez testified in 1528 that he had seen one of the half-burned vessels raised, but that the idea of reconstructing it could not be carried out because the Indians routed the Spaniards.[30]

[29] HC–MacN, I, 285.
[30] AGI, Patronato 57–1–1, fol. 14 (testimony, 1528); translation in AU–CC, Martín López 1528–1574, p. 43.

The Sad Night

The shaky position of the Spaniards in Tenochtitlán utterly disintegrated during the week following Cortés' return to the capital. Seemingly in an effort to patch up the strained relations between the Mexican emperor and himself, Cortés released a prominent hostage, Montezuma's brother Cuitlahuac. A vigorous enemy of the invaders, Cuitlahuac then hastened to call the native council into session, and that body deposed Montezuma and named Cuitlahuac the new ruler. With the hostage Montezuma no longer a curb upon the Mexicans, the Spanish position was immeasurably worse because of Cortés' action.

On June 25, less than twenty-four hours after Cortés' arrival from the coast, the Spaniards were attacked. That day they suffered between eighty and ninety casualties. The next day they could count an additional sixty to seventy dead and wounded men. Such a rate of attrition had to be stopped.

On June 27, while the Spanish manpower was kept within quarters, some of it being occupied with the construction of three armored battle chariots which were to press tank-like tactics of attack and demolition within the city, the howling Mexicans attacked with weapons and words. In the midst of the resultant bedlam, and most probably at Spanish insistence, Montezuma mounted a wall and tried to quiet his countrymen. With the same hatred and invective and weapons they had been directing at the invaders, the mob-maddened natives now turned upon their late ruler. Repeatedly hit by stones, Montezuma fell so badly wounded that death came three days later.

On June 28 the Spanish-made wooden war machines took the offensive. Accompanied by 3,000 of the ever-faithful Tlaxcalan allies, the strangely armed and armored Spanish force seemed intent upon securing positions that would facilitate an early withdrawal from the city over the Tacuba causeway. After a half day of bitter struggle, however, the invaders returned to their quarters, defeated. Meanwhile the Mexicans brought the war still closer to

the Spaniards by seizing a pyramidal shrine opposite Cortés' fortified position, and the Spaniards were able to retake that key point
from the natives only at the end of four bitterly contested assaults.
When Cortés directed an appeal to the Mexicans, their reply was to
the effect that they intended to fight until they had rid themselves
of the unwanted foreigners. Embittered, Cortés retaliated by burning a swath of three hundred houses on one street that night.

By the last three days of June the Spanish captain-general was
preparing for the inevitable evacuation. Certain of the men were
assigned to build a portable bridge, a necessity for rapid movement over a causeway. Meanwhile a combined battle and work
force sallied forth, once again with the armored war machines, to
prepare the avenue of retreat. On one occasion four of the eight
water breaches on the route to Tacuba were seized and filled. But
by the return of the Spaniards the next day to continue the work,
the Mexicans had removed the rubble. When next the breaches
were filled, guards were left to protect the gains. On June 30, with
the portable bridge and the route in as favorable condition as could
be expected and the position of the invaders in the city scarcely a
tenable one, Cortés knew it was time to retreat.

The order of march was established. The vanguard was to be led
by Sandoval and Ordás; Cortés, Olid, and others would command
the vulnerable, miscellaneous middle section; and Alvarado and
Velázquez de León led the rear guard. A select group was charged
with the care and operation of the portable bridge. Provision was
made for the transportation of the share of the treasure reserved
for the Spanish Crown; orders were given regarding the care of
long-held hostages who were being taken from the city. And the
rank and file of the Spanish force received permission to take whatever any man wanted from the pile of treasure that still remained.[31]

The maneuver of retreat was planned as a rapid and complete
disengagement from the enemy, and not as a slow, bitterly contested withdrawal. The narrowness of the causeway and the water

[31] *BDdelC*, II, 73–87; *HC*, I, 129–140; Salvador de Madariaga, *Hernán Cortés,
Conqueror of Mexico*, 335–343; and Wagner, *Cortés*, 293–299.

hazards posed by the sites from which the usual bridges had been removed made it utterly impossible for the cavalry to figure as a military asset in the operation. That the water neutralized the vaunted power of the horsemen is evident in Cortés' own statement that he had originally planned to remove all the horses via the brigantines. Meanwhile the extreme speed with which the movement had to be effected to be successful eliminated the prospect of effective use of the artillery. Understanding the neutralization of Cortés' cavalry and artillery as fighting effectives by such limitations in space and time, one more readily comprehends the timetable established for the withdrawal.

The night of June 30–July 1, 1520, was dark, cloudy, and rainy.[32] In the daylight hours immediately preceding the withdrawal, Cortés had undertaken a hurried last-minute reconnaissance of the total route to be traversed as he and a small body of horsemen pushed their way to the mainland and back again. The riders had experienced difficulty even then with the breaks in the causeway. Shortly before midnight the signal was given and the swift but stealthy movement got underway.

As the force made its way from the center of the city toward the Tacuba causeway, the engineers—for such we might well designate the corps assigned to the handling of the portable bridge— led the way. The first opening in the causeway, Tecpantzingo, was bridged. And here the bridge jammed and could not be moved after the infantry, cavalry, artillery, bearers of booty, and hostages and their custodians had passed over it.

Inferentially, at least, many writers treating this point suggest that had the bridge not become stuck the retreat would have been successful, with minimal losses by the Spaniards and their allies. Such reasoning is to be questioned. The fact that the Spaniards possessed only one portable bridge was in itself a handicap of im-

---

[32] *BDdelC*, II, 88. Orozco y Berra blames the rain and darkness for the Spanish defeat; see *Historia antigua*, IV, 454. The apologist of Cortés, also second-guessing, expresses the view that a daytime withdrawal would have resulted in fewer casualties for the Spaniards; see López de Gómara, *Historia*, I, 312.

measurable magnitude. Even if the bridge had not jammed at the very outset, it must be remembered that the total Spanish and allied Indian force, possibly numbering between four thousand and eight thousand in all, could move forward only in jerky, impeded leaps. While the center of the retreating column and the rear guard were crossing the bridge, the vanguard would have been forced to a grinding halt at the next watercourse. Then while the bridge was being removed from that location and carried forward over the already crowded causeway to the next point at which it was needed, the thousands of men would be so immobilized as to be sitting ducks for the attacking hordes of Indians, who manned canoes and harassed the flanks of the retreating column every inch of the way along the causeway. It is difficult to understand why the Spaniards believed that one portable bridge would suffice. Yet one must readily admit that construction of as many portable bridges as there were possible points at which they might be needed was probably beyond their capacity, given the shortages of time, materials, and skilled workmen that faced them in the last frantic, food-depleted days in Tenochtitlán. Nevertheless, had a program of multiple bridges been adopted and carried out—with the successive waves of engineers out in front of all the rest—it is likely that the speed and surprise which were conceived as major ingredients of the entire operation would have succeeded to such a degree that the event would not have gone into the record as the Sad Night.

Meanwhile the vanguard, led to expect the reappearance of the portable bridge, had halted at the edge of the Tolteacalli opening. At this point amid the crowding and confusion that attended the crossing of the water, of which the enemy took full and active advantage, there occurred the greatest slaughter Spanish forces were subjected to at any one moment in the entire conquest of Mexico. For those who escaped there were still other openings to be crossed ere the mainland could be gained, but the retreating force was better able to cope with the subsequent amphibious tests of its ingenuity and, in time, remnants began to straggle onto the mainland.

Both Cortés and Bernal Díaz wrote stirring accounts of the events of the night, and neither account can be read without an immediate appreciation of what enemy Indian domination of the waters of the lake contributed to the fateful outcome. The captain-general, in very few words, conjures up the frightful position in which his force, stripped of its naval power, found itself: "As there was water on both sides, they could assail us with impunity and fearlessly."[33] The more extended remarks of Bernal Díaz may well mirror the impressions of countless other foot soldiers in the ranks: "When I least expected it, we saw so many squadrons of warriors bearing down on us, and the lake so crowded with canoes that we could not defend ourselves. . . . As we went along the causeway, charging the Mexican squadrons, on one side of us was water and on the other azoteas [flat roof tops], and the lake was full of canoes so that we could do nothing." Although many years elapsed before he recorded his recollections of the events of those three or four hours, the hardened old warrior confessed that "to one who saw the hosts of warriors who fell on us that night and the canoes [full] of them coming along to carry off our soldiers, it was terrifying."[34] Both commander and common soldier acknowledged the might of the opposing naval power that was brought to bear upon them and their colleagues in arms.

Seldom in the recorded history of significant warfare can one find such naked helplessness as that evidenced by the retreating land force of Cortés in the presence of unchallengeable enemy naval strength.

[33] HC–MacN, I, 297.
[34] BDdelC–M, II, 244, 245, 246.

CHAPTER IV

The Beginning of the End

ALTHOUGH IT IS IMPOSSIBLE to determine with exactness the losses suffered during the withdrawal from Tenochtitlán,[1] the amount of influence this debacle had upon subsequent planning by Cortés can be appreciated only through recourse to the evidence, however conflicting that may be in matters of detail. Not long after the more fortunate of his followers had reached the comparative safety of the mainland and while they were pausing momentarily to rest, Cortés had his captains assist him in the compilation of a list of those who had been lost in the retreat. Whether or not this list, which may or may not have been written, survived the military operations of the conquest is not known. No writer of any period, past or present, has happened upon it. Yet the proof that such a list was constructed is well-nigh conclusive.[2]

The captain-general himself, reporting to his sovereign, indicated that 150 Spaniards, 45 horses and mares, and more than 2,000 Indian allies had been killed.[3] That this statement of losses sustained is decidedly on the conservative side is evident from the

[1] Orozco y Berra, attempting to resolve the impossible, presents a summary of the data offered by approximately a dozen different sources; see *Historia antigua,* IV, 455, note 1.

[2] LC–CC, Martín López 1529–1550, pp. 122, 130, 138, 145–146, 152–153, 159, 166 (interrogatory and testimony, 1540). Bernardino Vázquez de Tapia repeats himself in *Relación,* 42.

[3] *HC,* I, 142. MacNutt contributes to confusion by gratuitously inserting the word "over" before the number of Spaniards killed; see *HC–MacN,* I, 298.

86

document executed upon orders of Cortés in Tepeaca on August 20, 1520, less than two months after the events of the Sad Night. The tenth statement of the interrogatory, without being too precise, stated that more than 200 Spaniards and 56 out of a total of 80 horses and mares then in Spanish hands had been killed.[4] The reported loss of 70 per cent of all the horses poignantly indicates the disadvantage of horses and their riders in the peculiarly difficult physical setting of the retreat; one is struck by the utter futility of cavalry against Indians in canoes. The men in the canoes had bows and throwing spears; the men on horseback had swords and lances. The weapons of the canoe-borne Indians were effective at a distance, while those of the cavalrymen were absolutely impotent. Among the oddities that can be associated with Spanish warfare in the New World, cavalry victorious over naval units is definitely not one of them.

Herrera and Torquemada, the latter following the former, agree that 290 Spaniards and 4,000 Indian allies were lost.[5] Sahagún set the Spanish casualties at 300,[6] the number also contained in the Codex Ramírez.[7] Cortés' own principal apologist, López de Gómara, seemingly multiplies the captain-general's original figures by three as he states that 450 Spaniards and 4,000 Indian allies were lost on the Sad Night.[8] Diego Muñoz Camargo seems to follow López de Gómara at this point but permits further upward revision when he puts the words "more than" before the number 450.[9] According to Cervantes de Salazar the Spanish losses for the night were 600.[10] Martín López, in the course of a statement of his meritorious services during the conquest, indicated that approximately 800 men had been lost. Agreeing with him on that figure, as of 1540,

[4] Conway (ed.), *La Noche Triste,* 8.

[5] Herrera, *Historia general,* II, Part II, 270; and Torquemada, *Monarquia Indiana,* I, 503.

[6] Sahagún, *Historia* (1938), IV, 73.

[7] *Codex Ramírez,* in *Relación del origen de los indios que habitan esta Nueva España,* ed. Manuel Orozco y Berra, 116.

[8] López de Gómara, *Historia,* I, 312.

[9] Diego Muñoz Camargo, *Historia de Tlaxcala,* ed. Lauro Rosell, 236.

[10] Cervantes de Salazar, *Crónica,* 493.

were such conquistadors as Bernardino Vázquez de Tapia, Antonio Bravo, Andrés de Tapia, Andrés de Trujillo, and Diego Díaz.[11] The chronicler Bernal Díaz, lumping the losses during the evacuation of the island-stronghold with those occurring between Tenochtitlán and Tlaxcala, stated that more than 860 Spaniards died during that five-day period.[12] The heaviest report of losses is found in words of Juan Cano, who insisted that on the Sad Night and the subsequent march to Tlaxcala more than 1,170 Spaniards and more than 8,000 Indian allies were lost by Cortés.[13]

The foregoing representative statements clearly indicate that the losses suffered during the retreat from Tenochtitlán were excessively heavy, a fact that Cortés might well have hidden intentionally from the Crown. The testimony of such survivors of the ordeal as Martín López, Bernardino Vázquez de Tapia, Antonio Bravo, Andrés de Tapia, Andrés de Trujillo, Diego Díaz, and Bernal Díaz, agreeing in general terms that approximately 800 men, about 65 per cent of the total force, were lost on the Sad Night, leads us to accept that figure. Indian domination of the lake at the moment of the Spanish withdrawal had exacted a terrifying toll of a majority of the Spaniards, possibly as much as 70 per cent of the cavalry, and 100 per cent of the artillery. With artillery destroyed and infantry and cavalry so badly mauled in the engagement, the future demanded both a much-needed period of recuperation and a drastically different program of attack in any subsequent effort at reconquest.

Summer, 1520

Dating Cortés' decision that shipping would be required for the reconquest of Tenochtitlán is difficult. The astronomical losses his force had suffered must have written indelibly upon his

---

[11] LC–CC, Martín López 1529–1550, pp. 122, 130, 145–146, 152–153, 159 (interrogatory and testimony, 1540); MN–PyTT, Leg. 94, Información de los méritos y servicios de Diego y Francisco Díaz (1538, 1539). Vázquez de Tapia states (*Relación*, 42) that 425 survived from a Spanish force of 1,000–1,100 men.

[12] BDdelC, II, 97.

[13] Fernández de Oviedo, *Historia general y natural*, III, 551.

memory the vulnerability of his position on the causeway—his cavalry and artillery neutralized and his infantry harassed not only at the head and rear of the column but also on the flanks, owing to the Indian domination of the lake waters. The dramatic events of that one night might have conditioned Cortés' thinking so fundamentally that any plans for the reconquest of Tenochtitlán automatically and immediately included shipping.

One incident suggests that his plans for victory were taking shape at the time of his most decisive setback. Martín López records that as Cortés tabulated his losses on the night of retreat and defeat, the captain-general asked his officers if Martín López was among the living. When they replied that he was, Cortés was very pleased. Bernardino Vázquez de Tapia, recalling that he himself had witnessed the event, adds that Cortés did not make such personal inquiry about anyone else and clinches the significance inherent in Cortés' concern about Martín López as he remarks, "this witness is of the opinion that Our Lord inspired him [Cortés] to believe that by means of this Martín López the city would be regained which they had now lost."[14] Others who heard Cortés ask about Martín López and who saw his pleasure when told the shipwright was alive included Antonio Bravo, Andrés de Tapia, Andrés de Trujillo, and Lázaro Guerrero. The last-named so phrased his account of the event as to indicate that the escape of shipwright Martín López enabled Cortés the better to bear up under the loss of all the others. Guerrero said that "he saw the Marquis, before anything else, inquire how many men had been killed and when he learned it he was very sad and then asked for Martín López and the captains told him he lived, and he showed much pleasure and joy."[15] The decision concerning the means to be employed in reconquest seems to have been firmly established in the mind of Cortés even while he was still in the midst of stinging defeat and retreat. By the clear dawn of July 1, 1520, the man who

[14] LC–CC, Martín López 1529–1550, p. 130 (testimony, 1540); Cervantes de Salazar, Crónica, 493; and Alamán, Disertaciones, I, 107.

[15] LC–CC, Martín López 1529–1550, p. 166 (testimony, 1540).

had once ordered a fleet of brigantines built to guarantee safe retreat from the city probably knew beyond a shadow of a doubt that the construction of even more brigantines would be required to guarantee re-entry into that city.

From the western side of the lake the battle-weary wanderers worked their way clockwise around the shore line until they could strike out for Tlaxcala and much needed rest and recuperation. The choice of direction for the retreat along the lake shore was probably not accidental—the northwestern and northern shores of the lake were much less densely populated than were those on the southwest and south. During the month of July in Tlaxcala both the bodies and the spirits of the men were on the mend. Cortés meanwhile ordered Caballero, his lieutenant at Vera Cruz, to send him any seamen who could be spared from unfit ships. In pursuit of that order, Caballero sent seven men to the captain-general at that time.[16] Within about three weeks after the flight to Tlaxcala, it became the natural thing for Cortés to lead his force once more forth in battle array. All who were fit for duty joined him in an expedition to the southeast into Tepeaca.[17]

The Tepeaca campaign, an unbroken string of victories which probably happily recalled the early days of the invasion of the mainland, served at least two notable purposes, one of immediate importance and the other of long-range significance. Following the crushing defeat of the Sad Night, it was important that the commander test the mettle of his troops again and through victory renew self-confidence, without which even the thought of final and complete success would be chimerical. Tepeaca admirably enabled Cortés' force to regain its former fighting trim and élan. And as a service for the future, the victorious campaign, backed up by the garrison left in the town established at Segura de la Frontera, safeguarded the line of communication the invaders must maintain with the Vera Cruz garrison if further operations were to know final success. Only with the fortunate combination of the renewed spirit of his followers and the assurance that their line of communication

[16] *BDdelC*, II, 101–102.   [17] López de Gómara, *Historia*, I, 324.

with the coast was guaranteed could the captain-general begin the successive steps which were to end with the mastery of Mexico.

Convinced of the need of naval power and having assured himself of the fighting efficiency of his followers and that his line of communication with the coast could be maintained, Cortés was ready to launch the necessary shipbuilding program. One day, while in the city of Tepeaca, the captain-general addressed the following order to Martín López: "Proceed to the city of Tlaxcala with your tools and everything necessary and seek for a place where you can cut much wood—oak, evergreen oak, and pine—and fashion it into the pieces necessary to build thirteen brigantines."[18] These words, recalled and recorded by Martín López in 1528, are noteworthy as constituting one of the rare instances in which any reference is made to the types of timber employed in the brigantine construction. Interesting, too, is the forthright statement at the very beginning of this undertaking that there were to be thirteen brigantines, a number which is at variance with the figure given by Cortés in his second letter to the Emperor.[19]

Wide publicity was given the shipwright's assignment, as is evidenced by the testimony of eyewitnesses of the event. The blacksmith Hernán Martín was present and heard Cortés give the orders to López. Melchor de Alabes, Alonso Cárdenas, carpenter Andrés Martínez, Juan Ramos de Lares, Antón de Rodas, Francisco Rodríguez, and Rodrigo de Nájara testified that they had been present and had heard Cortés issue the orders to López.[20] Although further details concerning the circumstances under which the shipwright was notified of his new assignment are not available, it would seem that Cortés employed a general muster or some other such public occasion as the opportune moment. If so, the captain-general's purpose in making the announcement public might have been related to his continuing problem of morale, for it was extremely unlikely

[18] AGI, Patronato 57–1–1, fol. 2r (interrogatory, 1528); translation in AU–CC, Martín López 1528–1574, pp. 4–5.

[19] HC, I, 164.

[20] AGI, Patronato 57–1–1, fols. 5, 6, 7, 7r, 8, 8r, 13r, 14–14r (testimony, 1528); translation in AU–CC, Martín López 1528–1574, pp. 13, 18, 20, 22, 24, 26, 41, 44.

that the men could become enthusiastic over the prospect of a campaign against the island-capital without naval support. Furthermore, a public announcement about the shipbuilding program could well have served as the occasion to impress upon the men the importance of that project and the consequent necessity that some of them join the shipwright in this unsoldierly activity. Faced with the need of getting men to go with Martín López, the captain-general probably made an eloquent statement of the importance of the ships that were to be built. And extreme eloquence indeed might have been required to shift adventure-loving warriors, with high expectation of booty, into such prosaic pursuits as carpentering, blacksmithing, sail-making, and all the other routine endeavors necessary to the completion of the projected navy.

The date of the order to Martín López, though uncertain, may well be assigned to late September, 1520, possibly six weeks after the Tepeaca campaign had been inaugurated and some three weeks after the founding of the town of Segura de la Frontera. This conclusion is arrived at in the following fashion: Martín López, in 1528, signified that the time required for cutting the trees and fashioning the timbers in Tlaxcala and transporting the materials to Texcoco was five months. Counting back from the date of the arrival of the prefabricated vessels in Texcoco, thought to have been approximately the end of February, 1521 (see p. 119), one deduces that López was ordered out of Tepeaca into the forest of Tlaxcala in late September, 1520.[21]

Having received his orders, Martín López at once assembled his tools, purchased a quantity of supplies which he needed for himself and the three assistants he had with him, and proceeded to the city of Tlaxcala. Many years later, on July 9, 1565, when Martín López was approximately seventy-five years old, the shipwright contributed to confusion on this score when, serving as a witness giving testimony in support of the statement of services rendered by the

---

[21] AGI, Patronato 57–1–1, fol. 2r (interrogatory, 1528); translation in AU–CC, Martín López 1528–1574, p. 5. For a statement of the chronology of this phase of the conquest, see Maudslay, "Itinerary," in *BDdelC–M*, II, 325–326 (Appendix C).

Tlaxcalans during the conquest, he said he had not gone on the Tepeaca campaign because he was busily engaged on the brigantines in Tlaxcala. In the face of prior and contradictory statements by López himself and numerous other conquistadors, the statement of 1565 might be termed the confused recollection of a weary old man.[22]

The three assistants leaving Tepeaca with López, though not clearly identified on this occasion, most likely included his kinsman Juan Martínez Narices and the surviving Mafla, both of whom had assisted López in the earlier brigantine building in Tenochtitlán. Still other Spanish artisans assisted the shipwright, both in the forests and in the city of Tlaxcala. Identifying himself as a ship's carpenter by trade, Diego Ramírez signified that he took part in the building of the vessels. Alvar López, another carpenter, asserted that he had been one of those who helped the master shipwright. Lázaro Guerrero, whose warm friendship for Martín López had antedated the shipwright's coming to the New World by a decade, joined the group in Tlaxcala after the operation was underway. At the moment Cortés had issued the orders to López, Guerrero was absent from Tepeaca, having gone to Vera Cruz for some cloth the shipwright had stored at that point,[23] and the junket admits of considerable speculation. Was Guerrero merely after articles to supplement Martín López' wardrobe, or had Cortés taken steps to better the apparel of some of the troops and in consequence issued orders that part of López' surplus be put to use? Or could it have been that the shipwright was merely engaged in a legitimate and private practice of supplying his colleagues at a price? The ingenious López seems to have been a one-man quartermaster corps as well as soldier and shipwright!

[22] AGI, Patronato 57–1–1, fol. 2r (interrogatory, 1528); translation in AU–CC, Martín López 1528–1574, p. 5; and "Información recibida en México y Puebla el año de 1565, a solicitud del gobernador y cabildo de naturales de Tlaxcala, sobre los servicios que prestaron los tlaxcaltecas a Hernán Cortés en la conquista de México, siendo los testigos algunos de los mismos conquistadores," *Biblioteca Histórica de la Iberia*, Vol. XX (1875), 13, 113, 120.

[23] AGI, Patronato 57–1–1, fol. 5r (testimony, 1528); translation in AU–CC, Martín López 1528–1574, p. 16.

As soon as the shipwright had received his orders, he sent word to Guerrero to return immediately to Tepeaca. Upon receipt of that word, Guerrero set out, with some cloth; arriving at Tepeaca, he found that, although Cortés was still there, the shipwright had already moved to Tlaxcala. By the time Guerrero arrived in Tlaxcala—and there is no evidence that he wasted time on the way—López was hard at work upon the brigantines. This pattern of events in regard to Guerrero suggests interesting questions concerning the authority López enjoyed over manpower at that time. Did Cortés order him back from the coast and into the work on the brigantines, or did Cortés so delegate authority on the recruiting of manpower to Martín López that the latter ordered all the movements and work of Lázaro Guerrero? Given the tendency toward unified command so much in evidence on both earlier and later occasions, it is unlikely that Cortés had reduced his own authority by sharing it with López in matters of manpower procurement.

Some of the workers assigned to the crew assisting Martín López in Tlaxcala were obviously not volunteers. Diego Hernández, a carpenter, testified that "he had accompanied Martín López to Tlaxcala by instruction of Don Hernando Cortés to help him to cut the timber and to build the brigantines."[24] This individual, listed variously in the records as both sawyer and carpenter, is the same Diego Hernández who had worked dutifully upon the four brigantines in Tenochtitlán. The fact that he accompanied the master shipwright to Tlaxcala only on orders from Cortés might be taken as an indication of his reluctance to engage in shipbuilding activity again. Soldiering offered booty-gathering opportunities which must be sacrificed by anyone going into the forests, and, furthermore, bearing arms was more dignified than cutting timbers. Cortés could have had his difficulties in finding volunteers for the shipbuilding endeavor and probably was forced to assign men to the work. Carpenter Diego Ramírez and Francisco Rodríguez likewise asserted that they had gone with López to work on the ships only on

[24] AGI, Patronato 57-1-1, fol. 12r (testimony, 1528); translation in AU–CC, Martín López 1528–1574, p. 38.

orders from the captain-general. Though loath to go to Tlaxcala with the shipwright and identify himself with ship construction in 1520, this same Francisco Rodríguez, ere the close of the decade of the 1520's, was reminding Cortés of his shipbuilding services. In 1529 he instituted legal action against Cortés in an effort to collect 2,000 pesos in payment for his labor upon the brigantines.

Still another of the reluctant workers was Clemente de Barcelona, who stated that "Martín López asked him to accompany him to Tlaxcala to cut the timber for the brigantines, but he was unwilling to go, until later Don Hernando Cortés ordered him to go and he went, and when he reached Tlaxcala he found that Martín López had cut a certain quantity of timber and had begun to shape the framework of the brigantines."[25] This action of Cortés in ordering still another man to shipbuilding duty after the project was underway invites us to speculate whether Martín López had found the work slower and more laborious than expected, and was consequently in need of additional workmen. It also suggests that regular communications were maintained between Cortés in the field and López in the forest so that the captain-general might better know the progress of the naval project. Although we do not know how long the shipwright had been in Tlaxcala prior to the arrival of Clemente, we can surmise from the latter's remarks concerning the amount of work already achieved prior to his arrival that Martín López had wasted no time once he reached the forests of Tlaxcala. Still other workers with López in Tlaxcala included Andrés Martínez, Hernán Martín, Antón de Rodas,[26] and the seemingly ever-present Andrés Núñez.[27]

Shipwright López and his numerous assistants of 1520–1521 could point with pride, had they been so disposed, to the amount of recent and valuable experience they brought to this greatest shipbuilding project of the conquest. Of fourteen artisans who can

[25] AGI, Patronato 57-1-1, fols. 3r, 13–13r, 15–15r (testimony, 1528); translation in AU–CC, Martín López 1528–1574, pp. 8–9, 41, 47; and *CDIAO*, XXVII, 157.

[26] AGI, Patronato 57-1-1, fols. 7r, 8r (testimony, 1528); translation in AU–CC, Martín López 1528–1574, pp. 22, 26; and MN–PyTT, Leg. 95, Información de los méritos y servicios de Hernán Martín(1531).   [27] *BDdelC*, II, 139, 166.

be identified as associated with the work on the brigantines in Tlax-cala,[28] no fewer than eight of them had been associated previously with Martín López in building vessels in New Spain. His personal servant, the surviving Mafla brother, who also doubled as a skilled carpenter, had worked on the ill-fated brigantines of 1519–1520 and in all probability had labored also upon the unfinished caravel. For similarly faithful services on all three ship construction projects Juan Martínez Narices, the kinsman of the shipwright, also should be remembered. No one of the trio consisting of Pedro and Miguel de Mafla and Juan Martínez Narices lived to know the rewards of final victory.[29] With the deaths of these men who had been so close-ly and frequently identified with López was probably lost much of the light that could have been thrown upon all of the shipbuilding projects. Dying before the end of the conquest, they did not leave us any of the lengthy statements and the supporting testimony so commonly compiled by conquistador veterans concerning their services to God and king. In addition to these short-lived faithful cohorts of Martín López, two other persons, the ubiquitous soldier-workman Andrés Núñez and the self-confident Diego Hernández, aided López in every one of his shipbuilding assignments. Such a group, valuable in both their experienced work as artisans and their personal loyalty to Martín López, could easily have served as examples to the less experienced workmen. Four men, Antón de Rodas, carpenter Andrés Martínez, blacksmith Hernán Martín, and Juan Gómez de Herrera, had worked on one of the two prior proj-ects before joining Martín López on the thirteen-ship undertaking.

[28] This number is not to be construed as the total number of Spaniards ever related to the construction of the thirteen brigantines. Some workmen, as, for example, Melchor de Alabes and Juan Ramos de Lares, while not among the crew in Tlaxcala, did contribute to the final assembling and launching of the vessels in Texcoco; see AGI, Patronato 57–1–1, fols. 6r, 8 (testimony, 1528); translation in AU–CC, Martín López 1528–1574, pp. 18, 25.

[29] One of the Mafla brothers—which one is not made clear—lost his life in the debacle of the Sad Night. The remaining Mafla and Martín López' cousin, Juan Martínez Narices, perished in the course of the siege that preceded the fall of Te-nochtitlán; see AGI, Patronato 57–1–1, fol. 19–19r (interrogatory, 1534); transla-tion in AU–CC, Martín López 1528–1574, p. 60.

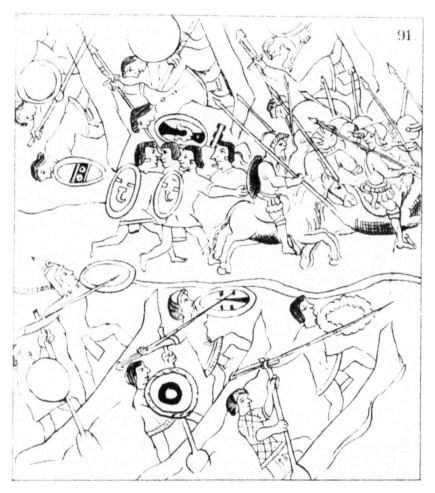

The Sad Night: Canoe-borne Mexicans attack the retreating invaders
(*From the Codex Florentino, Historia de las cosas de Nueva España,
Vol. IV*)

Western slope of Mount Malinche, Tlaxcala, probable source of brigantine timbers (*Photograph by the author*)

Río Zahuapan, testing place of the brigantines, looking upstream from the Tizatlán Ford (*Photographs by the author*)

These eight skilled artisans who had had prior and recent experience under the direction of Martín López were possibly the most valuable workers; nevertheless the five carpenters, Diego Ramírez, Alvar López, Lázaro Guerrero, Francisco Rodríguez, and Clemente de Barcelona, all brought needed and recognized skills, even though they were working under the direction of the shipwright for the first time. In the aggregate this handful of men who tackled a herculean undertaking in late 1520 constituted much more than simply so many workers in wood and metal. Theirs was a spirit of camaraderie born of common hardships and common goals, of related skills that individually could contribute but only collectively could achieve. Theirs was experience in working with a minimum supply of tools, of co-operating with and living among the natives, of directing the transportation of timbers over rugged terrain. In short, theirs was the courage and the capacity for working a modern miracle.

In addition to the requisite courage and professional capacity for doing the job ahead of them, the crew of workmen the shipwright assembled about him possessed the physical vigor of Spaniards in early adulthood. As of 1520 their ages were as follows: Diego Ramírez, forty-one; Alvar López, twenty-two; Lázaro Guerrero, about thirty-six; Diego Hernández, twenty-four; Francisco Rodríguez, twenty-one; Clemente de Barcelona, twenty-seven; Pablo del Retamal, nineteen; and Juan Gómez de Herrera, twenty-five.[30] These men averaged somewhat less than twenty-seven years of age; and Martín López himself was approximately thirty-two years old when he began work on the thirteen brigantines.[31]

Several of the men who served with the shipwright in Tlaxcala offer details concerning the supplies which López purchased for the common comfort of his Spanish workers and himself. The sawyer Diego Hernández testified, "Martín López purchased and sent

---

[30] AGI, Patronato 57-1-1, fols. 12–12r, 13, 15, 17 (testimony, 1528), 20r–21, 24, 30, 43r (testimony, 1534); translation in AU–CC, Martín López 1528–1574, pp. 38, 41, 47, 52–53, 65, 74, 92, 129–130.
[31] Conway (ed.), *La Noche Triste*, 86.

to Tlaxcala, where the said timber was to be cut, wine and vinegar and oil, which he shared with this witness and the other men who were helping him in the work on the timber." To the enumeration of the articles furnished by the shipwright for his workers, Francisco Rodríguez adds cheese and native clothing. A third co-worker, Clemente de Barcelona, indicates that Martín López informed them he had sent to Vera Cruz for the oil, vinegar, and wine.[32] One can but wonder about the circumstances that prompted the shipwright to purchase supplies for his workmen. Was Cortés in Tepeaca living so completely upon the countryside that he had no supplies to divide among the men he detached for this special duty with the shipwright? Was there no cache of such supplies in Tlaxcala? And why, when López turned to the stockpile of supplies on the Gulf coast, did he have to pay for them? In any event, in the light of the shipwright's previous experience with Spanish workmen on shipbuilding projects in New Spain, his action might be adjudged a stroke of genius. He knew that many of his crew were disgruntled with their assignment to manual labor, and he knew the task ahead of them demanded their very best. By giving them a few extras—and it is to be noted that wine, oil, and vinegar are in that category—he made hard work a little more palatable. Their mental and physical well-being taken care of, the men would have a will for work which better guaranteed the completion of the thirteen vessels. One suspects that Martín López was sufficiently a master of men that he knew the morale achieved and the work done would more than compensate for the personal expense he put himself to as he purchased such meaningful extras for his men.

Detached from the main Spanish force, the shipwright and his small crew were faced by serious problems in the matter of supplying their own wants. The knowledge that the daily pursuit of food would greatly reduce the work output of his manpower may have encouraged Martín López all the more to go out of his way to supply their wants. In 1534 López asserted that he,

[32] AGI, Patronato 57–1–1, fols. 12r, 13r, 15r (testimony, 1528); translation in AU–CC, Martín López 1528–1574, pp. 38–39, 41–42, 48.

both in Tlaxcala and Texcoco, provided all the skilled carpenters who were helping in the work with food, wine, vinegar, oil, cheese, and other provisions, at his own expense, as well as with supplies of all kinds, maintaining them as well as himself, because if at any time the Marquis gave them something, taken from the Indians, it was a case of giving them something one day and nothing for twenty, so that they practically had to maintain themselves.[33]

Lázaro Guerrero, who was both a workman and, in the words of Antón Cordero, a caterer for Martín López and the other Spanish shipbuilders, supplies the additional information that López sent out foraging parties to the neighboring Indian communities for food for the brigantine builders. Diego Ramírez recalled on a later occasion that the shipwright often had told his workmen that the food they were eating had been bought and paid for by his good money. Still another workman, Juan Gómez de Herrera, remarked that "Martín López . . . supplied the workmen . . . from his own stock and maintained them entirely the greater part of the time, because all the Marquis ever gave the workmen was Indian corn and fowls furnished by the Indians, and that only once in a while, and if it had not been for Martín López the workmen would have suffered great privations."[34]

Autumn, 1520

Identified with the Spanish cause for somewhat more than a year by this time, Tlaxcala was now to make its most noteworthy contribution to the success of the European invaders. Spread across the slopes of Mount Malinche and along the basin of the Río Zahuapan, this small, populous, independent province, surrounded by the territories of the Aztec empire, had posed the first real tests for Spanish arms. After the first departure from the Gulf coast, Cortés' expedition on reaching the interior had been faced in battle repeatedly by the Tlaxcalans in the eastern sector

[33] AGI, Patronato 57-1-1, fol. 18r (interrogatory, 1534); translation in AU–CC, Martín López 1528–1574, pp. 58–59.

[34] AGI, Patronato 57-1-1, fols. 21r, 25, 28 (testimony, 1534); translation in AU–CC, Martín López 1528–1574, pp. 67, 76–77, 85–86.

of their province, led by pock-marked, impetuous, and fiercely nationalistic Xicoténcatl the Younger. In September, 1519, the Indians, doubly disturbed as they faced strange, superior weapons and strangers who might well be gods, agreed upon honorable capitulation. Before the Spanish marched toward Tenochtitlán in early October, the Tlaxcalans had decided that identification with the invaders would serve their own best interests. So it was that when Cortés left the province it was friendly to him and had enriched his force by sending some six thousand warriors with the Spaniards. Significant and lasting social and military ties between the Tlaxcalans and the Spaniards were thus inaugurated.

Like other native armies in New Spain, those of the Tlaxcalans fought in established groups, each of which had its own leader and insignia. Spurred on in battle by music, the natives fought ably and courageously either in close combat with lances and stones or at a distance with bows and arrows. The Tlaxcalans served with the Spaniards during the initial entry into Tenochtitlán in November, 1519. Some remained in the Aztec capital with the invaders until the evacuation of the Sad Night; others accompanied Cortés and assisted him in his short-lived contest with Narváez. Even the Spanish debacle of the Sad Night did not undermine Tlaxcalan loyalty. The battered survivors, Indian and European alike, limped eastward to friendly Tlaxcala and recuperated. Then, with ship construction prominent in Spanish plans, loyal Tlaxcala made yet another contribution to Cortés' program.

With the city of Tlaxcala as his base of operations, López led his men into the nearby forests. The precise forest area which was exploited cannot be ascertained. In today's Tlaxcala, as in so many other regions of the Mexican Republic, the wooded areas have been cut and recut by successive generations until zones which once were richly forested have been so denuded and in recent decades have eroded so badly as to defy association with the idea of significant stands of timber. A leading Mexican geographer stated that the most eroded area in the entire country of Mexico, as of 1949, was the part of the state of Tlaxcala in the vicinity of Malinche, the peak dominating the region that supplied the brigantine timbers.[35] Given the topography of the terrain of Tlaxcala and the fact that López maintained headquarters in the city of Tlaxcala and originally assembled the vessels and tested them on the Zahuapan River a short distance upstream from the city, it is quite likely that the northwestern slopes of Malinche were visited by the Spanish timber cutters charged with the construction of the brigantines. Once the desired trees had been felled and the sawing and fashioning of the beams and planks accomplished, López had the timbers transported into the city of Tlaxcala.

One wonders what percentage of this work fell to the lot of the natives. When Spaniards, hoping for grants of land, royal appointments, or coats of arms, detailed their services during the conquest, they had considerable facility for understating the role played by Indian colleagues. Accordingly we do not know how many Tlaxcalans went into the forests with López and his men; nor do we know how many of them sawed trees, hewed timbers, and transported finished planks and beams back to the city of Tlaxcala. Even though specific proof is lacking, the magnitude of the task—the construction of thirteen brigantines by just about as many Spanish workmen in aproximately five months' time—implies the co-operation and assistance of countless anonymous natives of the region.

Some possible confusion centers about one significant aspect of the early work, namely, the amount of it performed in the forests and in the city of Tlaxcala respectively. In 1528 the shipwright stated categorically that "in certain forests he felled the timber and sawed and fashioned the beams and planks necessary for the building of the brigantines."[36] But twelve years later, still in litigation with Cortés over the brigantines, he stated, "Martín López went personally with his servants to the mountains to get the lumber for

[35] Jorge L. Tamayo, *Geografía general de México*, II, 513.
[36] AGI, Patronato 57-1-1, fol. 2r (interrogatory, 1528); translation in AU–CC, Martín López 1528–1574, p. 5.

these brigantines and he brought it to the city of Tlaxcala where he selected it and prepared it."[37] If it is true that timbers were trimmed, dressed, and converted into appropriate pieces for the projected vessels in the forests, one may assume that the cutting was done at such a great distance from the city and from such large trees that the transportation of the rough logs posed well-nigh insurmountable obstacles. Some reconciliation of the apparently contradictory evidence is seen in the likelihood that a preliminary, rough dressing of the logs in the forests might have been followed by the more skilled handling of the rough timbers at the base of operations in the city of Tlaxcala. By such a combination of procedures the bulkiness of the timbers to be transported to Tlaxcala would have been reduced, and at the same time the work of putting the finishing touches on the ships' beams and planks would have been centralized enough to promote efficiency in both the work and its supervision.

All of the foregoing statement of the work process in Tlaxcala is challenged by Alfredo Chavero who, interpreting the native-produced pictorial record of the events of the period known as the Lienzo de Tlaxcala, insists that Cortés ordered the timbers of one brigantine moved from the coast to Tlaxcala to serve as model for the shipbuilding work there. This interpretation credits the Tlaxcalans with almost all of the work of duplicating the timbers, and reduces the role of Martín López and several other Spaniards to mere supervision of the process.[38] Such a statement of the project in Tlaxcala flies in the face of too much evidence to the contrary to be given more than passing consideration.

The enthusiasm López entertained for his project and the kind of example he set for his workmen are seen in reports of the personal role played by him at this stage of the undertaking. Not content to direct the efforts and energies of others, the shipwright also did full days of work alongside his men. As he himself described it in 1534, while in Tlaxcala he was "doing the labor of two skilled men."

---

[37] LC–CC, Martín López 1529–1550, p. 120 (interrogatory, 1540).
[38] Vicente Riva Palacio (ed.), *México a través de los siglos*, I, 889.

Ten witnesses—the total number he presented—supported the truth of that statement by their testimony. Carpenter and co-worker Alvar López, from his vantage point as one able to judge a good day's work, bluntly said, "Martín López never rested until the brigantines were completed, directing and doing much of the work himself." Another fellow-worker, Lázaro Guerrero, not only supports Martín López' statement but explains the motivation be- hind his superhuman effort: "He toiled in everything connected with their construction, all day long, and often after dark and before dawn by the aid of candles, working himself and directing and encouraging the other workmen, with the zeal of a man who comprehended the urgency of the case."[39]

When the dressed timbers and lumber permitted final assembly, the vessels were put together at the edge of the Río Zahuapan. Most of the entire present-day state of Tlaxcala is in the drainage basin of this river, which rises in the mountains of Tlaxco in the northern part of the state. Carrying the northeasternmost waters of the Río de las Balsas system, which ultimately empties into the Pacific (near the sixteenth-century town Zacatula, a site of later Cortésian marine activity), the Zahuapan winds its way southward through the capital of Tlaxcala toward the state of Puebla. The Zahuapan and San Martín rivers unite to form the Río Atoyac which, in turn, is tributary to the Balsas.[40] It being the middle of the dry season at the time he wanted to test the small ships, quite probably February, 1521, Martín López had the stream dammed

[39] AGI, Patronato 57–1–1, fols. 18r, 21–21r, 44 (interrogatory and testimony, 1534); translation in AU–CC, Martín López 1528–1574, pp. 58, 66–67, 131.

[40] García y Cubas, *Atlas geográfico*, unnumbered page of text accompanying map XXVIII (Tlaxcala); Alfonso Luis Velasco, *Geografía y estadística de la República Mexicana*, XI, 16–17; Higinio Vázquez Santa Ana, *Apuntes geográficos é históricos del estado de Tlaxcala*, 10; Tamayo, *Geografía*, II, 348–349.

On November 4, 1937, a presidential decree provided for the establishment of Xicoténcatl National Park, which was to include a portion of the Zahuapan Valley that, among other things, concerned this shipbuilding chapter of the conquest. Un-fortunately the plan to erect the national park has not been implemented; see *Excel-sior*, September 21, 1951. The text of the decree of 1937, with a statement of the boundaries of the projected park, is in Antonio H. Sosa, *Parque Nacional Xicoténcatl, Estado de Tlaxcala*, 63.

so that enough water could be obtained to float them. This dam-
ming of the Zahuapan took place approximately three kilometers
upstream from the city of Tlaxcala at a point about one-half kilo-
meter below the small community of Tizatlán and opposite San
Esteban Tizatlán and in the immediate neighborhood of the small
chapel of San Buenaventura. It is in this vicinity, rather than in the
city of Tlaxcala itself, that the construction of the ships is thought
to have taken place. The dam was of such proportions as to with-
stand the passage of considerable time. Even now, prior to the
coming of the rainy season, natives of the area who are steeped in
the ancient history of their region can point out the earthen ram-
part which is reported to be the remains of the dam constructed in
1521.[41]

Whether López floated all thirteen of the vessels at once or assembled, tested, and then dismantled them one at a time, the handi-
work of the white men would have been a strange sight indeed to
the non-nautical-minded natives of Tlaxcala. Twelve of the vessels
measured between forty and one-half and forty-two feet each (between twenty-seven and twenty-eight cubits) and the thirteenth,
destined to be the flagship, measured forty-eight feet (thirty-two
cubits) in length.[42] The marked similarity, as regards length, between the thirteen brigantines and the first four vessels constructed
on the lake suggests that the initial vessels were such a marked success that the experience they represented was borne in mind as the
later fleet was constructed. In fact, Zamacois so records this as to
indicate that Cortés had ordered López to build the thirteen ships
on the same dimensions as those previously constructed in Tenochtitlán.[43]

[41] Vázquez Santa Ana, *Apuntes geográficos,* 27–28; and Sosa, *Parque Nacional
Xicoténcatl,* 134. The writer, in the course of visits to Tlaxcala in May and June,
1950, September, 1951, and July, 1953, never saw the Zahuapan River during the
dry season. At the height of the rainy season the dark, rushing waters at the Tizatlán
ford were only knee-deep.

[42] AGI, Patronato 57–1–1, fols. 2r–3 (interrogatory, 1528); translation in AU–CC,
Martín López 1528–1574, p. 6.

[43] Niceto de Zamacois, *Historia de Méjico desde sus tiempos más remotos hasta
nuestros días,* III, 532.

Whereas the foregoing assertion of the shipwright suggests that twelve of the thirteen vessels had the same dimensions and that the thirteenth, the somewhat larger flagship, was the only deviation from that standard, Cervantes de Salazar attributes a radically different idea to Martín López. It is said that Cortés, having realized he had to have a navy, thought in terms of six vessels. When the captain-general asked Martín López for his opinion regarding both the number and size of the ships, the shipwright urged the construction of at least twelve vessels to guarantee domination of the lake, some of them to be small ones for pursuit purposes, and some larger for ramming and other shock duty; one still larger ship, the thirteenth, would become the flagship.[44] Even though this suggestion seemingly was not followed as a whole (if we can depend on the later measurements López recited), the proposal is interesting as an index to the mind of the shipwright in regard to the tactical problems the navy could be called upon to meet.

Even though the workmen probably did not bother to mount the superstructures for the preliminary testing in the Tlaxcalan river, the assembling of the vessels can still be viewed as a significant undertaking. Once the tests had been passed, the ships were knocked down, to be transported timber by timber many leagues overland to the scene of their eventual operations. With the completion of the Tlaxcala phase of the shipbuilding program, the halfway point had been reached in the construction of the navy of reconquest.

When Martín López and his crew of brigantine builders left the Spanish camp in Tepeaca for Tlaxcala, much remained to be done before Cortés would use the navy he had ordered built. After the initial successes that preceded the founding of the Spanish garrison town of Segura de la Frontera, whose very name indicated its reason for being, Cortés and the bulk of his contingent continued for weeks and weeks to range through the Tepeaca countryside. The interval between the establishment of the town of

[44] Cervantes de Salazar, *Crónica*, 548–549.

Segura de la Frontera on September 4, 1520, and Cortés' return to Tlaxcala to muster his forces on December 27, 1520, is a period wherein precise dating of events must yield to speculation. Although numerous eyewitness participants indicate what happened, no precise chronology can be assigned the activities. Cortés, Bernal Díaz, numerous unpublished manuscript statements of services rendered by individual conquistadors, the earlier chroniclers, and the chronology derived by Orozco y Berra fail to throw much light on this period.

In a real sense the Tepeaca campaign was more a matter of occupation and consolidation of Spanish authority than a military expedition in the accepted sense. Although it was reported to the Crown that the invaders engaged the enemy in battle several times, the fighting side of the operation was unlike any other battling the Spaniards had known in New Spain, for Cortés was able to assert that in the course of the extended campaign his men did not suffer a single casualty, either killed or wounded.[45] Whether or not such reporting to his sovereign was strictly accurate, it is evident that the high measure of success in Tepeaca must have done wonders to restore the morale of the Spanish soldiery. The easy victories in Tepeaca also had guaranteed continued communications with the garrison force on the coast. By the time of the founding of Segura de la Frontera, Cortés clearly had determined to return against Tenochtitlán, otherwise a garrison town astride his line of supply and communication would have been unnecessary. By the time Martín López and his workers had been ordered to Tlaxcala, Cortés clearly had also determined the broad strategy he intended to apply in the siege of Tenochtitlán. Tepeaca, scene of the revived morale of the men and the disclosure by their leader of their future course of action, was a significant chapter in the over-all conquest.

Ere the Spanish widened their campaign westward from Tepeaca, Cortés received news from the coastal garrison that a small vessel commanded by an old acquaintance of his, Pedro Barba of Habana, had dropped anchor at Vera Cruz. In truth a certain

[45] *HC*, I, 150–151.

amount of subterfuge had been indulged in by Cortés' commandant on the coast to detain the ship, which had been sent out by Diego Velázquez to communicate with the Narváez expedition. It had but a small complement—thirteen men. The two horses aboard were probably intended to facilitate contact with Narváez once the vessel reached the mainland coast. Pedro Barba and his men soon joined Cortés in Tepeaca, and along with them came the sails, rudder, and compass of their vessel.[46] One can but suspect, in the absence of more conclusive proof than the rapidity with which this removal of men and materials to the interior took place, that commandant Caballero had been ordered by Cortés to be on the lookout for accidental re-enforcements of both men and much needed nautical equipment, the latter being a necessity for the efficient operation of the brigantines that were being built in Tlaxcala. Though no details are offered, the ship's gear must have been routed on to Tlaxcala. The men, meanwhile, were welcomed and incorporated into Cortés' force, with Barba being designated captain of the crossbowmen. Further relationship between such re-enforcements and the later nautical prosecution of the conquest is seen in the fact that Barba served as one of the brigantine captains and lost his life in the course of the fighting against the Mexicans.

Barba and his men represented the first of a series of accidental re-enforcements Cortés gained in the post-Sad Night period. The next small ship to approach Vera Cruz was expected, and its detention made easier, because Pedro Barba had passed along the information that a supply vessel, laden with cassava bread and other foodstuffs as well as such much-needed material as bowstring twine, would soon land on the coast of the mainland. So it was that Captain Rodrigo Morejón de Lobera, eight soldiers, and one horse shortly came to join the army under Cortés. Like Barba, Rodrigo Morejón de Lobera was to serve later as a brigantine captain.

While yet in Tepeaca, Cortés was notified by his coastal agents that two ships belonging to Francisco Garay had arrived at Vera Cruz. The first one—the ships arrived singly a few days apart—

[46] *BDdelC,* II, 115–117.

was commanded by Camargo, and aboard were somewhat more than sixty weary and indisposed soldiers who had failed in an effort to settle in the Pánuco area. The second vessel, commanded by the Aragonese captain Miguel Díaz de Aux, contained more than fifty men and seven horses, a contingent which originally had been intended as re-enforcement for the ill-fated Pánuco settlement.[47] All promptly joined Cortés in the interior.

The military manna from heaven continued to fall into the hands of the captain-general. Still another ship appeared at Vera Cruz; this one, captained by Ramírez the Elder, carried more than forty soldiers, ten horses, and a supply of crossbows and other arms. Ramírez was also in the employ of Garay, transporting additional supplies to the non-existent Pánuco settlement. Like their now numerous predecessors, the Ramírez contingent also moved inland to swell the fighting force at the disposal of Cortés. A sixth ship— the last to re-enforce Cortés in the period prior to the establishment of Texcoco as his base—climaxed this wave of good fortune. This vessel was not identified with discovery, exploration, or conquest. Its owner, Juan de Burgos, was a merchant, and the voyage upon which it was engaged was a prosaic trading mission. Out of Spain, via the Canaries, with Francisco Medel its master, the vessel was laden with numerous articles such as would be desired by a military commander in the position of Cortés: crossbows, three horses, muskets, powder, bowstrings, miscellaneous arms, and a variety of merchandise. The captain-general immediately took steps to purchase the entire cargo. Juan de Burgos, Francisco Medel, and the crew of thirteen accompanied the cargo and thenceforth were to be found in the service of Cortés.[48]

In an unbelievably short interval six ships, approximately one hundred seventy-five men, a score of horses, and a vague but appreciable supply of foodstuffs and military items had fallen to Cortés. Such re-enforcements contributed to almost every aspect of the operation that lay ahead: the soldiers and the horses quick-

---

[47] *Ibid.*, 122–123; and *HC*, I, 151.
[48] *BDdelC*, II, 124–125, 141.

ened the land campaigns;[49] and seamen and the ships facilitated the acquisition of supplies from the Caribbean islands; and later the nautical gear stripped from some of the ships contributed to the fighting efficiency of the fleet of brigantines on Lake Texcoco. There is no indication that Cortés' badly reduced artillery knew equivalent immediate improvement. But given the nature of the terrain and the measure of mobility that was desirable in the land warfare that lay immediately ahead, there was little need for artillery until the investment of Tenochtitlán was inaugurated.

With his long-range plans in mind and with confidence engendered by the unbroken successes in Tepeaca and the recent re-enforcements of men and supplies, Cortés decided to move westward to gain control of a pass that would permit his forces to move freely in and out of the Valley of Mexico. Accordingly he led his men against the town of Guacachula. Following the victory that put that place in his hands, he pressed on several leagues to take the town of Izúcar. By this time the captain-general and his men were poised at the southeast corner of the Valley of Mexico, once more sufficiently close to the island-city that prisoners of war were able to contribute to Spanish intelligence concerning the activities taking place within Tenochtitlán.

Having gone as far westward as he could without actually spilling into the Valley of Mexico, Cortés, because timing required a high measure of co-ordination between land and naval forces in the lake country and because a broadening of the area that the Spaniards effectively controlled to the east of Popocatepetl and Ixtaccihuatl would serve him well, soon saw fit to return eastward via Segura de la Frontera. He left here a permanent garrison of sixty men, as of mid-December, 1520. In Tepeaca again, Cortés sent orders to the coast that four vessels be dispatched to Santo Domingo to buy more horses and enlist additional men for the forthcoming operation against the core of Mexican power. Sufficient wealth was

---

[49] With the breadth of understanding that characterizes so much of his writing, Lucas Alamán clearly notes the interrelationship between the land campaigns and the program of naval construction; see *Disertaciones*, I, 109.

sent via the four ships not only to buy horses but also to purchase four additional vessels, which were to be laden with much-needed gunpowder, bows, horses, and men. With the establishment of the permanent garrison in Segura de la Frontera, Cortés sent the remainder of his force toward Tlaxcala, with the exception of a detachment of twenty horse which he personally led into Cholula. In Cholula he spent several days, explaining to the chieftains that he intended to make war upon Tenochtitlán and urging them to assist him in that undertaking. Assured of their future support, he, too, headed for Tlaxcala, where he and all the others who had been away for some months were surprised and pleased with the progress that had been made on the brigantines.[50]

Winter, 1520–1521

Although regularity of communication had enabled Cortés during the course of the Tepeaca campaign to keep informed concerning the construction of the brigantines, it was with evident pleasure that he learned firsthand that the shipwright and his men had a great deal of their work behind them by the time of the captain-general's return to Tlaxcala in the Christmas season of 1520. Cortés' recorded reference to the great diligence the workmen had employed in the joining and planking of the vessels indicates that the preliminary work in the forests was a thing of the past and that before Christmas, 1520, the work, centered in the immediate environs of the city of Tlaxcala, had progressed to the final operations prior to the assembly. With the assembly the builders would shortly be able to prove their work on the waters of the Zahuapan. Noting the stage of the naval construction program, Cortés felt it appropriate to send from Tlaxcala to the coast for nails, iron, sails, tackle, and other things which would be needed to finish the vessels. The captain-general also ordered all the blacksmiths on the coast to report to Tlaxcala for work on the brigantines. One such artisan who thus shifted the locale of his activities was Hernando de Aguilar. With no pitch available for the calking of

[50] HC, I, 153–164, 170–173.

the seams of the brigantines, Cortés ordered four sailors into the pine forests to obtain a supply—the Indians being totally ignorant of the process.

At this time most of the chieftains of Tlaxcala, including such men as Xicoténcatl the Elder and Chichimecatecle, reaffirmed their continued identification with the Spanish cause by offering to cut timber for the shipping and promising to do anything else that would further the war against the common enemy. Even that dyed-in-the-wool infantryman Bernal Díaz spoke with evident delight of the achievements of the shipbuilders.[51] From commander down to common soldier, the Spanish camp was permeated with enthusiasm and optimism concerning the future campaign—owing in large measure to the project headed by Martín López.

On December 27, 1520, Cortés mustered his force in the city of Tlaxcala and announced his plan to lead all the Spaniards except the shipbuilders westward to Texcoco, his intended base for operations within the Valley of Mexico. The army which was about to inaugurate a campaign for control of that strategically important region consisted of 40 horsemen and 550 foot soldiers (some 80 of whom carried either crossbows or muskets) with 8 or 9 fieldpieces and a scant supply of powder.[52] Naturally this muster did not count the sixty men on garrison duty in Segura de la Frontera or the unknown number then at Vera Cruz. The numbers given by Cortés on this occasion become an indirect but nonetheless real contradiction of previous figures stated by him. That an army well in excess of a thousand men immediately prior to the Sad Night, with the loss of one hundred and fifty to two hundred men on that occasion and the addition of about one hundred and seventy-five from the ships of Barba, Morejón, Camargo, Díaz de Aux, Ramírez, and Juan de Burgos, should now number but approximately six hundred is clearly preposterous, all the more so in view of Cortés' own statement that no casualties were suffered in Tepeaca. With a force not appreciably larger than the one he had originally brought to the

[51] *Ibid.*, 172–173; *BDdelC*, II, 138–139; and Orozco y Berra (ed.), *Codex Ramírez*, 202.   [52] *HC*, I, 173.

continent and with the vivid memory of a stinging defeat that might well have caused him to proceed with caution, Cortés entered upon the final phase of the land campaign for the domination of the center of Aztec power. On December 28, the day following the muster, the land force set out for Texcoco, arriving there the last day of the year.[53]

How did it happen that Texcoco was chosen by the captain-general as the seat of early operations within the valley? Cortés' own account of the conquest would indicate that he had seen the city but once prior to this time. On his initial entry into Tenochtitlán, he had bypassed the cultural capital of the Aztec Confederation as he moved from Cholula to the island-city via Amecameca and Iztapalapa. Clavigero is obviously in error in his statement that Cortés and his followers visited Texcoco prior to their initial entry into Tenochtitlán.[54] The following spring the hurried march to the coast to meet the Narváez threat, with time at a premium, surely did not see Cortés going out of his way to pass through Texcoco. However, on his return from meeting Narváez, Cortés did enter Texcoco, pausing there to learn of conditions in the island-stronghold before he again crossed a causeway leading to Tenochtitlán; but in view of the fact that the captain-general was rushing to the rescue of the hard-pressed contingent under Pedro de Alvarado, it was quite unlikely that he tarried long then. Following the retreat of June 30, 1520, over the Tacuba causeway, the remnants of the Spanish force straggled clockwise about the lake until, in the neighborhood of the northeast shore, some distance from Texcoco, they struck out due east for Tlaxcala. After the retreat Cortés had not returned to the Valley of Mexico, much less the city of Texcoco. Yet Texcoco was designated the base of future Spanish land operations, despite the commander's comparative ignorance of it and despite, too, the objections of some of the men.

A number of factors probably combined to make this city the logical choice of Cortés. First, no point on Lake Texcoco was nearer

[53] *Ibid.*, 175, 180.

[54] Clavigero, *Historia antigua de México*, III, 102–103.

Brigantines under construction (*From Diego Durán, Historia de los Indios de Nueva España y islas de tierra firme, México, 1867–80, Atlas, plate 30*)

The brigantines (*From the Codex Florentino, Historia de las cosas de Nueva España, Vol. IV*)

Tlaxcala, and nearness to Tlaxcala, synonymous with shorter lines of communication and with minimal problems of transportation both before and after the time for the prefabricated navy to be carried into the Valley of Mexico, must have meant much in determining the choice of sites for a base of army operations. The relative position of Texcoco in reference to Tenochtitlán was also an important consideration: it was more distant from Tenochtitlán than any other significant lake-district community, a fact which, coupled with the relative sparseness of population on the eastern shore of the lake (as compared with the southern and western shores), meant that the Spaniards would have a sense of physical security they could not know within any other lake-front town. The comparatively large size of Texcoco was in its favor as a long-term base for operations—Spanish army elements were destined to be in and out of it over a period of five months before the siege of Tenochtitlán was inaugurated—because it could guarantee comfortable lodgings for the Spaniards. The political significance of the city also might have been an attraction; since Texcoco was one of the three centers of the Aztec Confederation, Spanish occupation of it was an automatic blow to the continued unity of the tripartite native political system. The fact that the residents of Texcoco did not have a record of open hostility toward the Spaniards, as certain other centers of population did have, might have suggested that their disposition was such as to promote harmony, if not real co-operation, with the conquistadors. The city had the strategic protection of the dike of Nezahualcoyotl in reference to possible attack from Tenochtitlán; and its location at the mid-point between the northern and southern causeways of Tenochtitlán was bound to assist confused speculation on the part of the Mexicans regarding the ultimate direction the main Spanish thrust would take. In addition to these factors of importance to the army and the land phases of the war, Texcoco, as will be developed in detail later, was a well-nigh perfect setting for the final assembly and launching of the fleet of brigantines.

With Texcoco as headquarters, the invaders entered upon a series

113

of military actions within the Valley of Mexico. Some movements were intended to reassert Spanish military supremacy in limited areas in order to befuddle the natives sufficiently that when the time came for all-out warfare the loyalty of certain lake-front peoples to the authorities in Tenochtitlán would be in the realm of doubt. Such doubt would reduce the military effectiveness of the native defenders. Some movements were intended purely and simply as reconnaissance in force. Other actions were primarily to win allies for the coming showdown, still others basically for the procurement of supplies.

The land campaigns of the first five months of 1521 in the Valley of Mexico were as much a preliminary to the combined army-navy action of the final siege operation as the Tepeaca campaign had been a precursor of the return to the valley. The intimate relationship between what the army alone was doing and what the army and navy were to undertake later in combined operations is repeatedly in evidence. In even a kaleidoscopic presentation of the sequence of events in early 1521, one senses the masterly manner in which Cortés was controlling the tempo of a preliminary land operation dedicated to a mopping-up of the lake-front region which would be completed at precisely the moment the brigantines were ready for the inauguration of the siege itself.

After establishing and fortifying the position he wanted in Texcoco, Cortés sallied forth in a brief thrust against Iztapalapa. Returning to his base, he played host to representatives of various towns that wished to ally themselves to the Spaniards. Remaining in Texcoco, the captain-general next sent Sandoval on a brief expedition to Chalco after first leading his Spanish-Indian force to Tlaxcala to check on the progress of the brigantines.[55] It was but mid-January, and scarcely three weeks had elapsed since he had seen the brigantines himself, but Cortés demanded up-to-date intelligence concerning his own fighting potential so that he might regulate all the better the tempo of the campaigning underway in the valley. Both his concern about co-ordinating diverse and widely

[55] *HC*, I, 181–187.

separated activities and his capacity to do so present a side of the military genius of Cortés that has drawn but scant attention. Most writers treating the military aspects of the conquest, from sixteenth-century participants themselves down through the latest twentieth-century biographers of Cortés, have failed to see the forest for the trees. Seldom neglecting the smallest matter of detail, they have commonly been so much in pursuit of the separate threads of their narrative as to fail to sense the inherent element of co-ordination which demanded a high order of military administrative ability on the part of Cortés.[56]

Not long after Cortés had sent Sandoval to assist the Chalcans in their struggle with the Mexicans, the captain-general learned that the brigantines had been completed and were ready to be transported from Tlaxcala to Texcoco. The general enthusiasm for the brigantines and recognition of the need for them are obvious in the words of Bernal Díaz:

> As we were always longing to get the launches finished, and to begin the blockade of Mexico our Captain, so as not to waste time to no purpose, ordered Gonzalo de Sandoval to go for the timber, and to take with him two hundred soldiers, twenty musketeers and crossbowmen, fifteen horsemen and a large company of Tlaxcalans as well as twenty chieftains from Texcoco.[57]

As Sandoval and his force set out for Tlaxcala, the Spaniards under Martín López, accompanied by several tens of thousands of Indians led by such Tlaxcalan chieftains as Chichimecatecle, Ayotecatl, and Teuctepil, had already begun to convoy the brigantine materials from Tlaxcala toward Texcoco. Fulfilling every promise they had made to Cortés on the subject, the chieftains of Tlaxcala, along with the thousands of soldiers and carriers of provisions and cargo they provided, were of pivotal importance in the overland movement of the prefabricated navy. The magnitude of the under-

[56] For a fuller discussion of this aspect of the career of Cortés, see Chapter VII, pp. 190–196.

[57] BDdelC–M, IV, 24. Pedro de Alvarado is mistakenly given credit by one writer for conducting the brigantines from Tlaxcala to Texcoco; see Orozco y Berra (ed.), Codex Ramírez, 203.

taking is made clear when we learn that for the short-term expedition two thousand men were charged with the transportation of foodstuffs alone.

Leaving the city of Tlaxcala, the caravan of carriers, loaded down with the paraphernalia related to the brigantines, made its way westward via Hueyotlipán, which point was reached without coming upon Sandoval and his escort-guard. There the caravan paused. The Tlaxcalan chieftains, confident in their ability to deliver the brigantines, wanted to push on, but Martín López, loyal to orders from Cortés, insisted that they await the Spanish escort which the captain-general had promised. After waiting eight days in Hueyotlipán, the caravan was joined by Sandoval and his force. (Another view has it that the juncture between Sandoval's escort and the brigantine caravan was effected quite close to the western boundary of the province of Tlaxcala, such a point possibly being considerably to the west of Hueyotlipán.) The initial contact between the westbound expedition, with its natives of Tlaxcala and Huejotzingo, and Sandoval's force was effected by a Spanish detachment led by Francisco Rodríguez Magariño. Command of the operation, which seemingly had been a loose union of Spanish and Indian leadership to this time, was now vested in Sandoval.[58] Bernal Díaz, friendly to Martín López and interested in the brigantines, though in the aggregate he offers neither an extended account nor a penetrating appreciation of their role in the conquest, is manifestly wrong when he indicates that Martín López, rather than Gonzalo de Sandoval, confidant of Cortés and a proved military leader, served as commander in chief throughout the movement of the brigantines from Tlaxcala to Texcoco. It should be borne in mind that Díaz was not among those escorting the prefabricated navy.[59]

Sandoval established the following line of march for the caravan: 8 Spanish cavalrymen, 100 Spanish foot soldiers, and 10,000 Tlaxcalan warriors formed the vanguard; more than 8,000 native carriers with the ships' timbers, the relief carriers and those bearing

[58] AGI, Audiencia de México 98; AGI, Patronato 54-3-1; and López de Gómara, *Historia*, II, 12.   [59] *BDdelC*, II, 164.

the tackle, sails, nails, and other supplies, and 2,000 bearers carrying the provisions constituted the heart of the caravan; 7 Spanish
cavalrymen, 100 Spanish footsoldiers, and 10,000 Tlaxcalan warriors composed the rear guard; and along each of the extended
flanks was a force of an additional 10,000 Tlaxcalans. This immense
column of more than 50,000 men extended, in close formation, more
than two leagues in length.[60]

The route over which the brigantines were transported cannot
be traced with precision, although it is helpful to know that, prior
to the joining of forces at Hueyotlipán, López and the caravan had
moved from the city of Tlaxcala and Sandoval had come from
Texcoco via Zoltepec and Calpulalpan. However, it is not safe to
conclude, merely because Sandoval had moved eastward over that
route, that the return trip, with the brigantines, traversed the same
terrain. All the more doubt obscures the idea of automatic dupli-
cation of the route when it is remembered that Sandoval was
coupling a punitive expedition with his movement to meet the
brigantines and accordingly had treated certain peoples so roughly
that a revengeful band of natives might well have been anticipating
his return that way. One of the leading students of all the routes
used by Cortés and the Spaniards in the conquest of Mexico,
Manuel Orozco y Berra, maintains that in pursuit of the most level
and the least inconvenient route the caravan must have passed to
the north of the high peak of Telapón in traversing the mountain
range that guarded the eastern side of the Valley of Mexico.[61] José
María Luis Mora, applying logic to one of the hidden phases of the
conquest, concluded, for reasons of minimizing the physical ordeal
of the carriers, that the brigantines were brought to Texcoco via
the plains of Apám.[62] The views of Orozco y Berra and Mora are

[60] Orozco y Berra, *Historia antigua*, IV, 523–524. Needless to say, different sources
offer a variety of figures concerning the size of the escort. Bancroft comments on
this in *Mexico*, I, 580. One of the most extensive sixteenth-century accounts of the
transportation of the knocked-down ships is found in Cervantes de Salazar, *Crónica*,
594–598. Special attention is drawn by him to the work of Alonso de Ojeda as a
supervisor of that overland movement.
[61] *DUHG*, V, 856.   [62] *Ibid.*, 818.

117

not mutually exclusive. As one skirts the Sierra Nevada moving westward around the northern extremity of the range, there is a choice of cutting across the foothills of Telapón or, by going somewhat farther to the north, crossing the Plain of Apám. The shortest route with an established trail in the 1520's was possibly the one via Hueyotlipán, Calpulalpan, and Zoltepec.[63] If, on the other hand the caravan moved westward via Apám, it was probably felt that other advantages, such as more level terrain and more open countryside, outweighed the additional distance. The remnant force that retreated from the valley at the time of the Sad Night and the brigantine caravan both passed through Hueyotlipán; one cannot help but wonder what percentage of the route westward in 1521 was a repetition of the route eastward the previous year. Although the pattern of movement of the Spaniards in New Spain has produced a literature in itself, the authors seldom concern themselves with any route other than the one used initially between the coast and the island-capital. Despite the fact that many of these writers are romanticists at heart, they fail to appreciate fact-founded drama as they neglect the chapter of the conquest that found brigantines crossing mountains on the shoulders of men.[64]

Not far to the west of Hueyotlipán the caravan left the territory of the Tlaxcalan allies. Sandoval thought the increased threat to the brigantines sufficient reason for reordering the personnel of the expedition. In addition to so arranging the core of the caravan that the bulkier items, which in case of attack might constitute a bottleneck to the safety and a barrier to the defense of the caravan, were

[63] President Alemán, in his address to the Mexican Congress on September 1, 1951, announced that during the past administrative year a serviceable road had been constructed between central Tlaxcala and Texcoco, as part of the new short route between Vera Cruz and Mexico City; see *Excelsior*, September 2, 1951. Now every ten minutes a bus rolls westward out of Tlaxcala to Texcoco via Calpulalpan over a road that closely approximates much of the route over which the brigantines were transported; see advertisement in *Excelsior*, September 11, 1951.

[64] In vain does one look for discussion of the overland route of the brigantines in such writing as: José Segarra y Julea, *La Ruta de Hernán Cortés*; Harry A. Franck, *Trailing Cortez Through Mexico*; Luis Marden, "On the Cortes Trail," *National Geographic Magazine*, Vol. LXXVIII (September, 1940), 335–375; and Fernando Benítez, *La Ruta de Hernán Cortés*.

toward the rear, Sandoval also effected alteration concerning the order of the van and the rear. Following this restructuring, the expedition trudged westward for almost four full days. At the dawn of the fourth day, knowing that this day would see their laborious journey at an end and that their coming was anticipated and their achievement significant, those of the caravan who could do so put on their finest attire for the moment of triumph. To the accompaniment of trumpets and drums the two-league-long procession moved into the city of Texcoco, henceforth to be the base of operations for naval as well as military activities. Those who witnessed the event and later recorded it for posterity agreed it was awe-inspiring to gaze upon this fantastic expedition, which required six hours to pass a given point. It was probably in the closing days of February, 1521, that the ships' timbers came to rest alongside the shallow watercourse on which they were next destined to float. Well might the co-operative nature of this Spanish-Tlaxcalan enterprise inspire the cries that filled the air in Texcoco that day: "Viva, viva el emperador nuestro señor, y Castilla, Castilla y Tlaxcalla, Tlaxcalla!"[65]

From late February until the launching of the siege operation at the end of May, Texcoco was increasingly the center of multi-pronged Spanish endeavor. Still other recently arrived re-enforcements had to be absorbed; still more military columns sallied forth on missions of reconnaissance, procurement of supplies, chastisement of enemies, and support of allies; and still more naval activity centered about the final assembling of the brigantine fleet. More than ever before over a prolonged period, Cortés was called upon to demonstrate his capacity as a co-ordinator of military activities.

During this interval additional ships landed on the coast of New Spain. At this point I follow Cortés and Cervantes de Salazar rather than Díaz, for the foot soldier states there was but one ship, ignoring the vessels of Bastidas completely though proceeding to list some of his personnel with Alderete.[66] One ship brought His

[65] HC, I, 195–196; BDdelC, II, 165; and Orozco y Berra, Historia antigua, IV, 524–525.   [66] BDdelC, II, 188.

Majesty's Treasurer Julián de Alderete, a considerable but unspecified amount of arms and powder, and an unstated number of men, among them Antonio de Carvajal, who soon was named to the command of a brigantine. Almost simultaneously two other ships, the property of Rodrigo de Bastidas of Santo Domingo, also landed in New Spain. They carried men, horses, and equipment, all of which Cortés gladly added to his strength. The captain of the larger of the Bastidas vessels was Gerónimo Ruiz de la Mota, who soon shifted his marine talents to the command of a brigantine.[67] Early 1521 also saw a vessel belonging to the Licenciado Ayllón, a royal official on Española, augment Cortés' military power with men, horses, arms, and munitions.

The military detachments that sallied out of Texcoco on short excursions into the countryside were led sometimes by Cortés in person, other times by endlessly able Captain Sandoval. Once again we must resort to a kaleidoscopic presentation of the sequence of events, but we can direct attention to a number of land movements that were significant in the preliminary campaign for control of the hinterland area of the Valley of Mexico. Three or four days after the knocked-down brigantines arrived in Texcoco, Cortés undertook a counterclockwise sweep from his headquarters to Tacuba and then came clockwise from the terminus of the western causeway back to Texcoco, spending about three days on the road to Tacuba, six days in that city, and two days returning to his base. The captain-general himself indicated that the purpose of the trip was to talk with the enemy and to try to dissuade them from further warfare. However, he wrote later, "As my being there profited nothing, I decided, at the end of six days, to return to Tesaica [sic] and hasten the construction of the brigantines, so as to surround the enemy by water and land."[68] Failing to produce a diplomatic

---

[67] *HC*, I, 203; and Cervantes de Salazar, *Crónica*, 599.

[68] *HC–MacN*, II, 33–36. Bernal Díaz, who remained during this period in Texcoco with the garrison commanded by Sandoval, indicates that Cortés, even as he departed on the march to Tacuba, told both Martín López and Gonzalo de Sandoval to have the brigantines launched and ready to give battle within fifteen days; see *BDdelC*, II, 168. Díaz is difficult to accept in this instance for the very good reason

victory, the trip to Tacuba still served as another reconnaissance and contributed toward clearer definition of the military task that lay ahead.

Two days after Cortés' return to Texcoco (approximately on March 12) Sandoval, in response to an appeal from the natives, led a force to the aid of Chalco. Scarcely had he returned to Texcoco when a second appeal came from the same source, and so once more he went to Chalco. By such tactical employment of some of his men, Cortés continued to strengthen his strategic position, which was still further secured when certain provinces offered to become vassals of the King of Spain and allies of Cortés in the field.[69]

Spring, 1521

Leaving Sandoval and a sizable number of soldiers in Texcoco to guard the brigantines, Cortés set out with a strong force on April 5, 1521, on what was his final full reconnaissance of the lake shore communities and the approaches to the city of Tenochtitlán. As he himself expressed it, "Since I was to lay siege to the great city of Temixtitlan as soon as the brigantines were finished, I wished first to see the port of the city and the entrances and exits where the Spaniards might attack or be attacked."[70] The timing of this reconnaissance with the completion of the fleet is further evident from these words of the captain-general: "[It was] my intention to make a tour round the lakes, as I believed that after accomplishing this march, . . . the thirteen brigantines would be found complete and ready to be launched."[71] In the course of this slow, deliberate, clockwise movement around the margin of the lake, the Spaniards, during stubborn fighting in the area of Xochimilco, had still another opportunity to sense the important role the

---

that Cortés, with all the experience he had gained relative to the problems that attended the building of ships in New Spain, could not conceivably have envisaged the assembling and launching of thirteen vessels (not to mention the digging of a much-needed canal to get them into Lake Texcoco) in almost as many days.

[69] *HC*, I, 201–207; and *BDdelC*, II, 178.

[70] *HC–MacN*, II, 54.   [71] *Ibid.*, 42.

brigantines would have in the forthcoming amphibious operation against Tenochtitlán. At Coyoacán, which Cortés thought might well serve as his headquarters during the forthcoming operation, the captain-general is reported to have made an estimate of that setting as a base for brigantine operations. Late in April, Cortés was once more in Texcoco, hastening the completion of the navy which would permit the inauguration of the siege.[72]

The scantily told story of the completion and launching of the brigantines falls into two distinct parts—the work on the ships, and the work on the canal through which the vessels would move into Lake Texcoco. The two projects were undertaken simultaneously.

The site chosen for the final assembly and launching of the vessels was the bank of a narrow, shallow stream bed. The shipyard that was thus established, as the Tlaxcalan bearers deposited their cargo there in late February, lay approximately a half league from Lake Texcoco. That the shipyard was not directly on the lake front was exceedingly logical in terms of the Spanish position and the problems of the moment. Several writers have been so confused by the removal of the shipyard from the edge of the lake as either to refuse to accept the facts as stated by participants or to fail to understand them. Accompanying Chapter 77 of Durán's work, a plate (No. 30) shows Indians hewing logs and otherwise pushing the construction of the vessels under Spanish-Indian direction, and the activity is placed on the lake front, with several vessels already afloat.[73] On the other hand, the recent writer H. R. Wagner suffers such confusion when he is considering the canal required to connect the shipyard with the lake that he concludes the matter with these words: "No adequate reason for building it is given, why not have put the boats in the lake at once?"[74] Proof that the idea of assembling the vessels in a stream bed some distance from the lake was not merely a sudden whim of Cortés is evident from Bernal Díaz' record of the discussion, while the leader was still in Tlaxcala,

[72] HC, I, 213–216, 221; and López de Gómara, Historia, II, 26.

[73] Diego Durán, Historia de los Indios de Nueva España y islas de tierra firme, ed. José F. Ramírez, Atlas, plate 30.   [74] Wagner, Cortés, 344.

of the comparative merits of Texcoco and Ayotzingo as settings offering advantages for building and launching ships.[75] As demonstrated above, the interval between late February and late May found the Spaniards dedicated to a number of activities, every one of which contributed to the timetable of victory and every one of which demanded manpower simultaneously.

To order the final assembly of the brigantines on the open shore of the lake would have been synonymous with curtailing, if not eliminating, such activities as those centering about the procurement of supplies, the chastisement of enemies, and the reconnaissance of the valley. Even with the ship construction taking place in a relatively inaccessible spot removed from the shore, the Mexicans tried to sabotage the vessels on no fewer than three occasions. Had the shipyard been on the lake front, the Mexicans, with their thousands upon thousands of canoes, could have seriously hampered the efforts of the workmen by a sustained program of harassment, in which case, even if the vessels escaped outright destruction (and that is not a foregone conclusion), it is evident that the construction schedule would have been lengthened considerably. The enemy's harassment of the work would also have pinned down the artillery, the archers, and the musketeers so completely to an around-the-clock assignment of guarding the brigantines that none of the other undertakings which demanded sizable numbers of men for days at a time could even have been initiated, much less pushed with the vigor synonymous with success. Multiple, simultaneous demands upon limited manpower dictated that Cortés locate the shipyard some distance from the lake, sufficiently far that a builder could be precisely that at all times and not a combination of builder with tool in hand one moment and soldier with crossbow in action the next.

That details are scant concerning the progress of the ships at Texcoco is easily explained, for the soldier-authors Cortés and Díaz were not continuously in Texcoco in this interval to note and record in detail events related to the brigantines. However, we do know

[75] BDdelC, II, 140–141.

that Martín López was able to count upon the skills of experienced workmen who had been with him in Tlaxcala and that some additional Spanish artisans now joined his work force. Among the newcomers were carpenter Andrés López, Hernando de Aguilar, a blacksmith, Melchor de Alabes, Juan Ramos de Lares, elderly blacksmith Hernando Alonso, who hammered many nails into the brigantines, Antón Cordero, and Juan García, a blacksmith who made many nails and other metallic items required to complete the brigantines.[76] As for the building process, many of the comments of Morison about late fifteenth-century shipping in general, regarding tonnage, linear dimensions, draught, bolts, trunnels, the treatment given ships' bottoms, ballast, pumps, sails, outboard rudders, tillers, and pendants, might apply to the brigantines.[77]

The master shipwright, in charge of the work at Texcoco as completely as on previous occasions in other settings, asserted that the work of putting the brigantines together was begun as soon as the men and the materials arrived at that place. López de Gómara states that four days of rest separated the arrival of the supplies and the inauguration of the ship construction program. Martín López claimed to have spent five months on the project in Texcoco, an impossibly long interval in view of the arrival from Tlaxcala in late February and the beginning of the siege at the end of May; several of his workmen put the time they had labored in Texcoco as approximately four months.[78] The work included the most careful and complete calking job possible, something that had probably been

[76] AGI, Patronato 57–1–1, fols. 3r, 4r, 6r, 7r, 8, 8r, 12r, 13r, 15r (testimony, 1528), 21–21r, 27r–28, 30–30r, 33r–34, 39–39r (testimony, 1534); translation in AU–CC, Martín López 1528–1574, pp. 9, 11–12, 18, 22, 25, 26, 39, 42, 48, 65, 67, 83–84, 85, 92–93, 94, 101, 102–103, 117, 118; BDdelC, II, 165–166; G. R. G. Conway, "Hernando Alonso, a Jewish Conquistador with Cortés in Mexico," Publications of the American Jewish Historical Society, Vol. XXXI (1928), 11, 12, 25; and MN–PyTT, Leg. 94, Información de los méritos y servicios de Juan García (1550).

[77] Admiral of the Ocean Sea, I, 152, 160–166.

[78] AGI, Patronato 57–1–1, fols. 2r, 4r, 5 (interrogatory and testimony, 1528); translation in AU–CC, Martín López 1528–1574, pp. 5, 11–12, 14; and López de Gómara, Historia, II, 14.

bypassed in the hurried tests in the Río Zahuapan in Tlaxcala. At Texcoco every mast had to be put in place and every sail cut and fastened to the spars. In the bow of each vessel a gun had to be mounted. Texcoco called for precision and completeness such as had not been necessary in Tlaxcala, and every operation must have demanded the attention of the master shipwright. As the ship construction program advanced, it became necessary, in order to put the finishing touches on the vessels, to supplement the prefabricated fittings from Tlaxcala with some timbers cut in the neighborhood of Texcoco from forests planted a half century earlier in the days of the great Nezahualcoyotl.[79]

Three times by trying to destroy the unfinished vessels, the Mexicans indicated the awesome fear the earlier brigantines had struck in them. On one such occasion, when an evening patrol attempted to burn the shipyard, the Spaniards captured fifteen men.[80] Although such sabotage efforts may have delayed the completion of the ships, no real disaster was visited upon the fleet while still upon the ways. By the last week of April the launching ceremony was eagerly awaited.

The canal through which the brigantines had to move to enter Lake Texcoco was in itself a triumph of hurried workmanship. It is well-nigh impossible to assess the Indian contribution to the actual building of the ships, but the records are clear that the half-league canal was almost completely an Indian achievement. As soon as the placement of the brigantine materials determined the exact location of the shipyard, natives began to dig the canal. Apparently in charge of the canal project was the Texcocan chieftain Ixtlilxochitl, who directed the labor of some 40,000 Texcocans as they worked incessantly, in relays of 8,000 men each, for a period of seven weeks. For fifty consecutive days the natives were occupied moving earth and shoring the banks. Cortés indicates that the ditch,

[79] Fernando de Alva Ixtlilxochitl, *Historia Chichimeca,* in *Obras históricas de Don Fernando de Alva Ixtlilxochitl,* ed. Alfredo Chavero, II, 416.

[80] Orozco y Berra, *Historia antigua,* IV, 526.

when completed, measured twelve feet wide and twelve feet deep.[81] The depth cannot be associated with the draught of the vessels. Rather it would seem that in terms of the declivity from the shipyard to the lake itself the twelve-foot depth was probably necessary, at least at the point of the shipyard, with a gradual reduction closer to the lake, in order to use the lake level as a means of obtaining sufficient water to float the vessels. In other words, twelve feet represents the combination of declivity and draught.[82]

Today there is no clear evidence of the canal of Texcoco, although both Bustamante and Lorenzana claim to have seen traces of it in relatively recent times.[83] In 1938 the municipal authorities of Texcoco erected a monument and plaque at what is thought to have been the site of the brigantine launching. A simple, dignified shaft, standing approximately fifteen to eighteen feet high, bears at its top the Spanish words, here translated:

> Bridge of the Brigantines
> where
> Cortés launched the ships
> for the siege
> of the Aztec capital
> April 5, 1521

On the wall immediately behind the monument is a mutilated eleven-line tablet which offers a general statement concerning the siege of Tenochtitlán. The monument and plaque are to be found

[81] *HC*, I, 221–222. In agreement with Cortés is Cervantes de Salazar who states that both the depth and the width of the finished ditch exceeded twice the height of a man; see *Crónica*, 636. Also see Alva Ixtlilxochitl, *Historia Chichimeca*, II, 416; Fernando de Alva Ixtlilxochitl, *Décima tercia relación de la venida de los españoles y principio de la ley evangélica*, in Sahagún, *Historia* (1938) IV, 249, 254; and López de Gómara, *Historia*, II, 27. Thomas Gage surely read one of the early sources too rapidly as he recorded the number of canal workers as 400,000; see *The English-American—A New Survey of the West Indies*, ed. A. P. Newton, 56.

[82] In his choleric outpouring of vituperation and fiction, R. A. Wilson, after denying the existence of Lake Texcoco at the time of the conquest, insists that this canal was twelve inches deep, not twelve feet; see *A New History of the Conquest of Mexico*, xi, 434, 478.

[83] Bancroft, *Mexico*, I, 581, summarizes the statements of a half-dozen sources concerning the canal. The measure of agreement in the writings seems to stem from repeated dependence upon the words of Cortés.

at the south edge of town facing the street which leads from Tex-coco toward Mexico City. But, the monument to the contrary, there is no reason to accept April 5, 1521, as the date of the launch-ing of the brigantines. Both Cortés and Díaz make specific refer-ences to that date, but under circumstances which indicate the mop-up campaign was still underway and the ships were still under construction.[84]

Formal launching of the fleet upon the waters of Lake Texcoco took place on Sunday, April 28. Cervantes de Salazar writes the fullest and most colorful account of the launching activities, de-rived in large part from conversations in the 1550's with the brigan-tine captain Gerónimo Ruiz de la Mota. The account reports that the arroyo-canal did not have sufficient water to float the ships and it became necessary to build a series of dams, twelve in all, to im-pound the waters at intervals on the way from shipyard to lake; vaguely (perhaps with intention because of the author's inability to understand the operation) the mysterious inventions and machines required to achieve the needed water levels are men-tioned. With a dash of high wind and a bit of cloudburst, Cervantes de Salazar conjures up for the reader an occasion memorably re-plete with a sense of adventure and high destiny.

At the expenditure of considerable labor but with a minimum of danger to the vessels, the armada moved into Lake Texcoco. At the water's edge Fray Olmedo celebrated a mass and proceeded to bless the small ships before the assembled throng of native allies and Spaniards. The sails were unfurled, flags and pennants fluttered at the mastheads, and music burst forth. To the repeated roars of cannon fire were added the characteristic cries of exultation from natives and Spaniards alike. So great was the emotional outpouring that accompanied the dedication of the fleet which most had come to consider the key to the conquest that more than one rough hero of a dozen engagements shed tears of joy.[85] Alamán, one writer who attempts to make the brigantines seeable to his readers in a word

---

[84] HC, I, 207, and BDdelC, II, 190.
[85] Cervantes de Salazar, Crónica, 600–601.

127

picture, describes them as like a kind of modern gun-boat.[86] In less than eight months a navy had been created.[87]

Between July, 1520, and May, 1521, the reconquest of the Valley of Mexico was not only planned but in its preliminary stages achieved. Communications had been made secure; re-enforcements and additional supplies had been obtained. The valley had been invaded, and the campaign against the hinterland of the lake-dominated region had reached the mopping-up stage. Meanwhile a navy had been created for the amphibious operations that lay ahead. By May, 1521, only the welding together of fighting units, including an inexperienced yet all-important naval arm, delayed the inauguration of the climactic combat destined to introduce the concept of combined operations into sixteenth-century America.

[86] *Disertaciones*, I, 114.

[87] This estimate of the time consumed in the construction of the ships is advanced in the face of much contradictory evidence. Martín López asserted that he spent eleven months on the project; numerous workers on the vessels insisted that a full year was required. See AGI, Patronato 57–1–1, fols. 2r (interrogatory, 1528), 31, 34, 36r–37, 39r (testimony, 1534); translation in AU–CC, Martín López 1528–1574, pp. 6, 94, 103, 111, 118–119. With the vessels finished prior to May 1, 1521, it would have been necessary—with either the eleven or twelve months' schedule—for the work to have been inaugurated prior to the Sad Night. It should be added that, in the absence of calendars and in the presence of much hard work, the Spaniards are to be excused for such faulty time estimates as are so frequently encountered. The eight months' figure is advanced in the belief that López and his helpers left Tepeaca sometime in September, 1520, to begin the project.

CHAPTER V

The Key of the Whole War

ACROSS THE MANY MONTHS between the retreat of the Sad Night and the inauguration of the Battle of Tenochtitlán, Cortés repeatedly voiced the opinion that the brigantines constituted the pivotal factor in the operations he planned against that Mexican stronghold. His anxious inquiry about Martín López on July 1, 1520, immediately following the retreat from the island-city, hinted at his future plans. In Tepeaca, as he detached López and others from his field force to go to Tlaxcala to begin work on the vessels, Cortés declared that taking Tenochtitlán, his principal objective, was impossible without brigantines. Some months later, in Tlaxcala at Christmas time the captain-general, as he urged the native chieftains to co-operate with Martín López, told the Tlaxcalans that he could not dream of defeating the Mexicans without the brigantines. In the Valley of Mexico the moment chosen by Cortés for his final reconnaissance of the lake-front area was in close accord with the timetable for the completion of the fleet. As he mustered his forces on the eve of the siege, Cortés pointed yet again to the newly launched brigantines and declared before all his assembled men the importance of the navy's role in the forthcoming struggle.

The Brigantines—a Conjectural Reconstruction

A generic description of the brigantines of the conquest is as difficult as it is desirable. With the contribution of the vessels far from being a nebulous thing, one naturally expects specifics about them. Unfortunately no detailed description is available. However, the temptation to do a conjectural reconstruction of the vessels is strengthened by the existence of numerous pieces of the informational mosaic required to achieve something like a reasonably accurate representation. The description that follows, a welding together of numerous miscellaneous tidbits of information, is derived and presented in the manner that has so long characterized numerous valid historical studies of ancient shipping. Like those works, this synthetic description is likewise advanced with a combination of caution and confidence.

The over-all dimensions of the brigantines of the conquest can be approximated. The length is known, being about forty-two feet for each of twelve of the thirteen brigantines and forty-eight feet for the flagship. Our best index to the beam, beyond knowledge of the length, is the fact that the Texcoco canal through which they had to move to the lake proper had a width of twelve feet. Counterpoising that limiting factor, it must be remembered that a mast was mounted in the well, space was required for a double row of oarsmen—six on each side of the vessel—and minimum passageway had to be maintained for the free movement of gunners and bowmen about the ship. All such matters being taken into consideration, it is quite feasible to assume that the vessels had a beam of between eight and nine feet. Thus the brigantines, with the ratio of length to beam approximating five to one, might fall in the not uncommon class of five-beam vessels. This beam seems narrow in terms of space demands of the rowers, but as far as we can judge from available pictorial representations the propulsion seems to have been paddling rather than rowing. Instead of using long sweeping oars, with oarlocks, fixed fulcrums, and the resultant demand for considerable space inboard for sitting oarsmen, the men quite probably stood as they dipped their stubby paddles into the lake waters close alongside the ship. On the basis of the above dimensions and the information that each vessel carried twenty-five men, one may conclude that the brigantines probably drew between two and two and one-half feet of water. The limited salinity of Lake Texcoco surely was not a noteworthy factor in regard to the draught of the vessels. Owing to the added weight of the heavy gun on the bow, the effective distribution of the manpower, and the lack of supplies in the hold, the vessels probably had just that slight measure of drag which is desirable from the standpoint of ease of handling. Freeboard at the waist probably measured about four feet. While contributing to general sailing qualities, such a measurement was even more significant in terms of combat conveniences. It meant that the Spanish gunners and archers towered over their canoe-borne adversaries; it would insure, too, what may be termed eye-level action against the Mexicans on the causeways, the chinampas, and within the city proper. The freeboard at forecastle and poop possibly increased to between six and seven feet. The wooden rudders, of which we have neither word nor pictorial representation, quite likely were patterned on those of the caravels of the day.

Like the caravel and the still better-known galleon of that time, the brigantine was in general a well-decked rather than a flush-decked vessel, but the proportion of its castles, both fore and aft, to its total length was much less than was the case in either caravel or galleon. On the Cortés brigantines the well might have approximated 60 per cent of the over-all length, a surmise derived from several circumstances. In the first place, considerable space between the castles was needed for the paddlers. Secondly, neither of the castles was required to serve as living quarters or storage space, given the nature of the operations for which the ships had been built; the poop merely had to be large enough to support a mast and still allow room for a man at the rudder and for several fighting men, and the forecastle was primarily a support for the heavy gun, although it must also afford space for a couple of men, one of whom was quite probably a mud pilot—eyesight navigation being all-important in brigantine movements. Because of the presence of the gun, the bow could not and did not support a bowsprit.

The canvas on the brigantines was supported by either one mast or two—from the Codex Florentino one would conclude that about half of the vessels were in each category. Those that sported two masts had one standing amidships and the other on the poop. Vessels with but one mast had it mounted amidships. The number of sails employed seemed to equal the number of masts aboard, and in all instances the brigantines were square-rigged. Quite clearly the vessels were not overrigged. In many of their combat settings the Spanish brigantines were dead in the water as they supported the land forces during a thrust along the causeways or bombarded, fired, and otherwise razed peripheral portions of Tenochtitlán. Under such conditions, on each ship the twelve men deposited their paddles and became fighters and the sail was tightly furled aloft against the yards.

By virtue of their duty and their draught, the brigantines quite probably were not only single-decked but single-bottomed as well. Because of the extreme shallowness of the lake, the vessels must have been almost, if not entirely, flat-bottomed. In consequence of the common resort to the paddles, low bulwarks were probable, along with a freeboard but several feet above the surface of the water, and a rather straight gunwale. The square-sterned nature of the brigantine would also make for a straight gunwale.

In terms of the demands put upon the vessels, several protective features probably were in evidence. The shallowness of the lake waters and the extreme likelihood of occasional groundings logically could have dictated the employment of a false keel. Although a false keel would increase the draught ever so slightly, the reenforcement of the keel would lengthen the life of the vessel by reducing the prospect of over-all damage to the hull. In other words, groundings surely were anticipated and the brigantine probably was strengthened accordingly. In like manner, since ramming tactics were routine, the vessels probably had collision bulkheads, to strengthen that part of the vessel which otherwise might be damaged in a ramming action. In fact, in view of the comparative size advantage the brigantines enjoyed over the Indian canoes, the collision bulkhead easily could have essayed the role of a true ram. Collaterally, an actual ram not only was not needed in combat with the canoes but also would have been undesirable because of the added hazard it posed in regard to grounding.

The peculiar nature of Lake Texcoco and Tenochtitlán forced upon Martín López and his fellow shipbuilders certain departures from the lines and general construction of the then seagoing Spanish shipping; the brigantines represented the minimal modification necessary to meet the immediate situation. Offensively and defensively the ships were a tremendous addition to Spanish military power. Captain-general and men in the ranks alike had come to consider them *la llave de toda la guerra*—the key to the whole war.

The Skippers

As a parallel preparation to the activities that saw the navy take its place among the military effectives at the disposal of Cortés, the soldiers were mustered and arms and supplies were inventoried by the captain-general. One month before the siege began Cortés said he had the following:

  86 cavalrymen
 118 bowmen and musketeers
 700–plus foot soldiers with swords and shields
   3 heavy guns
  15 light field pieces
  10 cwt. of powder

From this force somewhat in excess of 904 men—Bernal Díaz says 928[1]—Cortés also had to man his fleet.

Beginning by designating the captains for the thirteen ships, the

[1] *HC*, I, 222. As in other statistical offerings, this is not the only array of figures available for this muster. Bernal Díaz said the Spanish force consisted of the following: 84 cavalrymen, 194 crossbowmen and musketeers, and 650 foot soldiers with swords, shields, and lances; see *BDdelC*, II, 221.

captain-general continued until every paddle was manned, every bow gun had a gunner, and every ship had a balanced complement of crossbowmen, musketeers, and infantrymen of the sword-shield-lance-bearing variety. At least twenty-two men have been listed as commanders of brigantines during the siege.[2] The following six names, it is felt, should not be so listed: Francisco de Briones, Juan de Mansilla, Juan Esteban Colmenero, Ginés Nortes, Hernando de Lema, and Alonso Pérez de Zamora.[3] A seventh person, Francisco de Verdugo, may be classed as doubtful since Bernal Díaz lists him as one of the three captains of land detachments fighting under the command of Olid during the siege.[4] However, if Verdugo is counted (Díaz did not serve with Olid and hence could be confused), the total stands at sixteen and embraces the following names: Pedro Barba, Pedro Briones, Antonio de Carvajal, Miguel Díaz de Aux, Cristóbal Flores, García Holguín, Juan Jaramillo, Juan de Limpias Carvajal, Rodrigo Morejón de Lobera, Andrés Núñez, Juan Portillo, Juan Rodríguez de Villafuerte, Francisco Rodríguez Magariño, Gerónimo Ruiz de la Mota, Antonio Sotelo, and Francisco Verdugo.[5] All the more because only a limited reconstruction of crew

[2] This total represents a compilation of the data available in *ibid.*, 224; Cervantes de Salazar, *Crónica*, 637–638; Dorantes de Carranza, *Sumaria relación*, 31–32; Herrera, *Historia general*, II, Part I, 20; Torquemada, *Monarquia Indiana*, I, 538; and Solís, *Historia*, 419. Cortés failed to name the ship captains.

[3] Except for Francisco de Briones and Juan de Mansilla, whose names are contributed by Dorantes de Carranza (*Sumaria relación*, 31), all of these men in the extremely doubtful category are listed by Bernal Díaz and no one else. Concerning Juan de Mansilla it should be added that if credence be given his own rather obviously boastful statement of 1525, he might seriously be considered the brigantine captain he claims to have been; see MN–PyTT, Leg. 95, Información de los méritos y servicios de Juan de Mansylla (1525). The removal of four of fourteen names from Díaz' group leads to his being the least reliable of all the listings. In fairness to Díaz it must be remembered he served with Alvarado on the Tacuba causeway and had little, if any, personal contact with brigantine captains during the siege. In later years his residence in Guatemala served to remove him from possible post-conquest contacts with most of the surviving ship captains.

[4] *BDdelC*, II, 228.

[5] With the exception of Miguel Díaz de Aux, Juan de Limpias Carvajal, and Andrés Núñez, this corresponds to the list of Cervantes de Salazar, whose source of information was Gerónimo Ruiz de la Mota, freely acknowledged in both published and unpublished sources to have been a brigantine captain. Dorantes de Carranza

lists is possible, it becomes desirable to know a bit better these skippers who made naval history in the course of the Spanish conquest of the New World.

Pedro Barba, a native of Seville, had come to New Spain in 1520, as a lieutenant of Governor Velázquez of Cuba, with a small vessel carrying men, horses, and letters for Narváez. Joining Cortés in the course of the Tepeaca campaign, Barba was welcomed and appointed a captain of crossbowmen. In the course of the land warfare between the time of his arrival and the launching of the siege against Tenochtitlán, he distinguished himself as a valiant fighter and a courageous leader of men. In a skirmish shortly before the opening of the siege he was wounded as he and his crossbowmen stormed a hill position in the vicinity of Chalco. While with Cortés on the last circuit of the lake, in April, 1521, Barba spent some time, during the stay in Xochimilco, directing his men as they feathered and put heads on their supply of arrows. On the very eve of the siege he was still identified with crossbows; it was he who divided the arrows and arrowheads among all the crossbowmen in anticipation of the amphibious thrust against Tenochtitlán. As the discussion of the naval operations will indicate, Barba, in his new role, continued his valiant fighting until, badly wounded, he fell a casualty of the campaign.[6]

Pedro Briones, a native of Salamanca and a veteran of the Italian campaigns, arrived in New Spain with Royal Treasurer Alderete just a few weeks before the inauguration of the siege. Of his services during the short interval before the amphibious assault nothing is known. Appointed a brigantine captain by Cortés, Briones did not so distinguish himself as to force his name and deeds into the record as constructed by the eyewitness historians. Whether his appointment was the result of friendship, his nautical background,

---

followed Cervantes de Salazar closely, as did Solís, though neither exactly duplicated his work. Herrera and Torquemada, on the other hand, copied him verbatim.

[6] *BDdelC*, II, 115–116, 192–193, 195, 207, 220, 224, 244; and Dorantes de Carranza, *Sumaria relación*, 221–222. Orozco y Berra, following Dorantes de Carranza, states that Barba came to New Spain with Narváez; see MOyB, "Conquistadores," 389.

or the captain-general's desire to appease a faction, one can but speculate.[7]

Antonio de Carvajal, a native of Zamora, likewise arrived in New Spain with Alderete in the spring of 1521 as the brigantines were being completed. Although it is known that Carvajal had reached the Indies at the age of eighteen, in 1513, it is not clear whether his years in the Antilles were identified with maritime matters. At the age of twenty-six, almost immediately upon his arrival in New Spain, he was named captain of a brigantine. In the absence of information concerning his prior career, one wonders if the appointment was based on already demonstrated capacity as a military leader, association with ships, or merely on his association with a powerful person, namely, the Royal Treasurer, whose favor Cortés must have desired to court.[8]

Miguel Díaz de Aux, a native of the mountain community of Aux in Aragón, arrived in New Spain, in command of a vessel bearing re-enforcements for the luckless Pánuco settlement sponsored by Garay, while Cortés was on the Tepeaca campaign. The reasons for his designation as a brigantine captain are not stated, but his proved ability as a leader of men, his long experience in the Indies, and his personal position might have influenced the decision. Miguel Díaz had been connected with the Indies for more than a decade prior to his arrival in New Spain. In the late summer of 1510 he, with others, was involved in litigation in Spanish courts concerning penalties assessed by the Casa de Contratación. In November, 1510, Juan Ponce de León, as governor of the island of San Juan [Puerto Rico], was ordered by the Crown to seize the property and Indians of Díaz. Rehabilitation came early the next year, with the insignia of the office of *alguacil mayor* of the island

[7] BDdelC, II, 188, 224, 337–338. Orozco y Berra, following Dorantes de Carranza, mistakenly states that Briones came to New Spain with Narváez; see MOyB, "Conquistadores," 390.

[8] MN–PyTT, Leg. 93, Información de los méritos y servicios de Antonio de Carvajal (1551); BDdelC, II, 188, 224; Dorantes de Carranza, *Sumaria relación*, 158–159; Edmundo O'Gorman, "Catálogo de pobladores de Nueva España," BAGN, Vol. XII (1941), 462–463; and Francisco A. de Icaza, *Diccionario autobiográfico de conquistadores y pobladores de Nueva España*, I, 72–73.

of San Juan restored to Díaz in late March. Two months later he gained royal licenses for two caravels which were engaged in carrying supplies to the island. Simultaneously Juan Ponce de León was ordered to restore to Díaz all the property and Indians that had been sequestered. In addition, the Crown granted him two *solares* and two *caballerias* of land on the island. Ere the first half of the year 1511 had passed, Díaz had been appointed *factor* of the island. Evidence is strong that he was pushing some kind of economic endeavor—he won an order from the Crown which required Diego Colón to allow him to transport forty slaves from Española to San Juan. Indicative of his position and wealth is the order of the Crown to the Casa de Contratación, in mid-1511, to permit Díaz to transport fifty marks of wrought silver to San Juan for use in his household. Additional licenses and orders involving exemptions from duties and other privileges bespeak his power and influence and that of his wife Isabel.[9]

Cristóbal Flores, a native of Valencia de Don Juan, apparently crossed to New Spain in company with Cortés, since his signature is found on the agreement reached between Cortés and the *regimiento* on August 5, 1519. Easily one of the most obscure of the brigantine skippers, Flores remained unknown prior to his appointment as a naval captain.[10]

García Holguín, a native of Cáceres, is thought to have entered New Spain in company with Narváez. He had resided on Cuba for

---

[9] *ENE*, I, 7–10 *passim*, 12–24 *passim*; *BDdelC*, II, 123–124, 224; Juan Francisco Andrés de Uztarroz, *Segunda parte de los Anales de la Corona, y Reyno de Aragón, Desde el Año MDXXI, hasta el XXVIII*, in *Conquista de México*, ed. Joaquín Ramírez Cabañas, 255–256; and Icaza, *Diccionario autobiográfico*, I, 73–74. Icaza, differing from the usual version that somewhat more than fifty men and seven horses came with Díaz, insists that he brought 150 foot soldiers, 20 cavalrymen, and a considerable amount of ammunition and artillery in two vessels, rather than the one he customarily is said to have commanded at that time. Bernal Díaz is the one basic source for the thought that Díaz de Aux captained a brigantine. Expressing the contrary view is Dorantes de Carranza, who writes, "As for Miguel Diez de Aux, I do not list him as a conquistador because he arrived after Mexico was won." See *Sumaria relación*, 450.

[10] *CDIAO*, XXVI, 15; *CDHM*, II, 546–548; Cervantes de Salazar, *Crónica*, 637; and MOyB, "Conquistadores," 411.

some time and was a debt-ridden landholder, owing money to Diego Velázquez, at the time he sailed to New Spain. Of his role in the pre-siege phase of the conquest nothing is known, though he is thought to have had wide maritime experience. His appointment as a brigantine captain might well not have altered his unspectacular life if fortune had not dictated that he should be the man to seize Cuauhtémoc and bring the siege to an end on August 13, 1521.[11]

Juan Jaramillo, a native of either Salvatierra, in Extremadura, or Villa Nueva de Balcarrota, accompanied Cortés to New Spain. His signature is upon the written agreement of August, 1519, between Cortés and the regimiento of Vera Cruz, and also upon the undated letter of the army to the Emperor in support of Cortés as captain-general. During the last circuit of the lake prior to the siege—in April, 1521—Jaramillo served as one of the captains under Cortés. As a brigantine skipper, on one occasion he distinguished himself by leading the rescue operation which prevented the loss of one of the vessels to the enemy natives.[12]

Juan de Limpias Carvajal, a native of Seville who had crossed to the New World late in 1513, landed in New Spain as a member of the original expedition of Cortés. Of his pre-siege duty no record is available. During the Battle of Tenochtitlán he served as a brigantine captain, quite possibly as a replacement for one of the initial group of skippers when a substitution had to be made.[13]

Rodrigo Morejón de Lobera, a native of Medina del Campo,

---

[11] *CDIAO*, XXXV, 128, 197, 528–529; *BDdelC*, II, 224, 295–299; *HC*, II, 46–47; Cervantes de Salazar, *Crónica*, 637–638; Dorantes de Carranza, *Sumaria relación*, 32. Without citing an authority, Orozco y Berra assigns him to the original Cortés force; see MOyB, "Conquistadores," 373.

[12] *BDdelC*, II, 196, 224, 262; *CDIAO*, XXVI, 15, and XXVIII, 489; *CDHM*, I, 431; Cervantes de Salazar, *Crónica*, 637; Dorantes de Carranza, *Sumaria relación*, 207; Eduardo Sánchez-Arjona, "Relación de las personas que pasaron a esta Nueva España, y se hallaron en el descubrimiento, toma e conquista della," *RABM*, 3ª época, Vol. XXXVI (1917), 421; and Luis González Obregón, *The Streets of Mexico*, tr. Blanche Collet Wagner, 55.

[13] *BDdelC*, II, 224; Cristóbal Bermúdez Plata, *Catálogo de pasajeros a Indias durante los siglos XVI, XVII y XVIII*, I, 112; Icaza, *Diccionario autobiográfico*, I, 20; and Cervantes de Salazar, *Crónica*, 709.

arrived in New Spain while Cortés was on the Tepeaca campaign. The *Santa María del Antigua*, the small supply ship he commanded, had been chartered in the service of Governor Velázquez to carry provisions to Narváez. His service as a brigantine captain was not characterized by any particular brilliance that would carry his name into recorded history.[14]

Andrés Núñez, who reached New Spain aboard one of the Garay vessels, succeeded to the command of a brigantine during the course of the Battle of Tenochtitlán, not having been among the originally designated group of captains. During combat a skipper abandoned his ship, and Núñez succeeded to the command. When the ignominious captain later tried to resume his command, Núñez stoutly refused to yield, saying the post had been forfeited. When the issue was presented to Cortés for settlement, the captain-general backed Núñez, who commanded the brigantine thereafter. Andrés Núñez the brigantine captain and Andrés Núñez the carpenter are two distinct personalities. Carpenter Andrés Núñez had already worked with Martín López on the first brigantines in Tenochtitlán before his namesake landed on the continent. Orozco y Berra is in error as he lists the carpenter with Garay and the skipper among Cortés' original force.[15]

Juan Portillo, a native of Portillo, arrived in the Indies sometime prior to entering New Spain with Cortés. Of his services before the inauguration of the siege nothing is known. He was the second of the two skippers to be killed in the course of the campaign.[16]

Juan Rodríguez de Villafuerte, a native of Cortés' home town of Medellín, came to New Spain with the captain-general. His name is among those affixed to the undated letter the army addressed to the Emperor in support of Cortés. From a statement of services

[14] *CDIAO*, XXVI, 393–394, and XL, 60, 66–68; *BDdelC*, II, 117; and Cervantes de Salazar, *Crónica*, 638.

[15] Herrera, *Historia general*, II, Part I, 42; and Ignacio de Villar Villamil (ed.), *Cedulario heráldico de conquistadores de Nueva España*, unnumbered page (No. 81); and MOyB, "Conquistadores," 379, 401.

[16] *BDdelC*, II, 224, 244; Cervantes de Salazar, *Crónica*, 638; and MOyB, "Conquistadores," 382.

recorded four years after the fall of Tenochtitlán, the major events of his first six years in New Spain can be gleaned. He participated in a full share of land campaigns, from the first landing on Cozumel through the final fall of the Indian island-capital. Along with Gonzalo de Sandoval, he was placed in charge of the vessels of the fleet in the early days while the town of Vera Cruz was being estab- lished; apparently this was his first distinctive and responsible post in reference to shipping. Participating in the actions against Tlax- cala and Cholula, he was with Cortés when the Spaniards made their initial entry into the Mexican capital. As the captain-general planned the withdrawal of his forces from the city, Rodríguez de Villafuerte was given command of a detachment of fifty men. At least one conquistador credits him with the selection of the route taken by the remnants of the Spanish army to Tlaxcala via Otumba. Rodríguez engaged in the Tepeaca campaign and served as captain of a contingent operating out of the base of Texcoco. He was with Sandoval on the excursions to Chalco and accompanied him as a member of the escort for the brigantines as they moved from Tlax- cala to Texcoco. Not only did he go with Cortés on the counter- clockwise reconnaissance to Tacuba, but he was also at his captain- general's side, in command of a detachment of sixty men, during the final circuit of the lake preparatory to the general hostilities. There is good reason to believe he was a personal friend of Cortés. When Cortés established the commands for the siege, Juan Rod- ríguez de Villafuerte was named commander in chief of the fleet. At that moment this veteran campaigner and proved leader of men was twenty-one years old. Throughout the two and one-half months' amphibious operation, according to his own claim, he had over-all command of the fleet of brigantines and the men serving aboard them as well as immediate command of the flagship, *La Capitana*.[17]

Francisco Rodríguez Magariño, a native of Mérida, entered

[17] MN–PyTT, Leg. 96, Información de los méritos y servicios de Juan Rodríguez de Villafuerte (1525); *CDHM*, I, 431; *HC*, I, 208; Conway (ed.), *La Noche Triste*, 95; Cervantes de Salazar, *Crónica*, 637; and *CDIAO*, XXVI, 476.

New Spain in company with Cortés. Prior to crossing to Cuba and enlisting in the expedition Cortés was forming, Rodríguez had resided for some time in the town of Puerto Real, Española. Married and the holder of an encomienda, he also served as alguacil mayor. Leaving his wife, home, Indians, and post behind, he sailed for Cuba and joined Cortés. By the time of the Sad Night his capacity as a leader of men was clearly in evidence. On that occasion, while commanding the detachment of sixty Spaniards charged with conveying and protecting the portable bridge, he suffered a severe head wound. When, immediately after the debacle of that memorable night, Cortés mustered his men and divided them into companies and appointed commanders, Rodríguez was given command of sixty Spaniards as the battered force made its way via Otumba to Tlaxcala. For the Tepeaca campaign he was assigned a force of 15 Spaniards and 100,000 Tlaxcalans—the latter a figure which, like many other statements of Indian warrior strength, one is inclined to consider absurdly high. When Cortés moved his base of operations to Texcoco, Rodríguez went with him. When the captain-general ordered Sandoval to Tlaxcala to convoy the brigantine materials to Texcoco, it would seem that Rodríguez Magariño was second in command of the escort-guard force. As soon as the convoy reached Texcoco with its unusual cargo Rodríguez was ordered to the coast to get a supply of nails, cannon, powder, and other munitions, at least some of which were needed for the brigantines. On the completion of the fleet, he was designated captain of a vessel, and he proceeded to fight his ship day and night during the siege operation, receiving a leg wound ere the city fell into Spanish hands.[18]

Gerónimo Ruiz de la Mota, a native of Burgos, came to the navy of Cortés with a background that included meaningful maritime experience. He captained the larger of the two vessels of Rodrigo de Bastidas that sailed from Santo Domingo to the mainland in

---

[18] MN–PyTT, Leg. 96, Información de los méritos y servicios de Francisco Rodríguez Magariño (1526); *CDIAO*, XXVIII, 493; Cervantes de Salazar, *Crónica*, 637; and Dorantes de Carranza, *Sumaria relación*, 182–183.

early spring of 1521, at the time the Spaniards, concentrated in Texcoco, were busy readying the brigantines and mopping up the valley prior to launching the amphibious assault upon Tenochtitlán. Named to command a brigantine almost at once upon his arrival in the camp of Cortés, he was about twenty-three years old when he entered upon that naval duty.[19]

Antonio Sotelo, thought to be a native of either Zamora or Seville, is considered to have entered New Spain with Cortés. No details are available concerning his life either prior to his duty as a brigantine captain or subsequent thereto. One wonders, as does Orozco y Berra, is he the Sotelo who, late in the siege, failed in his attempt to build a serviceable catapult in the center of the besieged city? If so—and as will be related in the narrative of the battle operations, men of the brigantines frequently participated in limited land operations during the siege—it can be added that Sotelo brought prior military experience with him, having served in Italy under Gonsalvo de Córdoba.[20]

Francisco Verdugo, a native of Arévalo and by marriage a kinsman of Governor Velázquez of Cuba, accompanied Narváez to New Spain in 1520. Although the brother-in-law of Velázquez and quite possibly an officeholder only because of the governor's power, Verdugo did not jump to obey his every order. In part it was owing to Verdugo's failure to follow an order sent by Velázquez that Cortés was not detained in Trinidad, in which town Verdugo served as *alcalde mayor* in 1518. At the time of his passage to New Spain with Narváez, he was twenty-three years of age and served as captain of the ship *La Portuguesa*. As yet another of the men of the different expeditions whose loyalty Cortés was intent upon having, Verdugo figured as a captain of soldiers prior to the beginning of the siege.

---

[19] *BDdelC*, II, 188, 224; *CDIAO*, XLI, 235; Cervantes de Salazar, *Crónica*, 599, 638; Dorantes de Carranza, *Sumaria relación*, 195–196; Villar Villamil (ed.), *Cedulario heráldico*, unnumbered page (No. 123); and Icaza, *Diccionario autobiográfico*, I, 72. Orozco y Berra lists Ruiz de la Mota as a member of Alderete's company; see MOyB, "Conquistadores," 405.

[20] *BDdelC*, II, 293–294; Herrera, *Historia general*, II, Part I, 20; and MOyB, "Conquistadores," 385.

He was a capable crossbowman and led a detachment in an assault upon a hill position during the circuit of the lake country in April, 1521. Though quite commonly listed among the brigantine captains, Verdugo is conspicuously absent from Bernal Díaz' list for the good reason that Díaz designates him as one of the captains with the land division led by Olid during the siege. About a month after the siege got underway, Díaz locates Verdugo in the camp of Cortés.[21]

Lest the listing of sixteen captains for thirteen ships be considered strange, it should be borne in mind that some supplementary appointments must have been made after the siege got underway. The death of Captain Juan Portillo in the only successful Mexican ambush must have necessitated one such appointment, since his vessel was not lost with him, and there was also the circumstance of the forementioned promotion of Andrés Núñez to the ship abandoned by its original skipper. If the number be in error, it is thought to err toward understatement rather than overstatement.

The captain-general's choice of the sixteen captains seems to have been guided more by a need for diplomacy and by his recognition of demonstrated leadership than by the amount of prior identification with the sea and ships. The diplomacy is in evidence when the backgrounds of some of the men are noted. Francisco Verdugo was a representative of the Narváez group, and his appointment identified the Narváez men with the naval endeavor to some degree. Significantly, he was also brother-in-law of Governor Velázquez. Two of the skippers, Pedro Briones and Antonio de Carvajal, were selected from the recently arrived Alderete group. In view of the fact that they arrived in New Spain too late to demonstrate their qualities of leadership in the land fighting preliminary to the siege, it would seem that their relationship to Royal

[21] CDIAO, XXVII, 434; BDdelC, II, 195, 228, 256; HC–MacN, I, 22–23; HC, I, 208; MN–PyTT, Leg. 95, Información de los méritos y servicios de Pedro Moreno (1561); Dorantes de Carranza, Sumaria relación, 182; and Icaza, Diccionario autobiográfico, II, 324.

Treasurer Alderete might have influenced Cortés as he named them brigantine captains. Gerónimo Ruiz de la Mota might have received his captain's assignment as the representative of a sizable group of men recently arrived in New Spain, as well as because of his prior maritime experience.

Four of the captains, Pedro Barba, Rodrigo Morejón de Lobera, Miguel Díaz de Aux, and Andrés Núñez, had previously either commanded or otherwise participated in small expeditionary forces related to larger enterprises that had failed. Barba and Morejón de Lobera commanded ships in the service of Governor Velázquez which were intended to aid Narváez; and Miguel Díaz de Aux commanded a ship related to the Pánuco venture of Garay. However, it cannot be concluded, merely because they commanded single-ship expeditions, that these men were ship captains in the normal sense. In fact the general pattern of the times would suggest that they, as commanders of expeditions, depended upon anonymous skippers to operate the vessels. Seven of the men, Cristóbal Flores, Juan Jaramillo, Juan de Limpias Carvajal, Juan Portillo, Juan Rodríguez de Villafuerte, Francisco Rodríguez Magariño, and Antonio Sotelo—somewhat less than half of the total number— were members of the original force that had come from Cuba under the direction of Cortés. But of this group only one man, Juan Rodríguez de Villafuerte, is clearly known to have been identified previously with ships, and his background was limited to a shadowy sort of short-term co-command of the Cuban fleet, along with Gonzalo de Sandoval, during the early summer of 1519 in the coastal waters of New Spain.

Recognizing fully the diplomatic purposes Cortés seemed bent upon serving as he selected the brigantine captains, the question still can be raised—why did he turn to a group of landlubbers rather than experienced pilots and reputable captains? Surely such professionals were available; when one counts all the ships whose personnel was incorporated within Cortés' force it is evident that approximately forty captains—not to mention lesser ships' officers —had entered New Spain. It is true that several such officers had

Views across Basin of Old Lake Texcoco from Peñón del Marqués (Tepepolco)

Toward the northeast and Texcoco

Toward the east (*Photographs by the author*)

Views across Basin of Old Lake Texcoco from Peñón del Marqués (Tepepolco)

Toward the northwest

Toward the west and Mexico City (*Photographs by the author*)

been sent back to Spain and that others surely had fallen in the course of battle, but it is still logical to believe that Cortés, had he so desired, could have had an experienced skipper on each brigantine. One must conclude that, in addition to the previously mentioned sense of diplomacy, Cortés, in not appointing experienced sea captains, was influenced by his cognizance of two unusual but exceedingly important aspects of the coming engagement—namely, the geographic setting of the future naval operations and the unique nature of the land-water campaign before them.

The fleet, it must be remembered, was not a seagoing navy. Called upon to operate on the limited waters of a lake—it was impossible to lose sight of land—a captain did not need the usual technical knowledge exacted of a seagoing skipper. The fine points of early sixteenth-century navigation were not demanded of him; he had no use for a compass or an astrolabe. He needed none of the special skill or courage or experience required to ride out heavy seas. He could get along without the specialized knowledge that would tell him exactly what supplies would be required for a long voyage, because he could put his ship into shore every day. One can imagine the air of professional superiority with which a bona fide skipper of seagoing ships would pass up such a command—all the more so since the vessels, powered by paddle as well as sail, would surely have reminded him of the Greek and Roman navies of bygone centuries rather than any vessel he had ever seen in modern sixteenth-century Spanish transatlantic service.

In the unique nature of the amphibious operation ahead of the conquistadors, little, if any, naval action in the accepted sense of combat between fleets was to be expected, because of the overwhelming naval superiority enjoyed by the invaders. Instead, the brigantines were to engage in close-in support of the armies on the causeways, serving to protect their otherwise vulnerable flanks. In a real sense the navy on Lake Texcoco played the role of cavalry (coincidentally the horses were not conspicuous assets in the siege operation), co-operating with and supporting and protecting the infantry. Accordingly, military tactics, rather than naval tactics

145

pure and simple, would serve a brigantine captain well. The proved land commander would fit easily into the picture, whereas the professional seagoing captain would be facing circumstances so strange to him as to force him, if possible, to repudiate a large measure of his past experience.

Representative Crewmen

The assignment of crews to the brigantines took place prior to the designation of the land forces of Alvarado, Olid, and Sandoval on Tuesday, April 30, 1521. No documentary proof can be cited to substantiate this conclusion, but when one considers the precise numbers of men that Cortés, on Tuesday, April 30, assigned as foot soldiers, crossbowmen, musketeers, and cavalrymen to the land forces commanded by Alvarado, Olid, and Sandoval, it is evident that the personnel needs of the navy had already been met because the total involved in the three land divisions did not account for all the manpower. And logically, it would have been less than sensible to organize the land forces, unit by unit, and then cannibalize them to furnish the brigantine captains with crews. Finally, since the formal launching of the ships had occurred on April 28, necessity, as well as logic, would dictate the naming of the ships' complements by that date. Bernal Díaz, whose chronology leaves something to be desired on occasion, implies the forementioned order of naval and army assignments.[22]

For once Cortés and Bernal Díaz are in agreement on a statistical point as they indicate that each brigantine was given a complement of twenty-five men: a captain, twelve rowers—six for each side—and twelve crossbowmen and musketeers, the bowmen and gunners being specifically exempt from duty as rowers. Such is the simplest statement of the distribution of men and duties. That some of the men doubled in other capacities is also evident—as pilots, as artillerymen charged with the firing of the cannon mounted in the bow, and as *veedores*. Assigning somewhat more than three hundred men—more than one third of the total force of Spaniards—to duty

---

[22] *BDdelC*, II, 223–228; and Herrera, *Historia general*, II, Part I, 21.

aboard those brigantines was no easy matter. Finding 156 experienced rowers might have been impossible. Finding even one man who *wanted* such backbreaking, degrading, essentially noncombat duty was unlikely. Faced with a shortage of experienced and willing men, Cortés assigned to the brigantines the seamen from his own and Narváez' fleets. Still lacking full complements of rowers, he next added those men who had been seen fishing and those who had resided in coastal towns of Spain—in fact all whose known backgrounds admitted of any association, real or imagined, with the sea. When finally the complements of all the crews had been filled, it was possible to assert that the majority of the men aboard the brigantines were possessed of some kind of previous shipboard experience.[23]

The degree to which Cortés dominated the manning of the ships is significant. By naming the crews prior to designating the captains, he achieved a tighter personal control over the composition of the navy than would have been the case had he named the skippers and then allowed them to enter into competition to fill their complements. The method employed probably also meant that the crews were more evenly matched in abilities than they would have been if the personalities and reputations of the individual skippers had entered into the issue; it surely meant crews whose primary loyalties were directed toward Cortés and the ships rather than toward the captains themselves.

If seagoing sailors were loath to take to the paddles, it can well be imagined that finding soldiers willing to take shipboard duty was even more difficult. However, two factors probably helped to attract the crossbowmen and musketeers: memory of the debacle of the Sad Night might well have inclined soldiers toward the navy on the theory that nothing could be worse than the land duty they had once known; and the express exemption from duty as paddlers enjoyed by the crossbowmen and musketeers gave their specialized fighting role a dignity and recognition that could not fail to appeal to the Spanish temperament. Given the difficulties that attended

[23] *HC*, II, 224; and *BDdelC*, II, 221–224.

the movement of field artillery in New Spain, plus the high ratio of loss of heavy guns during the retreat of June 30, 1520, one suspects that Cortés easily reached the decision to put most of his artillery aboard the ships. The artillerymen's love of their guns and their memories of the frustration that attended their fighting with such weapons on the causeways might have made comparatively easy the assignment of artillerymen to the navy.

In the absence of muster rolls for the various land divisions and the navy, it is difficult to record a parallel between the military and naval aspects of the fall of Tenochtitlán on the level of individual participants other than officers. We know the names both of the land commanders and of the brigantine captains, but as to the men in the ranks on the causeways and the men in the crews of the brigantines we are almost completely ignorant of names and battle assignments.

Only a small minority of those serving in the brigantine crews can be identified. Antonio de Arriaga, who originally had left Spain for Cuba in 1519 with a royal letter recommending him to Diego Velázquez and who entered New Spain in company with the Narváez expedition, served as veedor of the brigantine commanded by Gerónimo Ruiz de la Mota.[24] Alonso de la Reguera, who arrived in New Spain at the time that Cortés was in Texcoco readying the brigantines—and hence most probably came either in the company of Alderete or on one of the vessels of Bastidas—served as veedor aboard the brigantine commanded by Flores. Orozco y Berra mistakenly assigns him to the original Cortés force. During his short service in land campaigns prior to the launching of the siege, Reguera had been in a detachment led by Jorge de Alvarado.[25]

Just about the only paddler who can be positively identified is one Diego Díaz, another of the Narváez men. On the Sad Night he

[24] MN–PyTT, Leg. 93, Información de los méritos y servicios de Antonio de Arriaga (1548, 1559).

[25] MN–PyTT, Leg. 96, Información de los méritos y servicios de Alonso de la Reguera (1538); MN–PyTT, Leg. 94, Información de los méritos y servicios de Diego y Francisco Díaz (1538, 1539); MN–PyTT, Leg. 95, Información de los méritos y servicios de Francisco López (1539); and MOyB, "Conquistadores," 383.

fought his way out of the city with crossbow, sword, and buckler, sustaining three wounds as he did so. Later, during the imprisonment of Narváez on the coast of New Spain, Díaz exhibited continued loyalty to his former leader (as well as willingness to earn the 300 pesos promised him), when he and a couple of seamen planned to supply a vessel for the escape of Narváez to Cuba. In fact, the caravel *Maluenda,* on which Díaz had served as master, was the one on which the intrigue centered. In some manner the plot came to light, and for his part in it Díaz was tried and condemned to death in Vera Cruz on February 16, 1521. For some unknown reason he escaped that fate and from then on proceeded to serve Cortés loyally and faithfully. He participated in land campaigns prior to the launching of the brigantines. In addition to manning his paddle, Díaz employed a crossbow aboard ship. Such doubling as this, probably a quite common practice within the small navy, materially increased fire power beyond the basic number of crossbowmen, artillerymen, and musketeers who were assigned shipboard duty. Along with veedor Alonso de la Reguera, Diego Díaz served aboard the brigantine commanded by Flores. On one occasion during the battle the ship became stranded, and at once the Indians attacked in such numbers that all would have perished had Díaz not jumped into the lake and so righted the vessel as to permit it to float to safety once more. In the course of his stanch defense of his ship, Díaz suffered a head wound, but thanks to his efforts the ship and his comrades escaped.[26]

Pedro González Nájera, a signer of the undated letter sent to the Emperor by the army, was a member of the Narváez expedition. Orozco y Berra errs when he assigns him to the original Cortés force. He had brought with him a horse, two servants, and a son. Cortés ordered him to sell the horse and serve aboard one of the brigantines. One readily suspects that Pedro González Nájera,

[26] MN–PyTT, Leg. 94, Información de los méritos y servicios de Diego y Francisco Díaz (1538, 1539); and *CDIAO,* XXVI, 289, 291–293, 296–297 and XXVIII, 491. Among the witnesses whose testimony supported Díaz' statement of his services was a companion in arms aboard the brigantine, Alonso de la Reguera.

cavalryman, was among those who complained bitterly at the degradation and humiliation thought to have been part and parcel of the naval service. Yet such an assignment was to be expected in the light of his past association with the sea, because he had had a ship in transatlantic service in 1517. No available authority supports his own claim that he had charge of one of the brigantines.[27] It is quite conceivable that he might have been second in command and, as such, could have fought the vessel on occasion.

Illiterate Pablo del Retamal, with Cortés since his initial landing on the continent, served aboard the flagship *La Capitana* under Captain Juan Rodríguez de Villafuerte. He witnessed Martín López' heroic rescue of that vessel on the occasion when it became stranded while under heavy attack from the Mexicans and was abandoned by the skipper and most of the ship's company. At the time of his brigantine duty, Retamal was twenty years old.[28]

Alonso Nortes, who is thought to have entered New Spain with Narváez and who was among the signers of the letter of 1520 in support of Cortés, is known to have seen brigantine duty during the siege operation in the capacity of a soldier. His heroic action when several brigantines were sorely pressed by throngs of Indian canoes is lauded in the highest terms by chronicler Cervantes de Salazar.[29]

Juan de Mansilla, another Narváez man, served aboard the brigantine commanded by García Holguín. In his own statement of his services during the conquest, recorded in 1525 and showing its author to be not exactly a paragon of modesty of expression, Mansilla said, "I was appointed captain of one of the ships." Quite likely he was a junior officer under Holguín. During his naval duty, Mansilla, then eighteen years old, suffered a bad face wound, but even that did not terminate his service. On August 13, 1521, he was aboard the brigantine when Cuauhtémoc was made prisoner. His

[27] MN–PyTT, Leg. 94, Información de los méritos y servicios de Pedro González Nájera (1526, 1528); and MOyB, "Conquistadores," 413.

[28] AGI, Patronato 57–1–1, fols. 30–33 (testimony, 1534); translation in AU–CC, Martín López 1528–1574, pp. 92–100; and *CDIAO*, XXIX, 141–142.

[29] Cervantes de Salazar, *Crónica*, 711; and MOyB, "Conquistadores," 417.

own version of that event insists that it was he who seized and led the Mexican monarch to Cortés.[30]

Lázaro Guerrero, master of one of the brigantines in the Narváez fleet and a long-term friend of Martín López, was one of the most conscientious and persistent carpenters to dedicate his energies to the building of the thirteen brigantines before he was assigned, as master, to one of the twelve vessels other than *La Capitana*. Conflicting evidence suggests that Guerrero was between thirty-one and thirty-seven years of age at the time of his naval service under Cortés. Orozco y Berra fails to list him among the conquistadors.[31]

Martín López, native of Seville, had crossed to the Indies in late 1516 and was a member of the original Cortés expedition, entering New Spain with several servants, a considerable quantity of goods, and phenomenal capacity as a shipbuilder. After he had repeatedly shown himself to be a fine soldier in earlier phases of the conquest, it was his talent as a shipwright that was utilized almost constantly from November, 1519, through April, 1521, as he successively built the four brigantines on Lake Texcoco, almost finished the caravel on the coast, and supervised the construction of the thirteen-ship navy of 1521. When the amphibious operation got underway Martín López was aboard *La Capitana* in the capacity of master, serving in addition as pilot major for the entire brigantine fleet. He was then approximately thirty-three years old.[32]

[30] MN–PyTT, Leg. 95, Información de los méritos y servicios de Juan de Mansylla (1525).

[31] AGI, Patronato 57–1–1, fols. 5r–6 (testimony, 1528), 20r–24 (testimony, 1534); translation in AU–CC, Martín López 1528–1574, pp. 16–18, 65–74; and LC–CC, Martín López 1529–1550, pp. 161–168 (testimony, 1540); MN–PyTT, Leg. 94, Información de los méritos y servicios de Lázaro Guerrero (1542); and MOyB, "Conquistadores," 362–423.

[32] AGI, Patronato 57–1–1, fols. 1–18 *passim* (interrogatory and testimony, 1528) 18–48r *passim* (interrogatory and testimony, 1534); translation in AU–CC, Martín López 1528–1574, pp. 1–144 *passim;* LC–CC, Martín López 1529–1550, pp. 118–168 *passim* (interrogatory and testimony, 1540); and AGI, Patronato 63–1–15, fols. 1–13r *passim* (interrogatory and testimony, 1560); translation in AU–CC, Martín López 1528–1574, pp. 145–187 *passim;* MN–PyTT, Leg. 42, Núm. 13, Cédula de Martín López; CDIAO, XXVII, 164, XXVIII, 493, XXIX, 331; BDdelC, I, 386–387, 422–423, and II, 58, 138, 164–166, 168; Cervantes de Salazar, Crónica, 493, 548–

Other conquistadors who definitely served aboard brigantines include the following: Juan Fernández, of Seville, who served with García Holguín;[33] Alonso del Río; Antonio del Castillo, of Palos; Martín Monje, likewise of Palos, one of the crew of the brigantine captained by Francisco Rodríguez Magariño; Pedro Gómez, of Jerez; Bartolomé Tabarán; Juan de Santana; twenty-seven-year-old Juan Griego Girón; illiterate thirty-two-year-old Andrés López, of Seville; twenty-seven-year-old Antón Cordero, one of the brigantine builders at Texcoco; eighteen-year-old Martín de la Mezquita, of Seville, who served aboard the flagship; Pedro Moreno, an archer aboard the brigantine commanded by Francisco Verdugo; another bowman, Alonso Pérez de Zamora, who served under the command of Gerónimo Ruiz de la Mota; and the excellent horseman Juan Galindo, who served on the brigantine commanded by Antonio de Carvajal.[34]

549, 591, 597, 636, 646–647, 659, 699, 708, 709; Conway (ed.), *La Noche Triste*, x–xi, 84–86; Sánchez-Arjona, "Relación . . . ," *RABM*, Vol. XXXVI (1917), 423; Bermúdez Plata, *Catálogo*, I, 156; Herrera, *Historia general*, II, Part I, 38; Dorantes de Carranza, *Sumaria relación*, 215–216; Bancroft, *Mexico*, I, 490, 674–675; León de la Barra, "Geografía histórica . . . ," *BSMGE*, Vol. XLVII (1937), 73; and Guillermo Porras Muñoz, "Martín López, carpintero de ribera," in Instituto Gonzalo Fernández de Oviedo, *Estudios Cortesianos: recopilados con motivo del IV centenario de la muerte de Hernán Cortés (1547–1947)*, 307–329.

[33] MN–PyTT, Leg. 94, Información de los méritos y servicios de Juan Fernández (1536, 1558, 1561, 1572); and Sánchez-Arjona, "Relación . . . ," *RABM*, Vol. XXXVII (1917), 124. The manuscript statement of the services rendered during the conquest by Juan Fernández is one of the most significant individual records of any of the lesser figures in the navy of Cortés. Not only does it shed considerable light on the career of Fernández, it also includes supporting testimony from five other navy veterans, Alonso del Río, Antonio del Castillo, Martín Monje, Pedro Gómez, and Bartolomé Tabarán. Ambiguities in the wording of the different statements keep the document from shedding light upon that much-debated point: namely, was Cuauhtémoc coming to the Spaniards to surrender or was he fleeing at the moment of his capture?

[34] Alonso del Río: MN–PyTT, Leg. 94, Información de los méritos y servicios de Juan Fernández (1536); *CDIAO*, XXVIII, 491; and Bermúdez Plata, *Catálogo*, I, 163.

Antonio del Castillo: MN–PyTT, Leg. 94, Información de los méritos y servicios de Juan Fernández (1536); and Icaza, *Diccionario autobiográfico*, I, 250.

Martín Monje: MN–PyTT, Leg. 94, Información de los méritos y servicios de

The foregoing men, serving as paddlers, as masters, as crossbow-men, as veedores, and in other, unspecified capacities, are probably representative of the manpower of Cortés' navy. They mirror the various factions and groups that had come together to constitute the force of 1521. Some of them had been common seamen; others had been ship captains. Some had helped to construct the vessels, and, knowing them to be sturdy craft, identified themselves with them in combat. Others were foot soldiers and cavalrymen who had fought countless battles in the earlier land campaigns and who joined the navy reluctantly for the showdown engagement of 1521.

Juan Fernández (1536, 1558); and Sánchez-Arjona, "Relación . . . ," *RABM*, Vol. XXXVII (1917), 127.

Pedro Gómez: MN–PyTT, Leg. 94, Información de los méritos y servicios de Juan Fernández (1536); and *CDIAO*, XXVIII, 490.

Bartolomé Tabarán: MN–PyTT, Leg. 94, Información de los méritos y servicios de Juan Fernández (1536).

Juan de Santana: MN–PyTT, Leg. 97, Información de los méritos y servicios de Juan Santana (1531); *CDIAO*, XXVIII, 491; and MOyB, "Conquistadores," 421.

Juan Griego Girón: AGI, Patronato 57–1–1, fols. 36–39 (testimony, 1534) and AGI, Patronato 63–1–15, fols. 11r–13 (testimony, 1560); translation in AU–CC, Martín López 1528–1574, pp. 108–116, 182–186; and *CDIAO*, XXIX, 472, and XXVI, 98. It is not certain whether Juan Griego Girón and the Juan el Griego who was termed *contramaestre* as Francisco de Garay presented him as a witness in 1523 were one and the same person.

Andrés López: AGI, Patronato 57–1–1, fols. 39–41r (testimony, 1534); translation in AU–CC, Martín López 1528–1574, pp. 116–123; and MOyB, "Conquistadores," 394.

Antón Cordero: AGI, Patronato 57–1–1, fols. 33–36 (testimony, 1534); translation in AU–CC, Martín López 1528–1574, pp. 101–108; and Icaza, *Diccionario autobiográfico*, I, 148. Orozco y Berra erroneously lists Cordero among the members of the original Cortés force; see MOyB, "Conquistadores," 370.

Martín de la Mezquita: MN–PyTT, Leg. 95, Información de los méritos y servicios de Martín de la Mezquita (1540, 1559, 1573); MN–PyTT, Leg. 95, Información de los méritos y servicios de Pedro Moreno (1561); and Sánchez-Arjona, "Relación . . . ," *RABM*, Vol. XXXIX (1918), 92.

Pedro Moreno: MN–PyTT, Leg. 95, Información de los méritos y servicios de Pedro Moreno (1561).

Alonso Pérez de Zamora: MN–PyTT, Leg. 96, Información de los méritos y servicios de Alonso Pérez de Zamora (1540, 1559, 1583); and Icaza, *Diccionario autobiográfico*, I, 85.

Juan Galindo: MN–PyTT, Leg. 96, Información de los méritos y servicios de Alonso Pérez de Zamora (1540).

Most were young, as in truth were the majority in the entire expeditionary force. Some were literate; others could not so much as write their names. Coupled with their captains, such were the men of the brigantines.

The Naval Arm—a Comparative Analysis

The over-all significance of the brigantines in the plan of operation used by Cortés is apparent if the personnel and weapons assigned to the navy are noted in relation to the manpower and instruments of war dedicated to land operations during the amphibious assault upon Tenochtitlán. Within forty-eight hours after the launching of the brigantines, the mustering of manpower, and the inventorying of supplies on Sunday, April 28, 1521, every man was assigned to the captain with whom he was to be identified during the siege, and his duty specified.

The three land forces, divided quite appropriately in view of the fact that the city could be approached overland by only three causeways, were commanded respectively by the well-known captains Pedro de Alvarado, Cristóbal de Olid, and Gonzalo de Sandoval. Alvarado, with the town of Tacuba as his headquarters and the Tacuba causeway his battleground, was assigned the following: 30 cavalrymen, 18 crossbowmen and musketeers, 150 soldiers with swords, shields, and lances, and more than 25,000 Tlaxcalan warriors. For once there is remarkable statistical harmony between Cortés and Díaz, the infantryman agreeing with his commander in all particulars except the number of Indians, which he indicates as 8,000. The more acceptable number is the 25,000 given by Cortés, but even that is small when compared with Cervantes de Salazar's 30,000 plus, and Alva Ixtlilxochitl's 50,000. Conquistadors in general, and foot soldiers in particular, seemed incapable of giving the Indian his due in their accounts of the conquest.[35] Among those serving in the Tacuba division was Bernal Díaz. His identification with a land force during the siege provides us with some reason for

[35] *HC,* I, 223; *BDdelC,* II, 227; Cervantes de Salazar, *Crónica,* 646; and Alva Ixtlilxochitl, *Décima tercia relación,* in Sahagún, *Historia* (1938), IV, 255.

the curtailed consideration of the naval aspects of the operation we find in his reports.

Olid, with orders to establish his headquarters in Coyoacán, had the following assigned to him: 30 cavalrymen, between 18 and 20 crossbowmen and musketeers, between 160 and 175 soldiers armed with swords, shields, and lances, and more than 20,000 Indian allies. Again general agreement exists between Cortés and Díaz, although the latter once more plays down the number of Indians with his figure 8,000. Cervantes de Salazar lists 33 cavalrymen and agrees with Cortés regarding crossbowmen, musketeers, and foot soldiers, but raises the number of Indians to 30,000. Alva Ixtlilxochitl gives 50,000 as the number.[36]

Sandoval, who had brilliantly supported Cortés in a variety of undertakings up to this stage of the conquest, was heading a force which was initially to move against the Iztapalapa anchor of the southern causeway. Later this group was to be called upon to demonstrate its mobility and versatility. Sandoval commanded the following: 24 cavalrymen, from 14 to 19 crossbowmen and musketeers, 150 foot soldiers with swords, shields, and lances, and more than 30,000 assorted Indian allies. With unusual, though not perfect, agreement between Cortés and Bernal Díaz concerning the number of Spaniards involved in the division, Díaz once more lists 8,000 as the number of Indians. Cervantes de Salazar lists 33 cavalrymen, 17 crossbowmen and musketeers, 150 foot soldiers, and more than 40,000 Indian allies.[37]

From a total force of about 904 men, the three land divisions were assigned 599, according to Cortés. Díaz, asserting a total force numbering 928, listed 611 in the three land forces. It seems evident that the land divisions averaged approximately 200 Spaniards each. The accounting of Cortés left 305 men for the navy, that of Díaz, 317. While neither the captain-general's nor the infantryman's figures total exactly the 325 men needed by the fleet (13 vessels with

[36] HC, I, 223–224; BDdelC, II, 227–228; Cervantes de Salazar, Crónica, 646; and Alva Ixtlilxochitl, Décima tercia relación, in Sahagún, Historia (1938), IV, 255.
[37] HC, I, 224; BDdelC, II, 228; and Cervantes de Salazar, Crónica, 646.

25 men each), it is evident that neither figure is so far removed from that total as to suggest the navy was seriously undermanned. Parenthetically one cannot help but wonder if a recorded total short of the desired complement of 325 does not indicate the sharp reality of the difficulty Cortés faced as he found it necessary to force men into navy service. Be that as it may, it is still plainly evident that the navy, with more than 300 Spaniards, had 50 per cent more manpower than any one army division, and 33 1/3 per cent of the total Spanish strength. Viewed then from the standpoint that it was the largest, by far, of the four distinct fighting forces and included one third of the Spanish personnel, the usual statement of the historical record—whether by a sixteenth-century participant or by a twentieth-century historian—has invariably done violence to the contribution of a sizable segment of the entire Spanish force. Cortés told the conquering general's version of the conquest, Bernal Díaz the foot soldier's view; but no one, to date, has related the naval aspects, and, in consequence, one third of Cortés' force has been consigned unjustly to historical oblivion.

However impressive the quantitative approach is in regard to manpower, an analysis of the four fighting forces from the standpoint of weapons is even more decidedly in favor of the naval component. At the time of the muster of April 28, 1521, Cortés said he had 118 crossbowmen and musketeers; Bernal Díaz differed markedly as he listed 194 crossbowmen and musketeers. Cortés assigned 55 bowmen to the three land divisions. Using the captain-general's figures for both total personnel in that category and the assignments to the various divisions, it is evident that the three land divisions combined had less than 47 per cent of the crossbowmen and musketeers while the navy had more than 53 per cent of such personnel and weapons. If Bernal Díaz' figures are used—he assigned 52 of a total of 194 to the three army divisions—the three army divisions combined had less than 27 per cent of the crossbowmen and musketeers while the navy had more than 73 per cent.

The distribution of the cannon is still another index to the importance of the naval arm. As of the muster-inventory of April 28,

1521, Cortés found he had fifteen small bronze field pieces and three heavy iron guns. With each of twelve brigantines mounting a gun in its bow and the flagship carrying two cannons, the fleet accounted for fourteen of the eighteen former field pieces, leaving four cannon for the field artillery to be divided among three land divisions.[38] Almost 78 per cent of the fire power of Cortés' artillery was aboard the brigantines.

With one third of the total Spanish manpower, from 53 to 73 per cent of the crossbows and muskets, and 78 per cent of the artillery dedicated to the naval arm of the amphibious assault team, it is clear that Cortés was depending heavily upon the brigantines. Time and battle would determine whether the imaginatively bold commander was to be termed mere courageous opportunist or supremely successful strategist. Truly the brigantines were the key to the whole war.

[38] Cortés and Bernal Díaz, who maintained that each of the thirteen vessels mounted a single cannon, do not indicate how the remaining five pieces of artillery were distributed among the land divisions. Cervantes de Salazar, who states that *La Capitana* mounted two guns, accounts for the four remaining ones as he relates that Alvarado and Olid each had two cannon with their forces; see *Crónica*, 646.

CHAPTER VI

Trial by Water: Success

THE FOUR WEEKS between the assignment of the men to the various divisions and the opening of hostilities were ones of intense activity. Word went out to the chieftains of the numerous allies, specifying the numbers of men desired and designating the time by which they must be in readiness for military operations. Cortés tried to resolve, in preliminary fashion, the logistical problems posed by a siege operation of unknown duration, involving tens upon tens of thousands of fighting men in a unique geographical setting. The commanders of the land divisions must have spent time evaluating their fighting forces and formulating tactics in terms of their knowledge of their manpower, the military practices of the enemy, the restricted nature of the terrain (causeways) available to them, and the strategy established by the captain-general. Bowmen and musketeers must have put their weapons in final readiness. Lances had to be sharpened, new edges were wanted on the swords, and shields had to be strengthened. Gunpowder was distributed; arrows and arrowheads were fashioned. Texcoco must have been a beehive of almost ceaseless activity that month of May. Not least in importance was the effort required to whip heterogeneous manpower into an effective naval force.

The early weeks of May, 1521, probably found the brigantines frequently off Texcoco in the eastern waters of the lake engaging in shakedown cruises. Individuals who had not previously pulled paddles had to perfect that skill; and all the paddlers had to achieve the measure of co-ordinated teamwork which practice alone could produce. Seamen whose past experience had related only to ocean settings had to learn to handle sail in terms of both the pattern of winds characteristic of the valley and the sailing qualities of the strange new vessels. It was necessary, too, to harmonize the combination of sail and paddle. After countless skills had been acquired and equally numerous techniques had been mastered, which in the aggregate enabled a captain to feel proud of his crew and his crew confident of their ship, it was necessary for the individually polished fighting units to come together to master the concept of fleet action. The mere building of ships and the naming of crews did not produce a great new fighting force; the month of May, 1521, was required to effect that partnership of men and brigantines that would deserve the name navy.

Cortés' battle plan for the operation against Tenochtitlán was a combination of blockade, siege, and assault. He had thorough knowledge of the theater of operations, gained from long months spent in the island-city and equally long months on various sectors of the lake front. To achieve his end, the collapse of the power of Tenochtitlán, he carefully chose the positions which best would enable him to control the approaches to the city. In regard to the distribution of population, the native political alignments, and the economic orientation of the island-city in reference to the mainland, the southwestern and western shores of the lake were the most important. Control of the western shore pivoted on the town of Tacuba and the causeway between it and Tenochtitlán. Cortés dispatched Pedro de Alvarado and his division of Spaniards and legion of Tlaxcalan warriors to Tacuba. The southwestern sector centered about the southern causeway that had two approaches to the mainland, one to Coyoacán, the other to Iztapalapa. Effective control of this causeway, at least in early stages of the operation, would require Spanish forces at both points. Accordingly Olid and his force were dispatched to Coyoacán, with Sandoval scheduled to move somewhat later against Iztapalapa.

The land fighting was to be co-ordinated, with simultaneous thrusts from Tacuba, Coyoacán, and Iztapalapa against the Mexicans on the causeways. Alvarado and Olid quietly moved counter-clockwise around the lake to take up their appointed positions. Even as they did so, they shattered the aqueduct which supplied potable water to Tenochtitlán. (Customarily, by either inference or categorical statement, the view is advanced that all of Tenochtitlán's drinking water came from Chapultepec via the aqueduct. However, in consideration of the relatively late date at which the aqueduct was built, Linné holds that the island-capital had some springs of its own.[1]) Inconvenience in daily living was to bear down upon the Mexicans even before Sandoval moved by land and Cortés by lake to signalize the opening of general combat. At first, blockade preceded assault; later it paralleled it.

Little is known of life in Tenochtitlán during this period of the resurgence of Spanish power. Naturally, the kind of intelligence system which had initially instructed the natives about the presence of the invaders on the coast in 1519 could have kept them equivalently informed about Spanish activities after the Sad Night. In early 1521 the men of Tenochtitlán and their lake-front allies had fought back repeatedly and bitterly as the Spaniards re-entered the valley and pursued their program of general reconnaissance and limited conquest. The mounting losses of allies and shore terrain surely disturbed the Mexican leaders, who knew the weaknesses as well as the strengths of the geographic position of Tenochtitlán. Their fears of Spanish shipping, which had prompted the destruction of the four brigantines in 1520, were renewed when it became known that thirteen of the monstrous vessels were in the making. The series of efforts to sabotage the brigantines in the Texcoco ship-yard bespeaks uneasiness of mind in Tenochtitlán during the early spring of 1521, yet fear must have been tempered by the memory of the manner and magnitude of the Mexican victory of the Sad

[1] Linné, *El Valle*, 25.

The Engagement between ye Spanish Brigantines and the Canoes of the Mexicans.

Naval aspects of the Battle of Tenochtitlán (1) (*From Antonio de Solis y Rivadereyra, The History of the Conquest of Mexico by the Spaniards, London, 1753*)

The flagship in action. May 31, 1521 (From the Lienzo de Tlaxcala)

Night. And still another change had taken place in Mexican leadership, one which probably gave self-confidence to the dwellers of the island metropolis. After a reign of but a few months, Cuitlahuac, Montezuma's brother and successor, had died. In December, 1520, just before the Spaniards began to spill back into the Valley of Mexico, the young and vigorously anti-Spanish Cuauhtémoc, nephew of both Montezuma and Cuitlahuac, was selected as the new Mexican ruler. Submissive and loyal, the natives probably thought victory synonymous with Cuauhtémoc—but the name really meant "The Eagle That Fell."

Early Chronology

The Battle of Tenochtitlán was joined on the last day of May, 1521.[2] In the pre-dawn Sandoval moved westward from Texcoco toward Iztapalapa. A short time later Cortés had the brigantines lift anchor and move out into the lake, employing both sail and paddle as they did so. He intended to move the fleet in close support of Sandoval, who faced problems of terrain that suggested a combined operation by the land and naval forces.

As the fleet moved westward, its first opportunity to meet the enemy arose ere the ships could get into position to support Sandoval. Within a mile of the south shore of Lake Texcoco and possibly three miles east of Iztapalapa and six miles to the southeast of Tenochtitlán lay Tepepolco, one of the very few significant peñones in the lake. This island with rocky promontory—the very term peñón implies that—was an abrupt rise, and precipitous on its north shore, from the level of the lake, with a total area of but a minor fraction of one square mile. From its summit, several hun-

[2] Maudslay, following Orozco y Berra, establishes Friday, May 31, 1521, as the day hostilities were initiated. Cortés, petitioning for a coat of arms, said the battle lasted seventy-five days. Counting back from August 13, the day it ended, May 31 emerges as the day the siege operation was inaugurated. However, agreement on that date is not general. Bernal Díaz, for example, states the battle for Tenochtitlán consumed ninety-three days, which, in turn, would establish May 13 as the first day of hostilities. See *CDIE*, II, 200–201; *BDdelC*, II, 298; and Maudslay, "Diary of the Siege of Mexico," in *BDdelC–M*, IV, 375–377.

dred feet above the level of the lake, one could command a fine view of the southwestern sector of the lake country.[3] The day Cortés moved the navy westward toward Iztapalapa the peñón was crowded with Mexicans who were bent both upon signaling the capital city concerning the movements of the invaders and, if at all possible, on engaging the enemy naval force. Cortés decided to bring an end to the intelligence function of the peñón for the enemy, and in so doing committed his naval force to its first fighting function. So much was the idea of attacking the enemy on the tiny island an inspiration of the moment—the battle plan called initially for naval support of Sandoval's division—that by the time the decision had been made it was necessary to turn the fleet back toward the already bypassed peñón. Nudging the small ships close in against the island, Cortés ordered half the ships' complements to remain aboard the vessels; the others, approximately one hundred fifty men, went overboard, stormed the beach, mounted the hill of loose stones, and proceeded to defeat the enemy. Cortés in person led the landing party that cleared the enemy from the peñón. Later, despite the fact that twenty-five men in the landing force had suffered wounds, he termed the action a beautiful victory.[4]

The brilliant action against Tepepolco was completely outside the captain-general's plans, and it could scarcely have been called for even as a tactical necessity. The importance of the marine-like action against the pinpoint of land and the enemy handful thereon lay in the opportunity it gave Cortés to test his otherwise green amphibious assault team. The basic technique at Tepepolco—moving against an otherwise inaccessible point and then landing elements of the naval force for limited land action—was one that Cortés employed time and time again in the weeks ahead.

Immediately following the test given the navy as an assault force came its dramatic baptism in fleet action. From his vantage point

---

[3] In post-conquest years, Cortés petitioned the Crown for this peñón and, after the request was granted, its name was changed from Tepepolco to Peñón del Marqués. For the terms of the grant, see *CDIAO*, XII, 380–381.

[4] *HC*, I, 228.

atop the peñón, the captain-general soon discerned the movement of a tremendous fleet of Indian canoes. Countless small craft lingered cautiously in the wake of some five hundred of the biggest and best warrior-laden canoes[5] moving toward the brigantines, which were lying dead in the water with but skeleton crews aboard them. Cortés hastily ordered the landing party to re-embark.

In fleet formation the brigantines moved a short distance out into the lake, and then the paddlers once more lay on their paddles. It was early afternoon and there was not a breath of breeze to ruffle the sails which hung limply from the arms. In close formation—so close as to be able to take voice commands from the captain-general now turned admiral—the brigantines waited expectantly. The unity of the Spanish fleet was as perfect as if Cortés had been a professional navy man, as if he had read and absorbed those as yet unrecorded words of a celebrated sixteenth-century Spanish naval authority, "When the time for battle is at hand the captain-general should order the whole fleet to come together that he may set them in order, since a regular order is no less necessary in a fleet of ships for giving battle to another fleet than it is in an army of soldiers for giving battle to another army."[6]

The narrow canoes of the enemy continued to knife their way through the calm waters. At the last moment, however, they too drew up. A distance of two bow shots separated these navies representing widely different cultures. Tension probably grew apace as each awaited the action of the other in the hypnotic atmosphere of the listless air and the gleaming, glassy surface of the water. One can visualize both forces, silent, with every man scarcely drawing a deep breath, in the grip of that caution which anticipates action of far-reaching significance. The Mexicans, who had feared and out of fear had destroyed a fleet of four brigantines the previous spring, were fully aware of the menacing potential power of this new and larger Spanish fleet. The Spaniards, though they believed that the

---

[5] *Ibid.* Bernal Díaz reports more than 1,000; see *BDdelC*, II, 235.

[6] Sir Julian S. Corbett (ed.), *Fighting Instructions, 1530–1816,* 6–7, quoting Alonso de Chaves, *Espejo de Navegantes.*

brigantines were the key to the whole campaign against Tenochtitlán, must still have been conscious of their nautical limitations, for
the memory of the Sad Night could not easily die; in this spellbound
interval perhaps they awaited some heaven-sent advantage that
would guarantee the brilliant success and the immediate control of
the lake waters that would establish a psychological pattern of
inspiration for themselves and of fear and depression for the defenders.

Suddenly a stiff land breeze swept out of the southeast over the
poops of the brigantines. The moment of caution and calculation
was abruptly over. The order was given that signaled into action
the Spanish-manned ships of Cortés, supported by countless canoes
of Indian allies under the command of Ixtlilxochitl of Texcoco. The
thirteen brigantines, under full sail, went scudding over Lake Texcoco toward the massed canoes of the enemy. The Mexicans turned
their canoes cityward as swiftly as paddle would permit, but even
that was not soon enough to keep the Spanish ships from breaking
into and through them. It was a running battle—three long leagues,
Cortés said—with crossbows and muskets getting in telling blows,
with the brigantines ramming and capsizing canoes (as if so many
rowboats faced modern destroyers in unequal battle), with bow
guns striking fear in the Mexicans· if not dealing them physical
harm. So bloody was the battle that the waters of Lake Texcoco
were tinted red. As an increasing number of canoes were destroyed
and more and more Indians drowned, as the brigantines swept over
the lake to the very edge of Tenochtitlán itself, the magnitude of
the victory became apparent. In several short hours the waters that
had previously cast up dread memories for the Spaniards became
friendly waters, completely dominated by the Spanish fleet. The
significance as well as the unexpected magnitude of the victory are
evident in the words of Cortés—"the best and greatest victory
which we could have asked or desired."[7]

[7] HC–MacN, II, 67–68; BDdelC–M, IV, 110, note 1; López de Gómara, Historia,
II, 35; Cervantes de Salazar, Crónica, 656; and Alva Ixtlilxochitl, Décima tercia
relación, in Sahagún, Historia (1938), IV, 259. The completeness and success of the

In the fleet action on the waters between the Peñón of Tepepolco and the island-city of Tenochtitlán, the Mexicans missed a notable opportunity to embarrass, if not stop, the Spanish brigantines. Approximately midway between the peñón and the city on a north-south line the lake was traversed by the Nezahualcoyotl Dike. Though we do not know to what degree the dike had fallen into disrepair in the course of its seventy years of existence, it quite likely could have been so revamped—with the sluices narrowed to the point of making passage by the brigantines difficult—and then so manned by land forces as to challenge the approach of any vessel. In addition, other, fresh elements of the Mexican fleet—only a minor fraction of the canoes had been initially committed—could have ambushed the brigantines as they emerged from the sluices. The narrow passages through the dike also might have been filled almost to the surface with rubble, allowing their function in reference to the ebb and flow of waters to continue but killing the prospect of their being navigated by anything as large as a brigantine, or the Mexicans could have driven stakes beneath the water level to check the passage of the Spanish ships. These various tactics of Indian naval warfare—impaling the brigantines on stakes, stranding them in shallow waters, ambushing them from reed beds, and harassing them from land positions, served the Mexicans well on later occasions. Given the existence of the Nezahualcoyotl Dike, the defenders missed a golden opportunity to upset the timetable of the co-ordinated amphibious operation at its very outset. Once the Spaniards had moved from east to west through the dike, the Indians had no equivalent opportunity to nullify the ad-

---

pursuit that found the brigantines pressing up to the city itself would have warmed the heart of any professional navy man. When A. T. Mahan wrote, "Strenuous, unrelaxing pursuit is . . . imperative after a battle" (see *Navy Strategy Compared and Contrasted with the Principles and Practice of Military Operations on Land*, 267), he did not have this lake action in mind, but he could have searched all recorded history and not found a better example in support of his thesis. Despite the completeness of the defeat suffered by the defenders, with the resultant transfer of command of the lake waters to the attackers, there is no reason to believe, as does Zamacois, that the initial fleet action resulted in the destruction of almost all of the Mexican fleet; see *Historia de Méjico*, III, 784.

vantages inherent in the Spanish fleet, because all of the remaining operations centered on the land and water area to the west of the dike.

Since a departure from the basic battle plan had been productive of significant victory, Cortés, instead of resuming the original plan and going to the support of Sandoval, extemporized brilliantly in an effort to consolidate and even widen the unexpected gains of the first day. As the brigantines turned southward away from Tenochtitlán, after the pursuit of the canoes had been terminated and as twilight wore on, he ordered the fleet to put in on the east side of the southern causeway. His objective was the fortress of Xoloc at Acachinanco, the point at which the Coyoacán spur joined the Iztapalapa causeway. With the fortress in Spanish hands, Cortés could press more rapidly against the city proper; furthermore, control of the point of juncture would so speed Spanish control of the segments of the causeway between Acachinanco and Coyoacán and Iztapalapa respectively that the captain-general would soon be able to free one of the two divisions presently tied down by the two-pronged nature of the causeway. Even as the fleet had battled and given chase to the retreating canoes across the lake, Olid, from his station in Coyoacán, had been inspired by the brigantine success to press his attack against the Indians on the causeway leading toward Acachinanco. Meanwhile Sandoval was still battling in Iztapalapa.

With maximum fire power from the ships and minimum use of landing forces, Cortés moved against the important junction. Because circumstances found the vessels able to move close in against the targets and because the height of the buildings on the causeway encouraged rather than discouraged ship-to-shore fighting, the bow guns and most of the archers and musketeers remained aboard the ships. The totally different tactical problem posed by the Peñón of Tepepolco had demanded 50 per cent of the manpower of the fleet in ground operations, but in this new move only thirty men, a scant 10 per cent of the fleet personnel, were called upon to storm the causeway. Once the buildings that dominated the position had been taken, Cortés ordered the landing of three heavy iron field pieces. (According to Bernal Díaz, four cannons were taken from the brigantines to the causeway.[8]) The fact that Cortés terms them "three heavy iron field pieces" leads one to speculate whether the three heaviest cannon inventoried at Texcoco were actually aboard the fleet, in addition to the necessary bow guns for the brigantines. If they were, the brigantines had aboard, at least temporarily, more than 94 per cent of the artillery available to the Spaniards. It might well have been, however, that the heaviest cannon, which had proved awkward in previous land campaigns entailing much marching and which were known to be equally ill-suited for permanent use on such small ships, had been put aboard the brigantines only because they could thus easily be moved to some point of relatively fixed warfare such as the causeways promised to be. If, on the other hand, the "heavy pieces" taken from ship to shore on this first day of battle were bow guns of brigantines, it would indicate that those guns were easily mounted and dismounted.

With naval assistance, a landing had been effected behind enemy lines. Much as the cavalry in earlier engagements had enabled Cortés to apply a "divide and conquer" approach to doing battle with great hordes of the enemy, the brigantines now enabled him to increase the number of points of contact with the foe. Mobility on the causeways, without which successful offensive action was impossible, had been restored to the invaders by the navy.

The first day of fighting gave the navy still another opportunity to demonstrate its diverse roles. Shortly after the Spaniards had seized the fortress of Xoloc and had turned cannons on the Mexicans, who continued to press them on the causeway, a careless gunner accidentally set fire to the powder supply. Cortés at once detached one brigantine from the fleet and ordered it to Iztapalapa, a couple of leagues distant, to transport to Acachinanco all the powder in Sandoval's possession. The execution of these orders by the lone brigantine dramatically demonstrated the potential of the ships in matters of supply and liaison; and the mere fact that a

[8] *HC*, I, 229–230; and *BDdelC*, II, 236.

single vessel dared to make the trip clearly indicated the completeness with which the invaders had come to dominate a wide area of
the waters of Lake Texcoco by the close of the first day of battle.

The choice of the location of Cortés' headquarters was likewise
affected by the unexpected success made possible by the navy that
first day. Originally the captain-general had intended, following
the support he planned to give Sandoval's division, to move on to
Coyoacán. That site might have served quite logically as a general
headquarters because of its central location in reference to the positions of Alvarado and Sandoval, to north and south respectively.
But just as the initial idea of supporting Sandoval during the first
day of battle had been set aside, so the unexpected turn of events
dictated the location of the captain-general's headquarters on the
causeway at Acachinanco. That point not only became Cortés' base
but also served as the advanced base for the entire fleet. Cortés now
had an advanced land position which would require that some men
be stationed permanently on the causeway, yet to keep some of the
brigantine personnel permanently ashore would have meant the
weakening of the navy. Proof that Cortés did not intend such weakening is seen in his order to Olid at Coyoacán to send his force to
Acachinanco the following day, and in similar word to Sandoval
to send fifty of his men to Cortés on the causeway. Thus elements
of two land divisions, which alone could not have won such a
vantage point as Acachinanco so easily, so speedily, and so cheaply,
were able to take long strides toward the city because of naval
power.

One day of fighting had produced no fewer than three significant
actions for which the navy was primarily, if not entirely, responsible: a minor amphibious operation against the Peñón of Tepepolco, which tested and found good the fighting mettle of the navy
in amphibious operations; a major fleet action victory, which had
resulted in Spanish domination of the southwestern waters of Lake
Texcoco; and an unexpectedly rapid advance of the army toward
the city, with the seizure and establishment of Acachinanco as the
Spanish headquarters. In every one of the operations subsequent to

the raid upon Tepepolco, the canoes of the ally Ixtlilxochitl and his Texcocan warriors had swarmed over the waters in close support of the brigantines. Thanks to the navy, the Spaniards had demonstrated a measure of mobility that must have been as surprising as it was welcome to those whose prior experience had led them to appreciate the limitations of infantry, artillery, and cavalry in that aquatic setting. The speed and finesse with which Cortés had moved rapidly from one brilliant and unexpected gain to another during the course of the day clearly testified to the bold imagination and intuitive genius that stamped the commander as representative of an uncommon breed of military men.

Since all that had taken place was even more unexpected to the Mexicans than it was to the Spaniards, the defenders, faced by unusual weapons and tactics, were called upon to match daring with daring. That very night, the first night Cortés and the brigantines were at their base on the causeway, the Mexicans dared to do the unexpected in their turn. Precedent had indicated that the natives were not inclined toward nighttime fighting, yet at midnight the defenders suddenly unleashed a combined operation of their own against the Spanish position. Co-ordinating a renewal of the pressure along the causeway with an attack from the lake by a wave of canoe-borne warriors, they bore down upon the Spanish base. Despite initial fear and surprise, the Spaniards were able to beat off the attacks, winning a victory made possible in large part by the bow guns, archers, and musketeers of the brigantines.[9]

The next day, June 1, brought Cortés re-enforcements and more fighting. From Olid's division came fifteen crossbowmen and musketeers, seven or eight horsemen, and fifty foot soldiers armed with swords and shields.[10] In terms of Olid's original Spanish force at Coyoacán this transfer of personnel on the second day of the siege put 75–85 per cent of Olid's crossbowmen and musketeers, 25 per cent of his cavalry, and 30 per cent of his infantry with Cortés on the causeway. Subsequently even more of that division was to

[9] HC, I, 230–231; and Alva Ixtlilxochitl, Décima tercia relación, in Sahagún, Historia (1938), IV, 259–260.   [10] HC, I, 231.

come to the base on the causeway, but for the moment a large Spanish element had to remain in Coyoacán because of the affinity the entire lake-front region in that sector had for the Mexicans. The rear of the attacking force on the causeway had to be defended, hostile population intimidated, and the supply lines protected. Increasingly prominent in this regard, as more and more of the Spaniards were drawn onto the causeway, must have been the services rendered by the Indian allies.

Battle was joined once more as the Spaniards pushed relentlessly toward the city. On their right flank the soldiers on the causeway were protected by the brigantines. Not so on the left flank, however, for the brigantines had not been able to get through the causeway. Accordingly the left flank, in a manner reminiscent of both flanks on the Sad Night, was the object of ceaseless attack by canoe-borne Indians. But the strange circumstance which found opposing fleets separated by a narrow causeway was not to continue for long. In the vicinity of the Spanish base at Acachinanco, Cortés ordered an opening made through the causeway. Four brigantines were assigned to support the Spanish foot soldiers on the west side of the causeway. Speedily the four vessels pressed the enemy canoes back into the canals of the city. In this manner the navy extended the area of its operations on the lake and likewise the degree of completeness with which it protected the rear and flanks of the soldiers on the causeway. Within the lake area to the west of the Nezahualcoyotl Dike, the significant portion of Lake Texcoco in terms of the siege operation, the Spanish had gained dominance of the southeastern sector the first day of fighting; the second day saw them dominating the southwestern sector as well.

As early as the second day of combat, the brigantines took the war into Tenochtitlán, searching out the larger and deeper canals and using them to penetrate within the city proper. As the ships moved into the outskirts of the city, the naval force undertook to fire the houses.[11] The fragile and highly inflammable structures on

[11] *Ibid.*, 231–232.

the perimeter of the island-city had little chance against the incendiary policy of the navy. At a much later moment, after more than forty-five days—60 per cent of the siege—had passed, Cortés adopted for the land forces the same policy of leveling every building encountered.

Meanwhile Sandoval, pushing his way along the Iztapalapa causeway in the vicinity of Mexicaltzingo, came face to face with a situation which gave rise to still another use for the brigantine. Facing an unusally wide breach in the causeway, one of such proportions that foot soldiers and cavalrymen could not negotiate it without considerable danger, Sandoval reported his problem to the captain-general. Cortés at once dispatched two brigantines to his assistance. When the two ships, gunwale to gunwale, maneuvered into the breach they so filled it as to constitute a bridge over which the army could and did pass.[12] Such action as this suggests that the freeboard of the brigantines approximated the height of the causeway above the surface of the lake. When one recalls that the wide breaches in the Tacuba causeway had been the principal death-traps for the Spaniards during the Sad Night, one realizes that this seemingly insignificant temporary duty of elements of the navy as a pontoon bridge between sections of a broken causeway was an important added service of the navy, helping to reduce to a minimum the casualties suffered by the invaders. By the end of that third day of battle, Sandoval had united the majority of his force with Olid at Coyoacán and had personally pushed on to the general headquarters at Acachinanco with ten of his horsemen.

Ere the passing of the first week of battle, many facets of the navy's role in the siege had become fixed practices through successful repetition. The ships were put to supply and liaison duty; they protected the men encamped on the causeway during nightly respites from fighting; they protected the rear and flanks of the soldiers making daily thrusts along the causeway into the city; they entered, and their crews burned sections of, the Indian capital; and

[12] *Ibid.*, 232.

171

they dominated the waters to the east and west of the Iztapalapa causeway to such a degree that enemy canoes no longer ventured within a quarter league of the Spanish camp.[13]

Patterns of Action

Inevitably the student of the naval aspects of the siege against Tenochtitlán must join those who have studied the army operations in deploring the fact that the evidence available does not support a day-by-day chronological narrative of the operation. Refuge is taken, therefore, in a topical approach, with some attention to chronology, to the role naval power played in the activities of the late spring and summer of 1521 in the Valley of Mexico.

The encirclement of the Mexican capital, an operation to the success of which the navy was to make a heavy contribution, was not effected until approximately ten days of battle had passed. From his battle position astride the Tacuba causeway, the northern-most Spanish position, Pedro de Alvarado noted and reported to his captain-general that the inhabitants of the island-city were moving freely in and out via the northern causeway, thereby negating the blockade that had been set up on the southern side of the city. Cortés probably had hoped to see the islanders move to the mainland, where he felt the invaders might more easily meet and defeat them in battle, and therefore his failure to guard the last of the causeways may have been intentional; but it did not serve Spanish purposes for the natives to move *in* and *out* of the city, supplying their island wants yet declining to move so completely to the mainland as to offer the prospect of decisive battle. Indications by the enemy that they intended to remain in their island position led Cortés to order a complete investment of the city. Sandoval, with 23 horsemen, 18 archers and musketeers, and 100 foot soldiers, was ordered to establish his headquarters at the end of the northern (Tepeyac) causeway. Thenceforth every land approach to the city was in Spanish hands and it but remained for a widening of the

[13] *Ibid.*, 232–233.

theater of naval operations to make the blockade by water as complete as that by land.[14]

With Sandoval on the Tepeyac causeway, Alvarado on the Tacuba causeway, and a force under his own immediate personal command on the Iztapalapa causeway, the captain-general ordered a concerted three-pronged thrust against the city and in so doing demonstrated the need for the dispersal of the naval units in task-force fashion among all the land divisions. As this first co-ordinated drive along the three avenues of approach got underway, Cortés had all of the navy supporting the men on the Iztapalapa causeway and in consequence his force drove deeper into the city than did the divisions commanded by Alvarado and Sandoval. Realizing that naval power had contributed to his own greater success, Cortés decided to assign some of the vessels to each of the other camps. This action, testimony to the worth-while work the brigantines had been doing in his area of operations, was another proof of the fundamental fact that the geographic setting demanded combined operations for maximum effectiveness against the island-fortress. Seven brigantines remained with the garrison on the Iztapalapa causeway, three ships went to Alvadaro at Tacuba, and the other three went to Sandoval at Tepeyac. Bernal Díaz, whose restricted knowledge of the brigantine operations has been commented upon elsewhere, disagrees with Cortés concerning the disposition of the vessels, stating that six ships stayed with Cortés, four were assigned to Alvarado, and two went to support Sandoval's division. The thirteenth vessel, according to the same source, was decommissioned because it was exceedingly vulnerable to Indian attack due to its extreme smallness, and its complement was distributed among the remaining twelve, as replacements for casualties. As to the accuracy of this last statement, it may be pointed out that, in addition to Bernal Díaz' limited information concerning the brigantines and the obviously contradictory statements of Cortés, the dimensions given by Martín López and corroborated by a number of fellow

[14] *Ibid.*, 233–234.

workers on the brigantines discount the prospect of one vessel's being considerably smaller than the rest. Yet testimony of 1529 by Andrés López does insist that one brigantine, the smallest, had not been finished because it was overturned by flood in Texcoco.[15] Like Cortés' original Cuban ships, the brigantines on Lake Texcoco in 1521 are open to continuing dispute about number and size.

Among the six brigantines assigned to Alvarado and Sandoval were the two commanded by Cristóbal Flores and Gerónimo Ruiz de la Mota, who were charged with supporting the land divisions on the causeways and controlling the waters of the northwestern-most part of the lake, the sector between the causeways leading to Tacuba and Tepeyac. One day the two vessels were on the prowl in the canals of the city when the leading brigantine, that of Cristó-bal Flores, became stranded. Vigorously attacked by Mexicans, the crew of the immobilized vessel suffered heavy casualties, and indeed both they and the vessel might have been lost had it not been for the support forthcoming from Ruiz de la Mota, his men, and his ship. In time the stranded vessel was refloated. The episode did much to inject a note of caution into the future maneuvers of the brigantines. Among the other four brigantines sent to the divisional commanders were those commanded by Pedro Briones and Juan de Limpias Carvajal. (The unusual amount of information which permits us to pinpoint the area of operations of certain brigantines quite probably stems from Ruiz de la Mota's reconstruction of the battle for Cervantes de Salazar; we also have an account offered by Sahagún of the defending Indians in action against these brigan-tines in the northwestern part of the lake.[16]) With this distribution of the fleet among the three land commanders not only were more efficiently co-ordinated thrusts against the city promised for the future, but also the naval task forces came to dominate, for the first

[15] *Ibid.*, II, 2; *BDdelC*, II, 238; and LC–CC, Martín López 1529–1550, p. 94 (testimony, 1529).

[16] Cervantes de Salazar, *Crónica*, 661, 687, 688, 709; and Sahagún, *Historia* (1938), IV, 89–90, 92–93.

time, all the waters immediately surrounding the city, a circumstance that promoted the success of the land-water blockade which the captain-general had proclaimed. Effective blockade could now replace the paper portions of the previously partial blockade.

Despite the fact that the fleet had been divided three ways, Cortés maintained over-all command of it in the same sense that he was captain-general of all the land forces. This unity of command in naval matters is clearly exemplified by the blockade. In addition to giving orders to the brigantine captains regarding their role in support of the ground operations of the divisional commanders, Cortés told all the skippers to cruise about day and night in an effort to thwart the native efforts to provision the beleaguered city with canoe-borne supplies. In consequence, a number of the ships were detailed nightly for patrol duty, and, as in so many other naval activities, countless canoes of the Indian allies supported the brigantines.

As days passed, interception of supplies, destruction of canoes, and capture of prisoners added to the physical misery of the native garrison that long ago had been cut off from its normal supply of drinking water. Contact with the mainland becoming increasingly precarious for the island dwellers, the Mexicans turned more and more for food to the limited supply of small fish in the lake itself. In turn the brigantines disrupted that last resort. Although both Cortés and Bernal Díaz record the fact that the blockade reduced much of the defending population to the level of physical starvation, most historians, interested in the blood-and-thunder aspects of dramatic military events, have understated the significance of the blockade as a factor in the final victory. Whereas the Spanish land forces fought by fits and starts, sometimes having day after day of rest after many consecutive days of combat, there is no indication that the naval blockade was ever relaxed, much less momentarily called off, once it was instituted. Its completeness and relentlessness might well support the conclusion that the fall of Tenochtitlán was the result more of blockade and starvation than of Spanish military might and Mexican casualties in combat. Treating a topic on which no conclusive evidence is available, Alamán lists a total of 117,000 casualties for the defenders during the siege, of whom 50,000 were considered victims of starvation.[17]

One of the most significant and regular uses to which the brigantines were put was close support of the invading force on the causeways—the practice adopted on one side of one causeway the first day of battle. By the second day the ships were supporting the Spaniards on the Iztapalapa causeway on both flanks. With the assignment of six vessels to Alvarado and Sandoval, the men of their divisions likewise came to know the comforting presence of friends rather than enemies on their flanks. From experience both Alvarado and Sandoval had reason to know the potential of the brigantines. The former had been among the Spanish captains who accompanied Montezuma on a lake cruise aboard the brigantines constructed in Tenochtitlán in 1519–1520. More recently Sandoval had been extricated from a difficult position on a causeway through the assistance of brigantines, when shipping played bridge for foot soldiers, a procedure subsequently employed time after time with both brigantines and canoes acting as pontoons at the water holes. It could be expected that both the subordinate commanders to whom vessels were assigned were possessed of viewpoints that would permit, even facilitate, the early incorporation of naval forces within their operational plans. All three fronts found the naval units offering the same kind of tactical support to the ground forces.

When, with the dawning of a new fighting day, the Spanish foot soldiers would move toward Tenochtitlán, the accompanying brigantines so teamed with them as to guarantee the success of their combined operations. By protecting the flanks of those on the causeways, the ships contributed to the added military momentum of the ground force simply by enabling it to concentrate its fire

---

[17] *HC*, II, 2, 9–10, 20–21, 33; Alva Ixtlilxochitl, *Décima tercia relación*, in Sahagún, *Historia* (1938), IV, 266; and Alamán, *Disertaciones*, I, 117.

power forward against the enemy. The rapid forward movement of the infantry and cavalry was further facilitated by brigantine protection of the rear, preventing any possible landing of enemy canoe-borne warriors on the causeways to open a diversionary front. During the Sad Night and on several limited, later patrol actions on causeways without benefit of naval support, one of the maddening aspects of the fighting in which the Spaniards invariably found themselves pinned down and badly mauled had been the fact that the enemy, by attacking at both front and rear as well as on both flanks, had so forced a dispersal of Spanish fire power as to make rapid advance and minimization of casualties impossible. With naval support, however, the Spaniards, though weapons, organization, and tactics ashore remained virtually unchanged, gained fantastic mobility on the causeways and casualty lists were almost unbelievably reduced.

The fighting efficiency of the Spanish soldier was prolonged immeasurably because of the work of the brigantines. Prior to the creation of the navy, the problems posed by the geographic setting of the Mexican capital had meant continual hardship and danger to the invaders. For example, when trying to facilitate the withdrawal from the island-city in June, 1520, they were compelled repeatedly to fill in the watercourses. If they withdrew from a position to snatch even a few hours of sleep, they found the following morning that the Mexicans had opened the waterholes again and all the previous day's work had been in vain. Any time of day or night that they withdrew, even briefly, from an advanced position, their work was rapidly undone by the Mexicans. Accordingly, they were forced to hold continually any point taken if they wished to move on from it the next day. This meant spending the night in the front lines with no sleep and therefore a great reduction of physical strength and military effectiveness for the following day's fighting. The necessity of holding every inch of ground gained and of foregoing relief periods of real rest served as a special limitation on the length of any engagement the Spaniards might fight. Divisions subject to continuous round-the-clock hammering by a numerically superior enemy could not conceivably do battle for weeks and months at a time.

The brigantines changed all this. Because they enabled the ground forces to retake ground speedily, because they served as bridges and troopships for men momentarily blocked by stretches of open water, because they covered twilight-time retreats from the city after a day of fighting as easily as they facilitated sunrise penetrations into the city, because they kept enemy canoes a quarter league from the Spanish camp, the brigantines enabled the causeway-based soldiers to recoup physical strength with comparatively regular sleep each night. Thus a siege was made possible which lasted seventy-five days and brought the Spaniards victory, a siege which without the brigantines could not have continued that long and in all probability would have ended in Spanish defeat.[18]

Still another assignment the brigantines successfully carried out was the progressive razing of the city, an activity inaugurated the second day of the battle. As time passed and the destruction of buildings on the outer fringes of the city and better knowledge of the canal system made entrance into Tenochtitlán easier, the navy pushed farther and farther into the metropolis. Repeatedly it was recorded that the vessels penetrated to the center of the city; even allowing for the exaggeration usually attending such generalized statements, it is apparent that the time never came when the Spanish were to reduce their dependence upon the naval force. For example, on the memorable day when Gutierre de Badajoz and his small detachment of shock troops from the Alvarado division assaulted and took the famed Cue of Tlatelolco, the brigantines of Gerónimo Ruiz de la Mota and Antonio de Carvajal transported and otherwise facilitated the movement of Badajoz' land force across wide watercourses and into the heart of the northern sector of the metropolis. In late July, after more than fifty-five days of combat and at a time when three fourths of the area of the city was

[18] HC, I, 233–235 and II, 3, 7; BDdelC, II, 243–244; and Alva Ixtlilxochitl, Décima tercia relación, in Sahagún, Historia (1938), IV, 267.

already in Spanish hands, the part still held by the Mexicans, the easternmost sector, was particularly vulnerable to the brigantines and to them alone because it was the one cardinal point from which no causeway connected the city with the mainland.[19]

Considerable violence is done to truth if it is thought that all the naval support given Cortés and his forces derived from Spanish units. Even as Cortés had come to count upon the brigantines prior to the opening of battle, so also from the earliest moments he had planned to use the canoes of his allies as auxiliaries to his naval units. At the time of the muster that accompanied the launching of the brigantines, the captain-general ordered Ixtlilxochitl to gather together as many canoes as possible. Told that the canoes would be expected to accompany and co-operate with the brigantines and carry foodstuffs and military supplies for the fighting forces on the causeways, Ixtlilxochitl proceeded to amass a flotilla of 16,000 native canoes in which approximately 50,000 Texcocans saw duty. This tremendous array of native craft accompanied the brigantines toward the Peñón of Tepepolco and the first test of the Spaniards' ships. The Texcocan navy supported the brigantines during the fleet action of May 31 that saw the invaders win command of the waters of Lake Texcoco.

As time passed, the spectacular early successes of the invaders more and more inclined other natives, who initially had been sitting on the fence of neutrality, to align themselves with the conquistadors. One of the best contributions they could make—all the more so since the narrowness of the causeways restricted land movements, reducing the need for great hordes of warriors—was the swarm of canoes. When the Indians of Iztapalapa, Ochilobusco, Culuacan, Mezquique, and Cuitaguaca joined forces with Cortés, the captain-general initially and principally thought of their capacity for supplementing the blockade and harassment of Tenochtitlán and its inhabitants. No reasonably accurate estimate of the total number of native canoes supporting the invaders can be ad-

[19] *HC*, II, 5–6, 33–34; and MN–PyTT, Leg. 97, Información de los méritos y servicios de Diego de Salamanca (1547).

vanced, but we know that many canoes joined the brigantines in their support of the foot soldiers on the causeways and also as they entered and razed the city proper. On one occasion Cortés remarked there were 1,500 canoes manned by allies on each side of the causeway on which he was launching an offensive. Needless to say, the canoes were more capable of penetrating the city, with its myriad canals of varying breadths and depths, than were the brigantines at their best. Although Cortés himself made repeated references to the work of the canoes of his allies, the reporting of the naval aid of the Indians, even more than that of the land support they rendered the Spanish, is so couched in impersonal generalities as to guarantee that the Indian elements in the attacking naval force have never received the measure of credit due them.[20]

One of the strongest proofs of the capacity of the navy to exert pressure upon the Mexicans is seen in the fact that Cortés, even in the midst of a prolonged siege operation, was able to divert land forces from the siege for limited forays against the hinterland. When pro-Mexican elements of the Cuernavaca area struck out against Indian vassals of Spain in the region, the captain-general decided to detach Andrés de Tapia and a force of eighty foot soldiers on a punitive expedition against the hostile native elements. For approximately ten days these Spaniards were absent from the siege operation on that temporary additional duty. In like manner Gonzalo de Sandoval was sent out with eighteen cavalrymen, a hundred foot soldiers, and an indefinite number of Indian allies to pacify a region wherein neighbors of the Otomíes, allies of the Spaniards, were disturbing that native group. Such diversionary hostilities were inspired, quite probably, by Mexicans in an effort to break the Spanish stranglehold on the city, of which the brigantines were the most persistent factor. And it is to be noted that Cortés could not have detailed units of men to snuff out these minor conflagrations if so doing would materially have weakened his siege operation. The fact that he sent such sizable units off on

[20] HC, II, 8–9, 14–15, 28–29, 31–33; and Alva Ixtlilxochitl, *Décima tercia relación*, in Sahagún, *Historia* (1938), IV, 255, 256, 258–259.

tangential operations clearly indicates that the navy was bearing the brunt of the effective siege duty. Lastly, the fact that the siege was not noticeably prolonged by the temporary withdrawal of such sizable army units bears further mute testimony to the primary importance of the navy in the over-all operation.[21]

Illustrative Episodes

In addition to the forementioned general and recurring uses to which the brigantines were put in the course of more than ten weeks of battle, certain specific actions can be cited to illustrate further the naval activities during the siege. One such episode concerns the ambush prepared by the Mexicans and the counterambush devised by the invaders. The enemy began by stationing about thirty of their biggest canoes, crowded with warriors, deep in a bed of rushes. Some stakes were driven into the lake bed close by the rushes and sufficiently beneath the water level to escape detection but at the same time close enough to the surface to impede the free movement of the brigantines should they venture among them. The third element in the native trap, the bait, consisted of a number of ordinary canoes. Purposely moving in the open so that they might be detected and pursued by the brigantines as blockade-runners, the canoes lured two vessels into the well-planned trap one evening. While the brigantines were tangled with and nearly stranded on the stakes, the large canoes pounced upon them, wreaking death and destruction upon the crews and ships. In this affair Juan Portillo, captain of a brigantine, lost his life. Among the numerous Spanish wounded was Captain Pedro Barba, who succumbed several days later. As a climax to this signal success, the Mexicans even captured and made off with Pedro Barba's vessel, the only recorded ship loss during the entire siege operation. Cortés was so angered by this turn of events that he then set an ambush for enemy canoes which worked with equal success, the enemy losing many craft and experiencing a great number of casualties.[22] Although the Mexicans tried the technique of ambush on several later occasions, they never

[21] HC, II, 20–25.   [22] Ibid., 11–12; and BDdelC, II, 244.

again achieved the initial measure of success, possibly for two reasons: the first experience induced a greater degree of caution in the brigantine commanders, and the later allied canoe re-enforcements permitted the use of the smaller and shallower craft for operations in questionable waters. A significant historical truth emerges from the episode of the ambush and the counterambush: the Mexicans, no longer able to face the brigantines openly in fleet action, were forced, through the inferiority of their naval position, to resort to tactics relying largely on cunning and deception.

Another episode which pictures the navy in unique activity had to do with the near-loss of the flagship *La Capitana*, an occurrence of the first day's fighting which was a combination of cowardice bordering on treason and bravery that best can be described as above and beyond the call of duty. The villain was Juan Rodríguez de Villafuerte, skipper of the flagship and commander of the entire thirteen-ship fleet; the hero was shipwright Martín López, then serving as master aboard *La Capitana*. When the gust of wind arose that enabled the brigantines to rush in full fury against the fleet of Indian canoes, *La Capitana* led the chase—and in so doing violated the axiom which reads, "The captain-general should never be of the first who are to grapple nor should he enter into the press, so that he may watch the fighting and bring succour where it is most needed."[23] Probably in pursuit of the land practice of trying to capture or kill the leaders of the opposition, the Mexicans turned considerable attention upon the Spanish flagship. In some manner, as the result of either Mexican stratagem or conquistador ignorance of the waters, the ship grounded. During the bitter close-in fighting, with hordes of enemy warriors attacking the vessel and its crew, Captain Rodríguez de Villafuerte and most of the ship's complement abandoned ship. Seizing the authority that devolved upon him due to the irregular conduct of his superior, Martín López, at the head of a small band of loyal men, fought valiantly against the enemy. Sword and shield in hand, he grappled with the Indians who had boarded the vessel, then, having cleared the deck of

[23] Corbett (ed.), *Fighting Instructions*, 12, quoting Alonso de Chaves.

Mexicans, he took up a crossbow and carried the fighting to the enemy in telling fashion as he struck down the Indian commander. With the resultant withdrawal of the enemy canoes, López and his colleagues were able once more to refloat the brigantine.

All who witnessed the action and later expressed themselves concerning it agreed that Martín López demonstrated extraordinary heroism. Several eyewitnesses of the event magnify the heroism to unbelievable proportions as they insist that more than 5,000 canoes had centered their attention upon the Spanish flagship. Antón Cordero, himself aboard another brigantine and a witness to the action, praised the timeliness in relation to the victory; had the navy been worsted in its initial engagement, the resultant defeatism in the Spanish camp and optimism in the enemy camp might have changed the eventual outcome of the siege.[24] There is no accounting for Cortés' continual dependence upon the services of Rodríguez de Villafuerte after this event. It was only after considerable time had elapsed that Gonzalo de Sandoval was given over-all command of the navy,[25] although the affair of the flagship during the first day of fighting obviously warranted an immediate change of fleet commanders. Herrera states that after the episode Martín López served as captain of the flagship.[26]

Just as the fact that the siege operation was inaugurated by naval action is proof of the navy's importance to the plan of battle, so the fact that naval action brought the struggle against Tenochtitlán to a close is proof of the persistent importance of the fleet throughout all eleven weeks of the engagement. The surrender of Cuauhtémoc and his followers on August 13, 1521, was primarily produced by naval action.

By the closing days of the second week in August, a final victory for the invaders was plainly only a question of time: the thinning

[24] AGI, Patronato 57–1–1, fols. 20, 23, 32, 35, 38, 40r (interrogatory and testimony, 1534); translation in AU–CC, Martín López 1528–1574, pp. 62, 71, 97–98, 106, 114, 121; and LC–CC, Martín López 1529–1550, pp. 122–123, 130–131, 138, 146, 153, 159–160, 166 (interrogatory and testimony, 1540).

[25] HC–MacN, II, 123, 124–125, 128.

[26] Herrera, *Historia general*, II, Part I, 38.

of the ranks of the defenders was each day more noticeable; the full impact of long-term blockade had nearly stagnated the life of the city; the progressive destruction of the city continued apace. All of the island-capital except a fraction of the easternmost part had fallen into Spanish hands. As Cortés and the land divisions exerted pressure upon the defenders ashore, Sandoval, now serving as commander in chief of the brigantines, alerted the navy for the closing chapter in the long siege. The final day of battle, as had the opening day, featured combined operations.

Cortés was atop the Cue of Tlatelolco to observe the army and navy as they co-operated in battle for what was destined to be the last time. The order of the day obviously looked forward to the end of the conflict—the land forces were to move into those portions of the city which yet remained in enemy hands, and the navy, while systematically destroying the more aquatic parts of the enemy-held position, was to keep on the lookout for the possible flight of the Mexican leaders. A musket fired the shot that signalized the opening of the attack. The invading land troops pressed into the Indian-held sector; and the brigantines fell to destroying the outlying buildings. Suddenly out of a reed bed there emerged a flotilla of possibly fifty larger than average Mexican craft. In the swift action that followed, it fell to García Holguín to emerge from anonymity and write his name on the record of the conquest as he and the men of his brigantine seized Cuauhtémoc, the Mexican monarch.[27]

Across the years two versions of the capture of Cuauhtémoc have persisted. The Spanish accounts, derived principally from the words of Cortés and Díaz, indicate that Cuauhtémoc was in flight when overtaken, possibly bent upon reaching the mainland and continuing the war against the invaders on a new front. On the other hand, Sahagún, and others following him, state that Cuauhtémoc, bent upon sparing his people further suffering and reconciled to the idea of going to the Spanish captain-general to effect terms of surrender, was in fact en route to Cortés' headquarters

[27] MN–PyTT, Leg. 94, Información de los méritos y servicios de Juan Fernández (1536, 1558); HC, II, 42–47; and BDdelC, II, 294–296.

when approached and seized by Holguín and his crew. This particular point—i.e., was Cuauhtémoc in flight or was he approaching the Spaniards with the intention of surrendering—does not admit of easy and convincing resolution. Of the episodes cloaked in historical uncertainty in the story of the early years of the conquest of Mexico few have contributed to as much continuing disputation and publication in Mexican circles as has this issue concerning Cuauhtémoc. Be that as it may, the monarch of the Mexicans was seized. Proud of his feat, and quite probably looking for official favor, Captain Holguín refused to yield his famous prisoner to his superior Gonzalo de Sandoval. What could have continued as an unseemly quarrel between the two men was hastily terminated by the curt order from the captain-general that the prisoner be brought to him. With Cuauhtémoc in the hands of the Spaniards, the fighting ceased, the siege ground to a conclusion, and the invaders knew final victory.

To the very end the naval contribution of the Indian allies was noteworthy. Canoe-borne Ixtlilxochitl was not to realize his desire of personally effecting the capture of Cuauhtémoc; but even as the faster brigantine of Holguín achieved that end, the Texcocan chieftain demonstrated the efficiency of his canoes once more by seizing such leading Mexicans as a son of Montezuma and the wife of Cuitlahuac. As Holguín, representative of Spanish naval power, led his royal captive to Cortés, so Ixtlilxochitl, synonym of the native contribution to the naval might of the invaders, led his equally royal and but ever so slightly less important prisoners before the captain-general.[28] Through the closing moment of the extended combat operation, the joint Spanish-Indian naval effort had been both harmonious and successful.

[28] Alva Ixtlilxochitl, *Décima tercia relación*, in Sahagún, *Historia* (1938), IV, 280.

CHAPTER VII

Conclusions

THE THIRTEENTH OF AUGUST, 1521, marked the close of the Battle of Tenochtitlán, the end of the campaign for control of the Valley of Mexico, and the last day of naval warfare in the overall conquest of Mexico which was still to occupy Cortés, his captains, and his Spanish and Indian warriors for a number of years. No naval units and no naval action were destined to figure in the continuing conquest that dictated the fanning out of numerous expeditions from the seat of Spanish power in the valley.

The thrusts of Cortés, Alvarado, and Sandoval to the northeast into the Pánuco region of the Gulf coast called for no naval support. Such campaigns to the southeast as those of Sandoval in the Coatzacoalcos region, Luis Marín in Chiapas, Rodrigo Rangel among the Zapotecs and Mixtecs, Alvarado in Oaxaca and Guatemala, and Cortés in his pursuit of Olid were conducted entirely by elements of the artillery, cavalry, and infantry. Even the marine approach that Olid made to his fateful Honduran adventure did not find his ships a factor in any fighting. During the excursions of Montaño and Olid westward into Michoacán, soldiers shouldered the total effort, as they did when Francisco Cortés led men into Jalisco. The successive actions in the Colima district led by Rodríguez de Villafuerte and Sandoval were without any relationship to naval action; and so, too, were the thrusts of Rodríguez de Villafuerte and Sandoval to the Pacific coast in the Zacatula sector. The ever-widening waves of conquistador activity that radiated from infant Mexico City toward every point of the compass failed to include another naval episode.[1] Even the early days of the inauguration of Cortés' maritime interest and activity on the Pacific Ocean did not include naval action. Like a meteor flashing momentarily across the sky, the one brief, spectacular chapter of the conquest of Mexico that related to fighting ships made brilliant history, and then was finished.

Tenochtitlán and General Naval History

Uniquely significant in the conquest of Mexico, the naval aspects of the Battle of Tenochtitlán also constitute one of the most extraordinary actions in recorded naval history. In it one sees in kaleidoscopic panorama the sweep of naval history from ancient Salamis to contemporary Korea: ships under sail and oar, ramming, boarding, bombardment, fleet action, task force operations, blockade, liaison duty, marine-like raids by naval landing parties, close support of land operations, and psychological warfare.

Like Salamis in 480 B.C., the Battle of Tenochtitlán involved the mastery of a world—Salamis the control of the eastern Mediterranean world, Tenochtitlán the control of the Aztec world. For two years immediately prior to Salamis, Themistocles wisely directed the expansion of the Athenian navy; a year prior to Tenochtitlán, Cortés wisely ordered the creation of a navy for the conquistadors. Greek history, however, does not honor the shipwright counterpart of Martín López. When battle was initially joined at Salamis,

[1] HC, II, 49–247 passim; BDdelC, II, 313–446 passim, III, 9–105 passim; Bancroft, Mexico, II, 45–129 passim; Hubert Howe Bancroft, History of Central America, I, 617–703 passim, and II, 74–121 passim; Herbert Ingram Priestley, The Mexican Nation, A History, 44–46; and Rafael Heliodoro Valle, Cristóbal de Olid—Conquistador de México y Honduras. Some of the vessels furnished Olid as his armada was being organized in early August, 1523, are unique among Cortés-controlled shipping up to that date in that their cost is known. Prices on five vessels ranged from 400 to 1,000 pesos each, averaging 730 pesos per vessel; see Camilo García de Polavieja (ed.), Hernán Cortés—Copias de documentos existentes en el Archivo de Indias y en su palacio de Castilleja de la Cuesta, sobre la conquista de Méjico, 363.

Themistocles waited for and exploited the usual morning breeze; off the Peñón of Tepepolco Cortés waited for the wind that gave him equivalent advantage. Salamis and Tenochtitlán both occurred in periods when soldiers went to sea and naval warfare mirrored as fully as possible the use of the weapons and the tactics employed in land warfare. Combatants at sea in the sixteenth century, like those at Salamis, used such hand weapons as spears, swords, knives, javelins and bows—to which, of course, Cortés could add a limited number of arquebuses and cannon. At Salamis the quantitatively superior Persians lost to the qualitatively superior Greeks; likewise the quantitatively superior Mexicans lost to the qualitatively superior Spaniards at Tenochtitlán. The Greeks knew an advantage over the Persians in nautical skills akin to the shipping superiority the Spanish brigantine had over the Indian canoe. As at Salamis, the percentage of manpower ashore at Tenochtitlán dwarfed the fighting effectives afloat. Both battles demonstrated the strategical interdependence of land and sea warfare. However, in the final analysis, Tenochtitlán had an importance that cannot be assigned to Salamis: Tenochtitlán was synonymous with final victory, the conclusion of a war; Salamis was not. At Salamis a civilization was challenged; at Tenochtitlán a civilization was crushed.[2] Possibly in all history there is no similar victorious naval engagement that concluded a war and ended a civilization.

The strategy of Cortés, at Tenochtitlán, reminds one of that employed at Actium in 31 B.C. There, in the Ionian Sea, the contending commanders Antony and Octavius, renowned for their leadership of armies, recognized the significance of sea power and left their immense armies inactive while they boarded ships and battled

[2] Percy Arthur Baxter Silburn, *The Evolution of Sea Power*, 97; Sir Reginald Neville Custance, *War at Sea, Modern Theory and Ancient Practice*, 9, 16–18, 20–22, 27–28, 30, 108; Edward Kirk Rawson, *Twenty Famous Naval Battles; Salamis to Santiago*, 7; Fitzhugh Green and Holloway Frost, *Some Famous Sea Fights*, 3–4, 20, 31, 36, 39; Compton Mackenzie, *Marathon and Salamis*, 129, 131; Arthur MacCartney Shepard, *Sea Power in Ancient History—The Story of the Navies of Classic Greece and Rome*, 26–39, 55–65; and Vice-Admiral William Ledyard Rodgers, *Greek and Roman Naval Warfare—A Study of Strategy, Tactics and Ship Design from Salamis (480 B.C.) to Actium (31 B.C.)*, 85–94, 103–105.

upon the wave.[3] Similarly at Tenochtitlán, Cortés, pre-eminently a leader of land armies, bowed before the dictates of geography and the demands of broad strategy and incorporated naval power within his military effort, identifying himself with it personally as battle was joined.

The naval ties between Tenochtitlán and earlier days are dwarfed by the relationship the episode in New Spain has proved to have to subsequent events. Lepanto, in 1571, was reminiscent of Tenochtitlán in that the Christian warriors knew a favorable wind; picked arquebusiers stood upon the decks of the vessels; the enemy, broken and bewildered, was relentlessly pursued and cut to shreds; Don Juan placed added dependence upon his naval guns.[4] Quite commonly it has been stated that the short interval between Lepanto (1571) and the Spanish Armada (1588) brought a restructuring of basic concepts in naval warfare: the combination of sails and oars gave way to complete dependence on sail; ramming tactics and grappling and boarding yielded to fire power; and the idea that fighting afloat should mirror the techniques of land warfare gave way to distinctive concepts for naval warfare. However, the English meeting with the Armada still recalled Tenochtitlán in the sporadic fighting of the running variety that was spaced over an interval of several weeks and in the measure of consciously adopted tactics pursued by the victorious naval power.[5] The Battle of the Nile (August 1, 1798), which proved all too clearly that Napoleon's position in Egypt was untenable with the British in command of the waters of the Mediterranean, was but a restatement of the truth that Cortés' fleet on Texcoco eventually brought home to the Mexican defenders of Tenochtitlán.[6] Perry's naval achievement of 1813 on Lake Erie suggests at least two close parallels to the brigantines of Cortés: Perry's fleet was built of green timbers especially for use upon inland waters, and the construction of the vessels was con-

[3] Silburn, *Sea Power*, 58.

[4] Rawson, *Naval Battles*, 78, 79, 82, 83.

[5] Green and Frost, *Sea Fights*, 82–111 *passim*.

[6] *Ibid.*, 169–199 *passim*. The demonstration of the impotence of overseas land forces in the face of enemy control of intervening waters dates back to Salamis.

stantly endangered by the presence and power of the enemy.[7] Fifty years later the Battle of Mobile Bay (August 5, 1864), in shallow waters, among tortuous channels, shoals, and piles, and with the fighting including ramming tactics and fleet bombardment of land fortifications, cast multiple reflections of the action at Tenochtitlán.[8] In the Battle of Manila Bay (May 1, 1898), as in the initial fleet action between the thirteen brigantines and the Indian flotilla on May 31, 1521, the victor sustained no damage to ships and no injury to personnel. Both engagements were fights that, in a real sense, were not fights.[9] The naval disparity at Santiago (July 3, 1898), where the underdog Spanish force broke and ran and suffered annihilation, was not unlike the power picture at Tenochtitlán.[10]

The Spanish concept of the role of naval power at Tenochtitlán —with ships used primarily as instruments of unrelenting attack— suggests that the conquistador of the early sixteenth century was both the intelligent heir of ancient experience and the precursor of modern strategy and tactics.

Cortés—Strategist and Tactician

No military man of his century more fully forecast the mold of military activities of the twentieth century than did Hernando Cortés. The ways of war, then more art than science, still bore the stamp of the Middle Ages when Cortés was born. The closing years of the fifteenth century and the opening years of the sixteenth were ones of military transition,[11] and Cortés, a party to the transition, so applied his imagination and daring to the problems he faced as to become the accidental, but nonetheless real, precursor of the twentieth-century science of total war. The trends of current research on Cortés,[12] by their very omission of serious

---

[7] Rawson, *Naval Battles*, 389–417 *passim*.

[8] *Ibid.*, 493–498, 529; and Green and Frost, *Sea Fights*, 200, 213–215, 218, 222, 226–229.

[9] Rawson, *Naval Battles*, 637. [10] *Ibid.*, 666–667, 684–686.

[11] Sir Charles Oman, *A History of the Art of War in the Sixteenth Century*, 30.

[12] As illustrated in the studies published in connection with the four hundredth

consideration of the man as a military figure, imply that the military side of his career has already known definitive treatment. Yet virtually every writer who has treated his military work has centered comment upon the personal valor Cortés exhibited, and in so doing has automatically assigned him to the Middle Ages rather than to modern times. Any analysis, however, of the strategy and tactics employed by him in the Battle of Tenochtitlán, wherein he demonstrated a greater range of military talents than he was called upon to exhibit in all the prior and subsequent phases of his entire career, immediately tends to lift him above the limited military horizon of his day.

Cortés determined the manner in which he planned to bring the enemy in Tenochtitlán to battle in 1521 on the basis of a wealth of knowledge gained from his prior experience in the Valley of Mexico. The first time the invaders entered Tenochtitlán they did so in violation of the most basic strategic concepts that the geography of the lacustrine setting imposed upon a would-be successful invader. Riding on the crest of a wave of victories, all of which employed a common strategy geared only to land warfare, Cortés pushed into the fortress-city in a moment of military aberration. Once he was within the city and had soberly realized the magnitude of his disadvantage, he tried, through the building of the first four brigantines, to extemporize tactically a course of action which would partially atone for the strategic blunder. The burning of the brigantines and the calamity of the Sad Night combined to drive home to Cortés, as a lesson never to be forgotten, the realization that any

---

anniversary of the death of Cortés, such themes as his statesmanship, his inspirational influence upon the arts, and his relations with the Indians, to name but a few, have drawn the attention of numerous modern scholars. See, for example, Alberto María Carreño, "Cortés, hombre de estado," *BRAH*, Vol. CXXIII (1948), 171–183; José Subirá, "Hernán Cortés en la música teatral," in the Instituto Gonzalo Fernández de Oviedo, *Estudios Cortesianos*, 105–126; Jorge Campos, "Hernán Cortés en la dramática española," in *ibid.*, 171–197; Jaime Delgado, "Hernán Cortés en la poesía española de los siglos XVIII y XIX," in *ibid.*, 393–469; Manuel Ballesteros Gaibrois, "Hernán Cortés y los indígenas," in *ibid.*, 25–36; and Constantino Bayle, "Cortés, Padre de los Indios," in Institución de Servicios Culturales, *Estudios Hispanoamericanos—homenaje a Hernán Cortés en el IV centenario de su muerte*, 7–27.

future action in the valley had to be in strict accord with a carefully conceived plan of strategy. Accordingly, 1521 saw the invaders systematically setting out to construct a navy, mop up the lake-front communities in the valley, and then launch a combined operation against the island-city of Tenochtitlán. Both the time previously spent in that city and the forays and reconnaissances in connection with the mopping-up phase of the valley campaign enabled Cortés to determine with incisive realism the various positions the control of which would enable him to dominate the scene of imminent battle. When the base was set up at Texcoco and when the advanced bases were pushed into Tacuba, Coyoacán, and Acachinanco, Cortés was as aware as Napoleon ever was some centuries later that war is a business of positions.

Strategically Cortés sensed that the brigantines were the key to the situation. His force, like any other on the offensive, demanded mobility. Given the lacustrine setting of Tenochtitlán and the relative immobility of cavalry, artillery, and infantry in such a situation, it was the navy that tipped the scale sufficiently in favor of mobility to enable the invaders to realize tactically the offensive that was a strategic necessity if final and decisive victory was to be won. As the element which fostered and furthered offensive action in the lake country, the navy truly was the key to the whole war. The repeated comments of both the captain-general and Bernal Díaz concerning the pre-siege planning serve to support the idea that Cortés realized that his most basic strategic consideration must be an attack in the nature of a combined land and water operation against the island-city. In like fashion the importance of the actual contribution of the brigantines is evident in numerous post-victory comments by participants, indicating that the role planned for the brigantines had been fulfilled in actual combat.[13]

In the course of achieving and consolidating Spanish control of

---

[13] AGI, Patronato 57–1–1, fols. 4, 5, 6, 6r, 7, 7r, 8r–9, 9–9r, 12r, 23r, 27, 30, 33, 35r–36, 38r, 41–41r, 43r, 46, 48 (testimony, 1528 and 1534); translation in AU–CC, Martín López, 1528–1574, pp. 9, 14, 17, 19, 21, 22–23, 26–27, 28, 39, 73, 82, 91, 100, 108, 116, 123, 129, 136, 142.

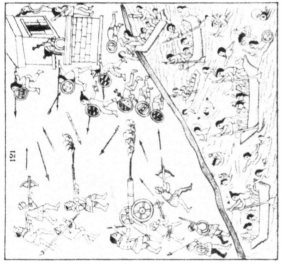

Naval aspects of the Battle of Tenochtitlán (II) (*From the Codex Florentino, Historia de las cosas de Nueva España, Vol. IV*)

Naval aspects of the Battle of Tenochtitlán (III) (*From the Codex Florentino, Historia de las cosas de Nueva España, Vol. IV*)

Lake Texcoco, Cortés demonstrated a masterful and intuitive grasp of the concept of applied naval power. He sensed that even prior to the inauguration of his own combined operation against the city, there had to be a transference of control of the lake from the Indians to the invaders. The fleet action of May 31, 1521, served that end. Not only did the Spaniards drive at the earliest possible moment for command of the navigable waters, but they also inaugurated at an early moment a strategical blockade of the water routes. Given the restricted dimensions of Lake Texcoco, it is difficult for us as observers to differentiate between the strategical or distant blockade and the tactical or close blockade, but in terms of the nature of the Spanish action of patrolling the lake at large rather than just the immediate waterfront of the city, the operation was closer to strategic blockade in both conception and application.

The issue of the relative areas of authority enjoyed by Cortés and the divisional commands regarding the brigantines seems to resolve itself quite simply. Unity of command, vested solely in Cortés, was apparent on the broad plane of basic strategy. Division of the command function, wherein Alvarado and Sandoval could demonstrate considerable ingenuity and individuality, lay in the area of tactical implementation of the strategy outlined by Cortés. This relationship between Cortés and his field commanders regarding naval matters was not unique; rather it was a simple extension of his longstanding approach to the conduct of army operations.

In the process of seeking out the enemy's fleet, Cortés demonstrated both capacity and caution in well-nigh professional portions. When he secured initial contact with the enemy to the east of Nezahualcoyotl Dike, at considerable distance from Tenochtitlán, he had the brigantines in excellent position to achieve a decisive victory. After the invaders won command of the lake on May 31, the defenders still had a sizable fleet in being, but the captain-general was never so eager to eliminate it that he pushed his own units into untenable positions. The restraint and patience demonstrated during subsequent weeks admirably complemented the dash and daring of the naval action of the initial day. Denied further fleet actions with the enemy's carefully husbanded maritime power, Cortés applied the less spectacular practices that furthered his strategy of attrition.

When the successes gained by Cortés' land division on the Iztapalapa causeway outstripped the gains of both Alvarado and Sandoval, owing in large part to the presence of supporting naval power, Cortés did not allow the concept of naval concentration to become a shibboleth. The man who read into his estimate of the situation a need to divide his army into three operating units easily saw the related truth that his naval might should be split into three task forces.[14]

In the manner in which he directed the tactical moves which supported his plan of strategy, Cortés was akin to nineteenth-century Napoleon, in being both the strategist of the precampaign map room and the tactician leading a combat force in the actual fray. The siege of Tenochtitlán was practically compelled to be characterized by a large amount of tactical innovation and ingenuity— because the daring of the strategy had to be implemented by equivalently imaginative and daring tactics. The rapidity with which Cortés junked one tactical plan and adopted another after the rout of the enemy on the first day of fighting was quite possibly due to his supreme awareness of how well it served his overall strategic aim. The close naval support commonly afforded the ground troops throughout the engagement smacked of later centuries, as did the total-war aspect of the progressive razing of the city which the navy inaugurated and the army later adopted. The marine-like raids of limited landing parties and the tightness of the blockade as operational techniques were more suggestive of the twentieth century than of Cortés' own sixteenth.

---

[14] To appreciate more fully the relationship between the practice of Cortés and more recent strategical theory, see statements concerning the latter in Mahan, *Naval Strategy Compared and Contrasted with the Principles and Practice of Military Operations on Land*, 22, 36, 120 note, 152, 164; Sir Julian S. Corbett, *Some Principles of Maritime Strategy*, 87–90, 93, 106, 134–135, 158, 169, 172–173, 182–183, 185, 204; and Colonel G. F. R. Henderson, *The Science of War—A Collection of Essays and Lectures, 1891–1903*, 39–42.

It is quite true that the accident of situation promoted the employment of certain of Cortés' most novel and successful tactics. But such a reduction of military success to a least common denominator of geographic determinism does not belittle the successful military figure; on the contrary it attests the elementary nature of his genius. Both as strategist and tactician, Cortés clearly demonstrated in the preliminary campaign for the lake-front region of the Valley of Mexico and in the Battle of Tenochtitlán that he had not only remarkable ability for estimating the situation but infinite capacity as well for achieving the end his planning logically embraced. He was much more than a valorous warrior of the stamp of the Middle Ages; he was also a brilliant strategist and tactician of the modern mold to such an extent that it is surprising that his military career, dotted as it is with lessons for professional military men of the present day, should be one of the least-known areas of significant modern military history.

Cortés' employment of combined operations, as he launched coordinated army and navy thrusts against Tenochtitlán, was one of the first and one of the most prolonged applications of such technique in recorded military history. On numerous occasions in both ancient and medieval periods, there had been partner-like relationship in army and navy actions in an over-all *campaign*, but seldom, if ever, had the relationship been so intimate as to find army and navy elements in a common *battle*. At Tenochtitlán, Cortés was closer to Normandy (1944) and Okinawa (1945) than he was to Lepanto (1571) or Austerlitz (1805). A logical reading of the geographical factor with which he had to cope, followed by a logical implementation in the field of the strategy dictated by geography, made the employment of the two-pronged attack against the island-fortress as natural as it was unique. Possibly no other military commander in all recorded history has been called upon to conduct seventy-five consecutive days of combined operations in such a restricted area as Tenochtitlán. The very limitations of the operation, in reference to space, should make it all the more attractive to those students of military history who may desire to turn

195

microscopic intensity of attention upon such a unique action. It follows that this genius of the sixteenth century was precursor to oft-repeated practices of World War II and the Korean conflict. In the realm of interservice co-operation and harmony, as well as the over-all unity of command which he essayed, Cortés, in the sixteenth century, achieved ends that are, in the mid-twentieth century, only hoped for in American operations and command.

The Brigantines and the Conquest

Long before the brigantines ever engaged in combat, long before they had been launched, even as they were being constructed, the vessels of the navy-to-be were described by Cortés as the key of the whole war. The uses to which they were put in the course of the siege operation against Tenochtitlán emphasize the accuracy of that designation.

In the first place, the brigantines shortened the war considerably. They permitted Cortés to wage total war against the defenders rather than merely the characteristic land warfare of that day. Total war included real blockade of the city, an operation which would not have been possible without the brigantines and which led to economic collapse for the capital and physical hardship for its defenders. Although the Mexicans never wavered in their determination to defend their civilization, the tactics of attrition realized through the blockade undermined their physical stamina to the point where it may be said starvation did as much to defeat them as did Spanish arms.

In the second place, considerable psychological importance attached to the brigantines. They raised the morale of the invaders and lowered the morale of the defenders. Consider the Spaniards for a moment. Many of them, when previously in Tenochtitlán, had been like so many mice under the paw of a gigantic cat; and the debacle of the Sad Night had demonstrated to them the tragic limitations of their infantry, cavalry, and artillery for warfare in this setting. Then the brigantines were built. To the conquistadors the ships were not only new and powerful weapons, signifying additional military force, but also a way of making mice into men and heroes once more. But for the defenders of the city, the brigantines were a nightmare come horribly true. The Indians had come to comprehend and find ways of guarding against the strange arms of the Spaniards one by one, and the lances, swords, horses, cross-bows, and muskets no longer constituted unusual physical or psychological advantage for the invaders. Then suddenly the Spaniards had the much greater and more powerful weapon, the brigantines, whereupon the psychological superiority of Spanish arms was renewed and augmented manyfold. When quite early in the operation Cortés divided the thirteen-vessel fleet, sending three brigantines to Alvarado and three to Sandoval after the latter commander had taken a position on the Tepeyac causeway, the Indians on all the approaches to the city and the Spaniards in all the land divisions came to feel the psychological effects of the brigantines.

In the third place, the brigantines contributed to a battle plan that saved many Spanish lives. While the land forces of the invaders pushed along the causeways toward the heart of the city, the brigantines were always but a short distance from the causeways, protecting the flanks and the rear of the invading forces. On occasion the brigantines moved in against the outskirts of the city and burned portions of it, thereby facilitating the advance of invading land troops within the city proper. On occasion, too, they hastened and protected the movement of Spanish troops when the retreating Mexicans had destroyed bridges; ships moved into the breaches and served to fill the gaps temporarily, much in the manner of pontoon bridges thrown by modern engineers across deep waters. No longer were the breaches the death traps they had been on the Sad Night. And possibly the most important service the brigantines rendered to an efficient, lifesaving battle plan was their guarding of the Spanish camps at night. Late each afternoon, protected by the brigantines, soldiers withdrew from the daily invasion of the city to their camps on the causeways. There the vessels so protected the camps that the enemy never ventured close; in consequence the soldiers could sleep undisturbed, to recoup energy for the next day's

197

fighting. As mentioned before, if the men had been forced to face the enemy on a night-and-day basis without relief and refreshment, it is inconceivable that their stamina would have lasted long enough to win final victory. Furthermore, with considerable credit due the navy, the Spaniards suffered during a battle of seventy-five days only a minor percentage of the number of casualties previously experienced in an approximately four-hour action in the same setting.

For us as modern observers, the brigantines provide a key to a more complete understanding of the conquest of Mexico as a whole. Earlier in Chapter VII an attempt was made to re-evaluate Cortés as a strategist and tactician in the light of fuller understanding of the complexity of the Tenochtitlán operation. There remains to be recorded an insistence that the brigantines did much to give to the Indian allies—Tlaxcalans, Texcocans, and others—of the conquest a stature that has never been realized. The contribution of the Tlaxcalans to the cause of the conquistadors cannot be stated fully by the present writer, but at least the sweep of the transcendently important service they rendered the Spaniards can be sketched. To the frequently made statement that without the Tlaxcalans the Spaniards could never have survived the debacle of the Sad Night and its immediate aftermath can now be added the assertion that without the Tlaxcalans the Spaniards could not have taken Tenochtitlán in 1521. Their work on the brigantine construction, for instance, cannot be lauded too highly: the direction and design that came from the Spaniards would have been meaningless without the muscle and material supplied by the Tlaxcalans. From the moment Martín López entered their forests searching for timbers to the moment the completed ships slid into Lake Texcoco, the Indians of Tlaxcala were ever-faithful servants and allies.[15] The Texcocans also made signal contribution to the cause of the Europeans; by

---

[15] See "Información recibida en México y Puebla el año de 1565 . . . ," *Biblioteca Histórica de la Iberia*, Vol. XX (1875), 13–29, 113–122. Tlaxcalan aid between 1519 and 1521 is summarized in Charles Gibson, *Tlaxcala in the Sixteenth Century*, 21–27.

digging the canal and later putting tens of thousands of men and thousands of canoes in support of the invaders, they gave assistance that ranks second only to that of the Tlaxcalans.

No former account of the Tenochtitlán operation makes even a fair general, much less a full detailed, statement of the Indian contribution to the Spanish cause. Given the complexity and duration of the operation, it is readily apparent that the logistical problems admitted of solution only because of the sustained support the Tlaxcalans, Texcocans, and other native allies extended to the Spaniards. Their assistance was vital in regard to food supplies that must be foraged, transported, and prepared; temporary housing that must be erected; broken causeways that must be repaired. Alone, the Spaniards could not have demolished Tenochtitlán literally stone by stone. Nor was the native contribution made only in the realms of services, supply, and combat engineering. Notable direct military support was also offered: thousands of their canoes supplemented the brigantines, taking the war into areas so restricted as to be beyond the reach of the big vessels; thousands of warriors did combat duty on the causeways, both in conjunction with the Spanish forces and in independent actions. Police duty behind the lines, a matter on which the available records are uniformly silent, also surely fell to the Indians, since it was a rare occasion when Cortés detached any band of Spaniards for temporary thrusts about the valley. It seems clear that the Indian allies did everything desired in the way of maintaining the lines of communcations with the coast and controlling questionable segments of the native population in the valley.

To the defenders of Tenochtitlán greatly added stature is also accorded when the contest that produced the city's fall is seen in the better perspective of the total war made possible by the brigantines. The personal bravery and the collective courage of those natives who fought against relentless forces and insurmountable odds have produced, it is true, many a paean of praise in Mexican historical writing. But quite commonly the grandeur of the defenders is too obliquely and inferentially presented: the story of the

199

dignity of their monarch in defeat and his subsequent torture at the hands of his greedy captors is recounted and his loyal subjects go unmentioned, or at best are left to bask in the reflected glory and greatness of their leader.[16] However, when it is realized that the increasingly ruthless and effective blockade of the city reduced every inhabitant to want and physical pain, there is magnificence in the continuing loyalty of the defenders to their ruler and their cause. The Spaniards could move back at will from the city to the causeway camps for a night's rest and stomach-filling meals. But for the defenders of Tenochtitlán, end of day did not bring battle's end; the unseen, relentless foe, starvation, continued to take toll from the Mexicans even as they slept. Time was ever the ally of the conquistadors once the aqueduct was broken and the blockade set. There is moral majesty attending the determination with which the Indians fought for their way of life under such circumstances. The brigantines were the one Spanish weapon for which the Mexicans had no answer and against which no measure of personal bravery could prevail, yet until the capture of their leader they never flagged in their role of defenders of Tenochtitlán.

One further aspect of the brigantines' total significance to the conquest has been commonly neglected by writers. In the decisive early years of the conquest, shipbuilding was one of the few activities engaged in by the personnel of Cortés' force that encouraged emergence of the artisan skills of many of the conquistadors. The construction of the thirteen brigantines, then, aside from its military importance to the victory at Tenochtitlán, gave men an opportunity to practice the civilian skills with which they could expect to make a contribution to the life of New Spain once the fighting phase of conquest was finished.

Too commonly the conquest is viewed completely as a blood-and-thunder saga. But when we see the conquistadors in more prosaic activities, hammer and saw in hand rather than sword and shield, we realize that fundamentally they constituted a civilian

---

[16] The following are illustrative: Alfonso Teja Zabre, *Tragedia de Cuauhtémoc*; and Héctor Pérez Martínez, *Cuauhtémoc—Vida y Muerte de una Cultura*.

army rather than a corps of professional soldiers. Most of them had known prior careers that would fit them into the constructive side of the Spanish imperial scheme of things: they had been ranchers on Cuba, merchant seamen, farmers in the Antilles, minor public officials. In their civilian pursuits they were soon to re-emerge in New Spain, but they were preceded chronologically by such artisans as the carpenters, the blacksmiths, and the sawyers, without whom the early ranchers would have had no branding irons, the seamen no ships. Lacking artisans, permanent settlement would have been discouraged by the absence of acceptable housing and the transference of the Spanish way of life to New Spain would have been incomplete and short-lived. Destiny had marked the carpenters, sawyers, and blacksmiths for great constructive achievement in the years ahead, but first of all they had to pool their civilian talents to further the military victory on which rested the realization of Spanish hope for the area. Diego Hernández with saw in hand, Hernán Martín bent over his forge, Juan Gómez de Herrera busily calking the hull of a vessel, Andrés Martínez fashioning masts, Lázaro Guerrero catering for a crew of workmen, and Martín López displaying a combination of skills as workman and masterful supervisor—such men epitomize a side of the conquest that is as important as it is understated in the usual account of an achievement which is presented, through over-simplification, only as military action.

Almost as soon as Tenochtitlán had fallen, Cortés, having heard the reports of Spanish exploring parties, developed a deep and continuing interest in the Pacific Ocean.[17] No issue, from the end of the siege until his final departure from the New World, drew his persistent attention and effort more completely than did the challenge of the Pacific. Repeatedly the conqueror of New Spain financed shipbuilding ventures and sponsored voyages of discovery and conquest. This seldom emphasized side of Hernando Cortés

[17] The very close relationship in time between the victory in the Valley of Mexico and the projection of plans embracing the Pacific is evident in Cortés' report to the Crown; see *HC*, II, 47, 50.

has begun to draw in recent years some measure of the attention it deserves.[18] Its full story is of course beyond the province of the present study, but the inspirational relationship of the naval chapter of the conquest to this later, less spectacular, and less successful chapter is readily apparent.

The oft-demonstrated capacity of the conquistadors to construct ships during the period 1519–1521 could not help but feed the captain-general's imagination and desires in regard to the Pacific.[19] Most of the men who were responsible for his unusual nautical achievements were still at his disposal after 1521. When a former brigantine skipper, Juan Rodríguez de Villafuerte, served at the coastal settlement of Zacatula in the dual role of commandant of the Spanish garrison and director of the earliest of Cortés' ship-building programs on the Pacific, Cortés was clearly relating past experience to future program. Certain others of the experienced artisans of the 1519–1521 period surely were parties to the Pacific projects. For example, when the carpenter Francisco Rodríguez went to court, in 1529, with his demand that Cortés pay him 2,000 pesos for his part in the construction of the brigantines for the siege at Tenochtitlán, that artisan rapidly followed up his first claim with a second demand—likewise for 2,000 pesos—this one for work he

[18] Illustrative of this recent literature are the following: Federico Gómez de Orozco, "Las primeras comunicaciones entre México y Perú," *Anales del Instituto de Investigaciones Estéticas*, Vol. II, Núm. 7 (1941), 65–70; Francisco de Ulloa, "Memorial sobre el descubrimiento y expedición cortesiana a las Californias," in *Cartas de relación de la conquista de América*, ed. Julio Le Riverend, II, 641–695; Max L. Moorhead, "Hernán Cortés and the Tehuantepec Passage," *HAHR*, Vol. XXIX (August, 1949), 370–379; Fernando B. Sandoval (ed.), "El Astillero del Carbon en Tehuantepec, 1535–1566," *BAGN*, Vol. XXI, Núm. 1 (1950), 1–20; Luis Romero Solano, *Expedición Cortesiana a las Molucas, 1527*; and C. Harvey Gardiner, "Tempest in Tehuantepec, 1529: Local Events in Imperial Perspective," *HAHR*, Vol. XXXV (February, 1955), 1–13. Sr. Romero Solano is currently working upon the Cortés-sponsored voyage of discovery to California.

[19] Luis Romero Solano shares this view. Opposite the reproduction of a portion of the Códice Durán he writes, "Cortés plans the strategy for the naval battle with which he had to reconquer Tenochtitlán, an episode unique in the history of the wars. . . . There he organized the elements with which he later equipped shipyards to explore the South Sea." See Romero Solano, *Expedición . . . 1527*, unnumbered pages [4 and 5]. In unequivocal fashion a writer on the Pacific phase of Cortés' career thus cites the Tenochtitlán phase as significant in the backlog of Spanish experience.

had performed on ships under construction at Zacatula.[20] Apparently in the realms of both intangible inspiration and tangible implementation, the success of the men of the brigantines served to influence a later chapter of Cortés' career.

As elements of conquest, however, the thirteen brigantines of the Valley of Mexico stand in unique relationship to Spanish military action throughout the Americas. The isolation of this naval action is all the greater when one remembers that in the whole period of the Spanish conquest of the New World no other conquistador had to call upon naval power to achieve his ends.

Of Fighting Ships and Fighting Men

With characteristic foresight, Cortés preserved the brigantines of 1521, counting them among the principal defenses of the new Mexico City which arose on the foundation stones of old Tenochtitlán. While he and his fellow conquistadors still were based in Coyoacán, he gave his earliest attention to the defenses of the new island-metropolis. In his fourth letter to Emperor Charles V, dated October 15, 1524, he reported:

Immediately after the capture of this city, I took steps to establish a fort in the water where the brigantines might be kept safely, and from where I might control the whole city should there be any occasion for it, and the exit and entrance remain in my hands. It was constructed in such wise that, although I have seen some forts and arsenals, I have seen none that equals it, and many others affirm the same as myself; and it has been built in this wise: on the side toward the lake [i.e., the east, facing Texcoco], it has two very strong towers, provided with loopholes: these two towers are joined by a building in the form of three naves, where brigantines are kept, and which have doors towards the water for going in and out; and all this building is provided also with loopholes, and on the end towards the city there is another large tower, with many rooms above and below for offensive and defensive operations. But, as I shall send a plan to Your Majesty to make this more clearly understood,[21] I shall give no more particulars about it, but, hold-

[20] *CDIAO*, XXVII, 157.

[21] An obvious reference to the so-called Cortés map of Tenochtitlán, which had been executed upon orders of Cortés by some unknown cartographer, surely a fellow

ing these with the ships and artillery, peace or war is in our hands as we choose. Once this building was finished, everything seemed secure for repeopling the city, so I returned there with all my people.[22]

From the foregoing the significance of the ships to the continuing Spanish control of the waters of Lake Texcoco is readily apparent. When, immediately following the siege of the island-fortress, Cortés and the majority of the conquistadors temporarily removed themselves to Coyoacán, the brigantines were left in Tenochtitlán, with Juan Rodríguez de Villafuerte in command of the detachment of men still assigned to the vessels.[23] From this it is evident that the navy was continued as a fleet in being to discourage the possibility of a rebirth of native resistance and to facilitate the rapidity with which the new Spanish city replaced the razed Indian capital. The departure of Rodríguez de Villafuerte with the force of Cristóbal de Olid on the excursion of mid-1522 into Michoacán invites speculation concerning the brigantines at that time. Was the prospect of Indian resistance so slight that it could be ignored; had another person simply been named to command the vessels; or had the construction of the dockyard for the brigantines made possible the release of some personnel previously assigned to them? Definite answers are not at hand but it can be stated with assurance, in the light of the established policy of holding numerous chieftains as prisoners, as well as from subsequent events, that Cortés had not dropped his guard so completely as to write

---

Spaniard, in days shortly after the fall of the city to the invaders. It was published in Europe as early as 1524 and has known frequent reproduction and interpretation in succeeding centuries. As intended, it admirably supplemented Cortés' word picture of his plan of defense for the new city. A bibliography concerning this famous map is in Lowery, A Descriptive List of Maps, 26–27. In recent years a reproduction of the map has been distributed widely by the William L. Clements Library of the University of Michigan. The interpretation of the map made by Ignacio Alcocer has been generally accepted; see his Apuntes, between 12 and 13.

[22] HC–MacN, II, 202. For a discussion of various opinions concerning the location of the arsenal as well as speculation concerning its ultimate fate, see Artemio de Valle-Arizpe (ed.), Historia de la ciudad de México según los relatos de sus cronistas, 145–151.

[23] MN–PyTT, Leg. 96, Información de los méritos y servicios de Juan Rodríguez de Villafuerte (1525).

off the brigantines as no longer important. By early autumn of 1524, as he readied an expedition which he personally led overland toward Honduras, he looked to the defenses of the new city, which even then counted some 30,000 households, most of which obviously were Indian; in addition to providing the guard detachment with sufficient cannon, ammunition, and manpower, he ordered that the brigantines be readied for possible use.[24]

At least one episode in the early post-siege period illustrates graphically the continuing importance of the brigantines. A pair of Spaniards, returning from a reconnaissance of Michoacán, brought a brother of chief Cazonci with them to Cortés' headquarters at Coyoacán. Desiring to impress the Indian so that upon his return to his home country he would work for peaceful submission to Spanish power, Cortés proceeded to demonstrate before him the full array of Spanish military might. Artillery and muskets were fired; infantrymen marched; cavalry units galloped in simulated battle. Having displayed his land might, Cortés next took the guest in a canoe on a tour of the water defenses of the city, finally showing him the brigantines whose past exploits were common knowledge even in distant Michoacán. After minute inspection of the vessels and their sails and paddles by the Tarascan guest, Cortés ordered some forty to fifty Spaniards to launch one of the brigantines. They proceeded to maneuver the ship. A well-impressed Indian returned to Coyoacán that day with Cortés.[25] This episode of 1522 indicates several things: the brigantines were considered an integral and important part of the total defense of the new city; the nautical skills of the conquistadors were being maintained; and, judging by the fact that the ship had to be launched for the demonstration, the brigantines were probably kept normally out of the water, a circumstance which would tend to prolong the period of their usefulness. With care bestowed upon them, the brigantines may well have

---

[24] HC, II, 109, 129.

[25] Whereas Cervantes de Salazar details all aspects of this episode in his Crónica, 796–798, 800 note 1, Cortés fails to report the naval phase of his military display; see HC, II, 54–55.

been in fairly good condition decades later when Cervantes de Salazar saw them.

For a long time the arsenal which centered about the dockyard of the brigantines played its role in municipal affairs. It was located at the eastern end of the street of the Calle de las Atarazanas (the street of the arsenals), at that point which previously had served the Mexicans as the port area for canoe traffic on the eastern side of old Tenochtitlán. The Calle de las Atarazanas constituted the eastern prolongation of the street which, on the west side of the great plaza, led to Tacuba.[26] Early cabildo records are dotted with petitions for and grants of *solares* to conquistadors and early settlers along the Calle de las Atarazanas, sometimes also called the Calle de los Bergantines (the street of the brigantines).[27] In 1533, Alcalde Antonio de Carvajal, himself an old brigantine skipper, and *Regidores* Gonzalo Ruiz and Juan de Mansilla, the latter also a veteran of naval service, made an interesting and significant report to the cabildo of Mexico City. The trio had been authorized to seek a likely site for La Merced Monastery. They reported that due to the already strong tendency to build along the streets leading to Tacuba and Chapultepec, in which region there were also three monasteries, the section of the city in the vicinity of the arsenal was being depopulated. Accordingly they recommended that the new monastery be a square-shaped structure in the neighborhood of the arsenal.[28] So there came to that section of the city the name and structure which later so dominated the area immediately to the east of the great plaza as to eclipse the name of the arsenal that sheltered the brigantines.[29]

In the late autumn of 1528 the military post of *alcaide de la atarazana*, which continued the Cortesian concern about the defense of the city, was given added significance when the then alcaide, Lope de Samaniego, was accorded the powers and pre-

[26] Linné, *El Valle*, 126.

[27] *AdeC*, I, 7–8, 11–12, 62, 64, 70, 75, 166, 171; III, 56; IV, 130, 136, 148–149, 151, 153–154, 166, 180.

[28] *Ibid.*, III, 52–53.

[29] José María Marroqui, *La Ciudad de México*, II, 476.

rogatives of a regidor in the municipal government of Mexico City. If anywhere, one would think that in the interests and actions of Samaniego the continuing story of the brigantines could be traced. Such, however, is not the case. Nowhere, either in his official role in the cabildo or in his personal statement of his services, does one find the key to further information about the former fleet. Except for periods during which he was absent from the city, Samaniego served on the cabildo well into the term of Viceroy Antonio de Mendoza, and never did he either introduce or discuss the brigantines in official business of the municipality.[30]

Early in the long viceregal term of Antonio de Mendoza, attention was directed once again to the defenses of the capital city of New Spain. In the course of discussions within the cabildo the view was expressed, in the autumn of 1537, that the arsenals served no useful purpose in their present location and hence should be transferred to the street leading to Tacuba.[31] Although the recommended transfer did not occur then, it is evident that a decade and a half after the victory at Tenochtitlán a number of factors (e.g., the pattern of growth of the city, the arrival of many Spaniards who neither knew nor could easily imagine the past pattern of military action in the lake country, the perceptible shrinkage of Lake Texcoco, and the long record of peace) combined to promote the obsolescence of the López-built fleet of brigantines. Without being accorded equivalent care, the brigantines had been reduced to the category of museum pieces.

Like the ships themselves, the more prominent men who had

[30] *AdeC*, I, 187, 188–191 *passim*, 193–211 *passim*; II, 4–26 *passim*, 160–195 *passim*; III, 7–12 *passim*, 13–67 *passim*, 69–104 *passim*, 105–137 *passim*; IV, 3–59 *passim*, 61–109 *passim*, 111–182 *passim*; and MN–PyTT, Leg. 97, Información de los méritos y servicios de Lope de Samaniego (1531). For early chronology listing the alcaides de las atarazanas, see Marroqui, *La Ciudad de México*, II, 476–477.

[31] *AdeC*, IV, 98–99. The year 1537 also found Samaniego addressing a communication to the Spanish Crown on the desirability of transferring the site of the fortress of Mexico; see *CDIHIA*, I, 85–87. Andrés Cavo indicates the Crown was interested in shifting the fortress of Mexico City as early as 1527 or 1528; see *Los tres siglos de Méjico durante el gobierno español hasta la entrada del ejército trigarante*, ed. Carlos María de Bustamante, 57.

fought on the brigantines saw little if any further nautical duty during the conquest of Mexico. Pedro Briones, inconspicuous as a brigantine skipper during the siege, went to Honduras as *maestre de campo* for the ill-fated Cristóbal de Olid. Four years after that expedition, he was hanged in Guatemala as a mutineer, an ignominious end to a colorful career.[32]

Antonio de Carvajal continued to serve in the conquest, alternating as a horseman and as a captain of infantry in expeditions into Pánuco, Tututepec, and Soconusco. For decades, beginning about 1525, he was prominent in municipal political life, serving variously as regidor, procurador, and alcalde. For his services in the conquest, he received the village of Zacatlán of the Bishopric of Tlaxcala in encomienda. In the late 1520's he was counted among the most bitter enemies of the then partially eclipsed Cortés. In 1530 he was granted a coat of arms. A property owner of some note in the vicinity of the viceregal capital, he included ranching among his interests. His Spanish wife, the former Catalina de Tapia, bore him one son and nine daughters. Charged by the Indians of Zacatlán with abuses and the collection of excessive tribute, Carvajal was sentenced by Royal *Visitador* Diego Ramírez in 1555, but on appeal the decision was reversed. The doughty old conquistador was still alive in 1571, by which time he was in his late seventies.[33]

Before entering upon more peaceful pursuits as a settler in New Spain, Miguel Díaz de Aux continued in the ways of the warrior for some years, participating in campaigns into Oaxaca, Michoacán, Pánuco, Colima, and Zacatula. Thirty years after the fall of Tenochtitlán he was still in New Spain, the year 1551 finding him bitterly contesting the right of Visitador Diego Ramírez to extend his *visita*

[32] *BDdelC*, II, 188, 224, 337–339, 342, 344, 384, 385; III, 22; and *CDIAO*, XIV, 239, 243, 248, 253, 259 ff.

[33] *BDdelC*, II, 188, 224; *CDIHIA*, II, 76; *CDIAO*, XXVII, 298, 436, 457; XXVIII, 97–98, 287–288; XLI, 257–259; MN–PyTT, Leg. 93, Información de los méritos y servicios de Antonio de Carvajal (1551); *ENE*, VIII, 4–8; IX, 14; XI, 123; Icaza, *Diccionario autobiográfico*, I, 72–73; and *AdeC*, I, 25–67 *passim*, 69–76 *passim*, 157–186 *passim*, 204–209 *passim*; II, 10–15, 57, 132–149 *passim*, 151, 205; III, 13–66 *passim*, 135; IV, 3–59 *passim*, 61–107 *passim*, 111–158 *passim*, 159–183 *passim*, 185–223 *passim*, 225–264 *passim*, 265–321 *passim*, 323–354 *passim*; and V, 313.

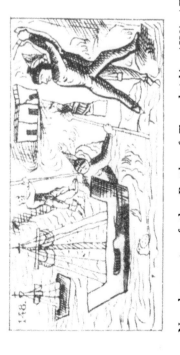

Naval aspects of the Battle of Tenochtitlán (IV) (*From the Codex Florentino, Historia de las cosas de Nueva España, Vol. IV*)

Naval aspects of the Battle of Tenochtitlán (V) (*From the Codex Florentino, Historia de las cosas de Nueva España, Vol. IV*)

to include the village of Meztitlán, which the conquistador held in encomienda.[34]

The immediate post-siege activities of Cristóbal Flores are unknown, but he did interrupt his residence in Mexico City in the late 1520's to serve with Nuño de Guzmán during the latter's campaign into Nueva Galicia. Settling in Mexico City, where he acquired several pieces of property, Cristóbal Flores was prominent in municipal politics during the mid-1520's, serving variously as regidor and alcalde of the new Spanish community. By the close of that decade he was prominent among those in opposition to Cortés. His death occurred sometime prior to June 1, 1539.[35]

García Holguín, famed as the brigantine captain who seized Cuauhtémoc on August 13, 1521, cannot be identified with further military activity in the Aztec area after the fall of Tenochtitlán. He settled in Mexico City and became the owner of several pieces of property, including ranching and milling interests. In addition he served variously as regidor and alcalde in the administration of Mexico City during the first decade of its political life. On one occasion he went to Michoacán as a royal investigator. The early 1530's found him among the followers of Pedro de Alvarado in Guatemala, and, although it is not clearly established, he had probably served previously in Alvarado's campaign of conquest in that area. After Alvarado had readied a sizable fleet on the Pacific, García Holguín was dispatched to check on the stories current about Pizarro's rich find. When the ex-brigantine skipper returned from his mission with a confirmation of the accounts of Peruvian wealth, Alvarado moved his fleet in that direction, in January, 1534. So it happened that García Holguín, without further naval duty, did know additional maritime experience in the post-conquest

[34] *BDdelC*, II, 123–124; Icaza, *Diccionario autobiográfico*, I, 73–74; *ENE*, VI, 69–71, 125; VII, 115, 117, 122–125; Walter V. Scholes, "The Diego Ramírez Visita in Meztitlán," *HAHR*, Vol. XXIV (February, 1944), 30–38, and *The Diego Ramírez Visita*, 69 ff.

[35] *CDIAO*, XIV, 416, 422, 427, 430, 441; XXIV, 288; XXVII, 6; *AdeC*, I, 4–20 passim, 88–112 passim, 113–155 passim, 157–186 passim; and José López-Portillo y Weber, *La Conquista de la Nueva Galicia*, 184, 241.

period. This episode suggests that the captor of Cuauhtémoc had acquired considerable nautical experience prior to his brigantine duty of 1521.[36]

Juan Jaramillo continued his military contribution to the conquest by enrolling in expeditions destined for Oaxaca, Pánuco, Honduras, and the Río Grijalva area. For services rendered in early phases of the conquest of Mexico, he was granted the village of Xilotepec in encomienda. With Jaramillo's marriage to Marina, the famed interpreter, in October, 1524, Cortés designated him *encomendero* of the towns of Olutla and Tetiquipaque in the province of Coatzacoalcos. A rich resident of Mexico City, Jaramillo concerned himself with its government, serving terms as regidor, *alférez*, alcalde, and *alcalde de la mesta* between 1525 and 1540. Following the death of Marina, by whom he had a daughter, named María, Jaramillo married Beatriz de Andrade, who bore him no children. For a while during the colonial period a street of the viceregal capital bore this conquistador's name. On July 20, 1538, a coat of arms was conferred upon him. In 1540 he left Mexico City to join the famed but relatively fruitless expedition of Francisco Vázquez de Coronado, of which he later wrote a generalized account. The date of the death of this honored, wealthy, and powerful citizen of Mexico City is not known.[37]

Juan de Limpias Carvajal went on numerous land expeditions, including those into Pánuco and Honduras, after the fall of Tenoch-

[36] *CDHM*, II, 546–548; *CDIAO*, XXVIII, 392; *AdeC*, I, 69–112 *passim*, 113–155 *passim*; II, 75–150 *passim*, 172, 199; and Bancroft, *Central America*, II, 125–129.

[37] *CDIHIA*, II, 197, 199; *CDIAO*, XIV, 304, 315; XLI, 188–189, 210; *ENE*, III, 31–32; Arthur S. Aiton (tr. and ed.), *The Muster Roll and Equipment of the Expedition of Francisco Vázquez de Coronado*, 15; Dorantes de Carranza, *Sumaria relación*, 207, 448; Sánchez-Arjona, "Relación . . . ," *RABM*, Vol. XXXVI (1917), 421; Icaza, *Diccionario autobiográfico*, I, 4; *AdeC*, I, 3–23 *passim*, 88–112 *passim*, 162–163; II, 60–62 *passim*, 175; IV, 159–184 *passim*, 185. González Obregón, *The Streets of Mexico*, tr. Wagner, 54–55; Orozco y Berra, *Historia antigua*, IV, 122; and MacNutt, "Marina," in *HC–MacN*, I, 329 (Appendix I). For an English translation of Jaramillo's narrative of the Coronado expedition, see "Account Given by Captain Juan Jaramillo of the Journey which he made to the new country, on which Francisco Vazquez Coronado was the general," in George Parker Winship (tr. and ed.), *The Journey of Coronado: 1540–1542*, 222–240.

titlán, but saw no additional naval duty in the course of his campaigning. For services rendered as a conquistador, he was granted an encomienda within the Bishopric of Oaxaca. He was still in possession of it in early 1560, by which time he had fathered a family of unknown size.[38]

Sooner than most of the conquistadors who later differed with Cortés, Rodrigo Morejón de Lobera became a bitter enemy of the captain-general. During the course of the campaign Cortés led into Pánuco after the fall of Tenochtitlán, the ex-brigantine skipper, considered a gentlemen by some of his colleagues, was seized by Cortés, who considered him a thief. After being held prisoner four or five months, he was sent away from New Spain in the expedition of Francisco de las Casas to Honduras in pursuit of Olid. In that distant land Morejón de Lobera died.[39]

On January 18, 1531, as Nuño de Guzmán placed Francisco Verdugo in charge of two brigantines, Andrés Núñez was designated a brigantine captain. In this manner, one full decade following his naval service before Tenochtitlán, Núñez was again concerned with ships. It cannot be clearly established whether it was Andrés Núñez the captain or Andrés Núñez the carpenter who shared the encomienda of Tequixquiac with Martín López and was the ranching partner of the shipwright.[40]

Of all the brigantine skippers, none knew a more significant post-siege connection with shipping than did Juan Rodríguez de Villafuerte. Immediately after the cessation of hostilities on San Hipólito's Day, 1521, this ship captain was placed in charge of the men who were detailed to guard the fleet at ruined Tenochtitlán. A short time later he campaigned in Michoacán as a member of the Olid force, elements of which pushed on into Colima and thence to Zacatula on the Pacific. After brief excursions to pacify the regions

---

[38] *ENE*, IX, 2, 20; XV, 1; *CDHM*, II, 546–548; Dorantes Carranza, *Sumaria relación*, 209; Sánchez-Arjona, "Relación . . . ," *RABM*, Vol. XXXVI (1917), 429–430; and O'Gorman, "Catálogo de pobladores de Nueva España," *BAGN*, Vol. XIII (1942), 150, 503–504.

[39] *CDIAO*, XXVI, 393–394.

[40] *ENE*, II, 9–10; IX, 2, 26; and *AdeC*, II, 198.

of Opelcingo, Coaquatlan, and Mesceloacan, Rodríguez de Villafuerte returned to Zacatula, which thenceforth was to be a significant base for the maritime schemes of Cortés. He not only commanded the Spanish garrison that settled the town of Zacatula, but also had charge of the shipbuilding activity which was of prime importance in terms of the wider interests and plans of Hernando Cortés. In mid-1526 Rodríguez de Villafuerte met with other municipal procuradores in Mexico City, the inference being that he was serving as a procurador for the town of Zacatula. At the close of the 1520's he was busily pressing a claim for 100 pesos against his former close friend, Cortés. He was still alive and in New Spain in early 1536, but the date of his death is unknown. Indirect information regarding his family, fortune, and death is seen in word that his daughter, Aldonza de Villafuerte, had inherited and was holding as of January, 1560, the encomiendas of Acapulco, Çaçapotla, Xaltiamgus, Cuyuca, Maxcaltepec, Atlala, Acamalutla, Yacapal, and Naguala, all of which the conquistador had originally held.[41]

Following the siege of Tenochtitlán, Francisco Rodríguez Magariño saw no more military duty. Perhaps the serious leg wound suffered at that time precluded further such strenuous activity, though on orders from Cortés he joined the group detailed to build a road to facilitate the movement of pack trains between Vera Cruz and the interior. Very little else of the post-conquest career of Rodríguez Magariño is known. The document conferring a coat of arms upon him in August, 1537, indicates he was residing in Mexico City at that time. It is apparent that he fathered a considerable number of sons and daughters, at least some of whom were subsequently considered wealthy.[42]

[41] MN–PyTT, Leg. 96, Información de los méritos y servicios de Juan Rodríguez de Villafuerte (1525); CDIAO, XXVI, 257, 263; XXVII, 155; XXVIII, 325; ENE, IX, 2; XV, 84; Conway (ed.), La Noche Triste, 95; R. H. Barlow (ed.), "Relación de Zacatula, 1580," Tlalocan, Vol. II, No. 3 (1947), 259; and Francisco Fernández del Castillo, "Tres Conquistadores y Pobladores de la Nueva España," in Vol. XII of Publicaciones del Archivo General de la Nación, 57.

[42] MN–PyTT, Leg. 96, Información de los méritos y servicios de Francisco Rodríguez Magariño (1526); CDIHIA, II, 344–345; and Dorantes de Carranza, Sumaria relación, 182–183, 441.

Gerónimo Ruiz de la Mota, one of those who had brought experience as a ship master to his role as brigantine skipper, seems not to have been further identified with shipping in the post-siege period. Ere settling down to long residence in Mexico City, he accompanied the Cortés-led march into Central America and also served on occasion as a royal investigator in previously subjugated provinces, in the course of which latter duties he is reported to have traveled a thousand leagues. In Mexico City he was closely identified with the political and economic life of the municipality for many years, serving repeatedly as regidor, alcalde, and alcalde de la mesta. His wide property holdings included the encomienda of Chiapa, numerous plots of land in Mexico City, and ranching interests. He and his fellow ex-skipper, Antonio de Carvajal, were close friends. Like most of the conquistadors, Ruiz de la Mota was the bitter enemy of Cortés less than a decade after the fall of Tenochtitlán. He married a daughter of his companion in arms Francisco de Orduña and fathered a family of six daughters and five sons. Cervantes de Salazar, who met the ex-brigantine captain three or more decades after the siege operation of 1521, relied heavily on Ruiz de la Mota as he wrote in his *Crónica* concerning the fleet, and he termed the old conquistador a sagacious and well-read man of grand and true memory. In 1559 Ruiz de la Mota requested and was granted a coat of arms. Beyond January, 1560, at which time he still held Chiapa in encomienda, his career cannot be traced.[48]

Although Francisco Verdugo's role as captain of a brigantine before Tenochtitlán is only doubtfully presumed, there is no doubt about the fact that his subsequent career associated him with shipping. It was undoubtedly some prior experience on Verdugo's part that led Nuño de Guzmán in 1531 to put two brigantines under his

[48] *CDIAO*, XXIX, 441–443; XLI, 235; *ENE*, IX, 10; MN–PyTT, Leg. 93, Información de los méritos y servicios de Antonio de Carvajal (1551); MN–PyTT, Leg. 93, Información de los méritos y servicios de Antonio de Arriaga (1559); Cervantes de Salazar, *Crónica*, 638; *AdeC*, I, 64, 157–181 *passim*, 204; II, 27–71 *passim*, 82, 204; IV, 4, 62–109 *passim*, 111, 136, 265–321 *passim*; Icaza, *Diccionario autobiográfico*, I, 72; Villar Villamil (ed.), *Cedulario heráldico*, unnumbered page (No. 123); and Dorantes de Carranza, *Sumaria relación*, 195–196.

jurisdiction, at least on paper. He saw service as one of Guzmán's captains and as his treasurer during the campaign into Nueva Galicia. In post-conquest years, Francisco Verdugo occupied a place among the foremost enemies of Hernando Cortés, as he served Nuño de Guzmán and others in opposition to the great Extremaduran. His enmity must have been based partially on the fact that he was reduced to poverty when the half interest he had in the encomienda of Yautepec was taken from him and transferred to the extensive holdings of Cortés. He settled and reared a family of unknown size in Mexico City, participating actively in the political life of the community as he served on several occasions as a member of the cabildo. His ranching interests must have been persistent, if not extensive, because he repeatedly registered a variety of cattle brands. As late as December, 1566, after some forty-five years of residence in New Spain, he was still sufficiently active to concern himself about the condition of a road that was then under construction. The date of his death is not known.[44]

Martín López, whose art made possible the ships and who assumed command of a brigantine under unusual conditions during the siege operation, lived in Mexico City for more than a half century following the victory of 1521. After a few additional land campaigns, including one into Pánuco, realizing that promises made by Cortés during the critical early days of the conquest were not to be fulfilled, he quit soldiering, settled in Mexico City, and gravitated toward the growing camp of enemies of Cortés. Embittered, he had nothing to do with the Cortés-inspired shipbuilding project at Zacatula on the Pacific in the mid-1520's. In 1528 he initiated an unsuccessful suit against Cortés, seeking some 8,000 pesos for his shipbuilding efforts of the 1519–1521 period. As a by-product of the litigation of 1528, he found himself the following year on the margin

[44] *CDIAO*, XIV, 361, 413, 417, 419, 422, 424, 429, 431, 438; XXVII, 36, 158, 433–435, 457; XXVIII, 317; *ENE*, II, 9–13, 142, 148; IX, 13; X, 161–162; *AdeC*, I, 69–88 *passim*, 157–191 *passim*, 193–211 *passim*; II, 3–24 *passim*, 107, 199, 208, 209; IV, 4; Dorantes de Carranza, *Sumaria relación*, 182, 443; López-Portillo y Weber, *La Conquista de la Nueva Galicia*, 120, 138, 203–204, 213, 220, 236; and Icaza, *Diccionario autobiográfico*, II, 324.

of a bitter perjury suit. With the arrival of the first *audiencia* in New Spain, López went to Tehuantepec as a minor official and so administered matters in that region as to undermine Cortés' authority and sabotage his most important Pacific shipbuilding project. Before the end of 1529 he left Tehuantepec, returned to Mexico City, joined Nuño de Guzmán, and marched off to Nueva Galicia on a campaign which occupied him for a couple of years. Returning from that duty, he found himself impoverished and the object of bitter litigation directed at him by Francisco Maldonado, an agent of Hernando Cortés.

By 1534, married to a Spanish woman and beginning to found the family which was destined to be large by mid-century, López decided to renew his court battle with Cortés regarding his insufficiently rewarded services during the conquest. Again failure attended his effort to force a financial settlement. Holder of one half of the town of Tequixquiac in encomienda, he constantly fought off poverty and sought royal preferment. Viceroy Mendoza ignored his petitions with regularity, but Mendoza's successor did give López a brief royal assignment in the late 1550's. Ever complaining and ever loyal, he was alive as late as 1573. No record of his death can be found. Recognized throughout the years of his long life as the man who engineered the ships which paved the way for victory at Tenochtitlán, López realized little tangible reward for such memorable service. One exception was his coat of arms, on which the brigantines were featured.[45]

Francisco Cervantes de Salazar, churchman and educator in mid-sixteenth-century New Spain, was possibly the last person to record an eyewitness account of the brigantines. Dr. Cervantes de Salazar crossed from the mother country to Mexico City in 1551,

[45] AGI, Patronato 57–1–1, fols. 1–18 *passim* (interrogatory and testimony, 1528) 18–48r *passim* (interrogatory and testimony, 1534); translation in AU–CC, Martín López 1528–1574, pp. 1–144 *passim*; LC–CC, Martín López 1529–1550, pp. 118–168 *passim* (interrogatory and testimony, 1540); and AGI, Patronato 63–1–15, fols. 1–13r *passim* (interrogatory and testimony, 1560); translation in AU–CC, Martín López 1528–1574, pp. 145–187 *passim*; UC–CC, Maldonado contra López, 268 fols.

remaining there the full quarter century until his death in 1575. Exactly when in that interval of three to five decades after the fall of Tenochtitlán he saw the brigantines is not clear. In the course of his description of the grandeur of Mexico City somewhat after the mid-point of the sixteenth century, he employed these words:

Continuing for some distance in the same direction [eastward], the church of Sanctisima Trinidad is reached, and a good way farther out we come to the fortress known as the Atarazanas, the alcalde of which is Bernardino de Albornoz, regidor of Mexico. Below these Atarazanas are *ad perpetuam rei memoriam*, lying in orderly manner, the thirteen brigantines which the Marquis ordered Martín López to build, and with which this city was conquered. It is a pleasure to see them, and even after the lapse of so much time, they are as sound as when they were built. This fortress stands on the edge of the lake, which is in itself a beautiful sight, owing to its size and the rocky islets that arise out of it, and the picturesque fishing canoes on its waters. The fortress is mean, and it would be advisable to make it as strong as the importance of the city merits.[46]

---

in 4 vols.; UC–CC, Docs. Various Suits, 67 fols., *passim;* UC–CC, Misc. Docs., 1–206 *passim;* LC–CC, Martín López Osorio, *passim;* AC, Libro 1° de bautisimos de la cathedral, desde noviembre de 1536 hasta octubre de 1547, *passim;* AGI, Escribanía de Cámara 178 B, fols. 1–9r; MN–PyTT, Leg. 42, Núm. 13, Cédula de Martín López; *CDIAO,* XXVII, 164, XXVIII, 493, XXIX, 331; *ENE,* X, 215–217; XI, 5, 20; XIV, 148, 153; *CDHM,* I, 434; *AdeC,* I, 8, 62, 148, 170, 183, 184; *IEPANM,* I, 98–99, 141–142, 181, 221, 230, 245, 255–256, 280, 325; II, 42–43, 48–49, 74, 83, 111; *BDdelC,* I, 386–387, 422–423 and II, 58, 138, 164–166, 168; Cervantes de Salazar, *Crónica,* 493, 548–549, 591, 597, 636, 646–647, 659, 699, 708, 709; Conway (ed.), *La Noche Triste,* x–xi, 84–86; Sánchez-Arjona, "Relación ...," *RABM,* Vol. XXXVI (1917), 423; Bermúdez Plata, *Catálogo,* I, 156; Herrera, *Historia general,* II, Part I, 38; Dorantes de Carranza, *Sumaria relación,* 215–216; Bancroft, *Mexico,* I, 490, 674–675; León de la Barra, "Geografía histórica ...," *BSMGE,* Vol. XLVII (1937), 73; and Porras Muñoz, "Martín López, carpintero de ribera," in Instituto Gonzalo Fernández de Oviedo, *Estudios Cortesianos,* 307–329.

[46] Cervantes de Salazar, *Crónica,* 318. I have used the English translation of this material found in G. R. G. Conway, *An Englishman and the Mexican Inquisition, 1556–1560,* 81–82. The first written reference to the brigantines by Cervantes came in his second dialogue in *México en 1554,* tr. and notes Joaquín García Icazbalceta, ed. Julio Jiménez Rueda, 74–75. It was possibly a decade or more later when he wrote: " ... the brigantines still exist; and thus today, more than forty years since they were built, they are in the arsenals of Mexico, whole and sound." See *Crónica,* 554. Cabildo action of 1557 indicates the brigantines were long considered significant in the defense of the city; see *AdeC,* VI, 275.

With the Cervantes de Salazar report on the one-time fleet, the brigantines passed into that special historical oblivion reserved for unsung ships.

For a few years immediately following the fall of the seat of Aztec power, at a time when energies were consumed in the establishment of Mexico City and in the widening conquest, the Spaniards were so busy with affairs of the moment that they seemed without inclination to recognize and honor the significant achievements of their own recent past.[47] In a short time, however, historical perspective joined with Spanish love of fiesta to fasten significance upon San Hipólito's Day—and that moment when a brigantine facilitated the seizure of Cuauhtémoc.

Two weeks before the seventh anniversary of the conclusion of the conquest of Tenochtitlán, the cabildo of Mexico City, on July 31, 1528, authorized the observance of a fiesta on August 13, and in August, 1529, annual celebration of the anniversary was decreed. The highlight of the social side was the bullfight. In early celebrations, of seven animals, two were scheduled to be killed, with the carcasses going to charitable institutions. The commemorative ceremonies involved the evening of the twelfth as well as the day of the thirteenth. On the twelfth, the municipal banner was removed from its accustomed place in the cabildo and was carried at the head of the procession that wended its way to the Church of San Hipólito. Following a vesper service, the procession returned the banner to its customary place. The day of the thirteenth another procession formed, and once more the municipal standard was given the place of honor. After this second pilgrimage to the Church of San Hipólito, the standard was returned to its customary place to await the next celebration.[48] Scarcely had the people of Mexico City inaugurated the festival when the Crown dignified

[47] For example, the *AdeC* are silent on this subject throughout the middle years of the 1520's.

[48] *AdeC*, I, 176, 180; II, 8–9; and Cervantes de Salazar, *México en 1554*, tr. and notes Joaquín García Icazbalceta and ed. Julio Jiménez Rueda, 183–190.

and regularized it with the passage of legislation on the subject. On May 28, 1530,[49] Emperor Charles V indicated that the municipal standard should be carried by a regidor, that the vespers and mass should be conducted in the Church of San Hipólito, and that all royal officials should attend the ceremony.[50]

The festival of August 13 vies with that of Corpus Christi for distinction as the earliest fiesta introduced into New Spain by the Europeans, and surely the former was the first celebration resulting from the clash of the New and Old World cultures. Though it continued to be observed until the close of the colonial period, with some changes introduced in the course of time, the ceremony celebrating the winning of Tenochtitlán was never given any noticeable nautical twist, even in the early years when the continuing presence of the brigantines in the arsenal of Mexico City served to remind the citizenry of their notable contribution to that victory.[51] Rapid and complete was the decline of the brigantines in importance.

The one purpose for which the brigantines had been constructed, the capture of the seat of Aztec power, had been accomplished. The mopping-up expeditions that radiated from the Spanish posi-

[49] This was but the first of a series of official actions on this subject. The last seems to have occurred on August 16, 1642.

[50] Recopilación de leyes de los reynos de las Indias, II, 69r, 70 (Book III, Title XV, Law LVI).

[51] Like many other festivals characterized by humility and simplicity in early years with but a minor social side thereto, San Hipólito's Day knew a gradually shifting emphasis in its celebration. The initial minor expenses, such as 25 pesos salary for the bearer of the standard and a few pesos for trumpeters and drummers, gave way to such expanding expenditures that the cabildo found it necessary to appropriate 3,000 pesos to cover official expenses. In addition, extravagant social affairs, some of which are said to have cost the host, the bearer of the muncipal standard, thousands upon thousands of pesos, highlighted the activities of the occasion. In time the well-formed processions of horsemen gave way to loosely formed carriage parades. The dignity and honor of marching through the streets bearing aloft the municipal standard paled, and the bearer of the honored device took to holding it out of a carriage window. By the middle of the eighteenth century, the procession surely was badly attended—because the viceroy found it necessary to impose fines of 500 pesos on individuals who did not have valid excuses for their failure to participate. See AdeC, II, 10, 60, 62, 122, 125, 189; III, 45, 46, 49–50, 94, 119; IV, 90, 92, 96, 136–137, 141, 246; Cervantes de Salazar, México en 1554, tr. and notes Joaquín García Icazbalceta and ed. Julio Jiménez Rueda, 186, 190; and Artemio de Valle-Arizpe, Por la vieja calzada de Tlacopan, 135–141.

tion in the Valley of Mexico meant continued usefulness for the infantry and cavalry, but all too rapidly the navy that had no future sank into oblivion. In the early years of Spanish reconstruction, the arsenal on the eastern side of the city included the fleet of brigantines among the equipment the citizens could turn to in defense of their new city, should the Indians rise and attack their Spanish masters. But as years passed and no occasion for use arose, as causeway defenses reduced dependence upon the naval arm, as succeeding waves of Spanish population so altered the ratio of conqueror to conquered as to lessen the prospect of strife in the lake country, the brigantines gradually and inevitably disintegrated. Need had brought them into being; ironically, their own adequacy to the need hastened their disappearance. But no one who would give proper perspective to the high point of battle in the conquest of Mexico would deny that between their coming and their going the brigantines had helped immeasurably to create one of the most momentous chapters of the European conquest of the Americas. Its unique drama cannot be challenged: this most significant naval action in the waters of the Western Hemisphere took place a mile and a half above sea level, almost two hundred miles from the sea, on a lake which today has so almost completely disappeared that only a trace of its former extensive waters serves as a reminder of the decisive and fantastic role of naval power in the conquest of Mexico.

Glossary

The following words are defined in terms of the specific uses to which they were put in the body of this study.

ALCAIDE DE LA ATARAZANA—the warden or official in charge of the arsenal; in Mexico City he was granted the powers and prerogatives of a regidor (which see) as he participated in the government of the municipality.

ALCALDE—a municipal official whose duties combine administrative and judicial functions; commonly thought of as the approximation of our mayor, though certain duties resemble those of our justice of the peace.

ALCALDE DE LA MESTA—an official within the cattle raisers' organization whose duty it was to play the role of judge and settle disputes between cattlemen.

ALCALDE MAYOR—an official in colonial Spanish America with a combination of administrative, judicial, and economic responsibilities; as a royal appointee he might govern a town, other than the capital of a province.

ALFÉREZ—a military title for the person serving as standard-bearer in the infantry or cavalry; on occasion he exercised a command function.

ALGUACIL MAYOR—a peace officer whose duties approximated those of a sheriff.

AUDIENCIA—a leading agency of colonial government, primarily judicial in function but also possessed of administrative responsibilities; numbers of judges varied, depending on the size and significance of the area involved.

CABALLERÍA—the piece of land given a cavalryman for the services rendered by him during the conquest or early occupation of a region;

a variable measure of land which frequently approximated 400–500 acres.

CABILDO—the municipal council consisting of the alcaldes and the regidores (councilmen) assembled in meeting to consider municipal matters; also the meeting place of the municipal council.

CHINAMPA—a small, rectangular, man-made island used in the Valley of Mexico for the cultivation of flowers and foodstuffs; popularly referred to as floating gardens.

CONTRAMAESTRE—a ship's officer possessed of considerable authority and frequently second only to the captain.

ENCOMENDERO—the holder or master of an encomienda.

ENCOMIENDA—the fiduciary interest of a Spaniard in Indian laborers entrusted to him for a specified period of time upon certain conditions.

FACTOR—in military operations the official charged with the distribution of supplies to the soldiers; in political life an official charged with collecting the tribute and other revenue due the Crown.

MAESTRE DE CAMPO—a military title approximating colonel.

PESQUISA SECRETA—a secret inquiry into an official's administration; a secret marshaling of evidence concerning an official which is to be presented to higher authorities.

PROCURADOR—an advocate, attorney, or delegate designated to represent the interests of his constituents; colonial Spanish American municipalities frequently sent procuradores to Spain in behalf of municipal interests.

REGIDOR—a municipal councilman.

REGIMIENTO—the total number of municipal councilmen considered as a unit.

SOLAR—a plot of ground or lot intended as a building site.

VARA—a linear measurement approximating 33 inches.

VEEDOR—an overseer or supervisor.

VISITA—the inspection of an official's conduct of his office during his tenure in the post.

VISITADOR—the judge or inspector authorized to conduct a visita.

Bibliography

NOTES ON CERTAIN SOURCES

As a preface to the formal bibliography, the writer wishes to comment briefly on certain materials which (1) opened previously unexploited vistas of the conquest of Mexico through 1521, (2) humanized a major sequence of events with rich detail on individual participants, and (3) offered a particularly balanced account of the siege operation of 1521.

One block of manuscript materials of basic importance to the present study, the transcripts, translations, and photostats of the late G. R. G. Conway of Mexico, merits special attention.

The late G. R. G. Conway, a wealthy engineer-industrialist whose long career in Mexico brought him into personal contact with every president of that country in the first half of the twentieth century, had a persistent and deep-rooted interest in Mexican history. In the course of more than a quarter-century pursuit of his avocation, his attention moved from English contacts with New Spain in the sixteenth century to a variety of subjects within the first half of the colonial period. For approximately two decades he built his extensive holdings of manuscript and published materials. For a score of years he paid competent paleographers to produce transcriptions of manuscripts reposing in Spanish and Mexican archives. Much of the work in Seville was directed by the indefatigable Irene A. Wright. In like fashion competent translators worked over many of the transcribed manuscripts. Whenever possible the present writer has used microfilm copies of the original manuscripts. Numerous occasions arose, however, when close study of Conway's transcriptions and translations took place in reference to the text of the original manuscripts. In consequence of such study, high regard is voiced for the remarkable measure of accuracy in the Conway materials.

In time, scores of volumes of transcripts and translations resulted. In his own limited writing and more extensive contributions as editor, Conway set some of the fruits of his interest in Mexican history before the reading public. Although his published works do not inspire the present note, it might be added that volume after volume appeared in very limited editions in Mexico.

In the course of systematizing the great mass of transcripts and translations, G. R. G. Conway had the typed materials grouped topically and chronologically and bound, bearing titles of his own invention which generally served as rough guides to both content and time period. This handling of his great volume of photostats, transcripts, and translations seems to have evolved gradually and hence no categorical statement can be made that concerns every item. For example, not every transcript and photostat was translated.

Carbon copies of the typed materials had been made, and Conway eventually had more copies than he cared to continue to house in his library in Cuernavaca. On repeated occasions, beginning about 1929, carbon copies of such volumes of transcripts and translations, along with volumes of photostats, were presented to certain institutions outside Mexico. The Library of Congress, the University of Cambridge, and Aberdeen University were the recipients of such gifts. The typed volumes did not exist in four copies each, hence it was not possible to have complete collections in each of the libraries of Cuernavaca, Washington, Cambridge, and Aberdeen.

Since the death of G. R. G. Conway in 1951, the Cuernavaca library has ceased to be available to scholars, hence any citation of sources referring simply to it would confound rather than help the reader. Logically the question arises—why not cite the archival sources in all instances? But one finds that some materials that once were at one's finger tips in Spanish and Mexican archives are no longer there.

Confusing the situation further, a hush-hush sale of manuscripts occurred in New York City several years ago that was not without relationship to both the Conway transcripts and the missing archival materials. In two groups, totaling some ninety-four items, a noteworthy array of sixteenth- and seventeenth-century manuscripts was sold to one buyer at a price only a millionaire could afford to pay. To date, those materials, now in the United States, have not been available to researchers.

Confronted with the problem of unavailable items that repose in the United States and of materials in Mexico that are no longer available for study, the writer has cited the items in relation to institutions to which the public has access. Under present circumstances, then, it becomes necessary to include two British university libraries and the Library of Congress, as well as the archives in Seville and Mexico City, in the sources of pertinent materials.

Brief descriptions of the Conway items related to the naval phase of the conquest and shipwright Martín López follow:

(A) MARTIN LOPEZ, CONQUISTADOR— DOCUMENTS, 1528–1574

This material falls under three headings: (1) Martín López' 13-item interrogatory of 1528 and the related testimony of sixteen witnesses; (2) Martín López' 37-item interrogatory of 1534 and the related testimony of ten witnesses; and (3) Martín López' 18-item statement of services of 1560 and the related testimony of seven witnesses.

Items (1) and (2) were unified in 1547 as a result of a request made by Martín López in 1544. Originally this material of 1528 and 1534, in the certified text of 1547, ran to 48 folios and reposed in Seville under the classification of AGI, Patronato 1–2–4/24 (now 57–1–1).

Item (3), brought together with the foregoing by Conway, originally approximated 16 folios and in Seville had the classification of AGI, Patronato 1–3–10/1 (now 63–1–15).

Occupying two volumes in the Conway collection, the transcript is in one volume and the translation in the other. It is available, in translation only, at Aberdeen.

(B) MARTIN LOPEZ, CONQUISTADOR— DOCUMENTS, 1529–1550

This material falls under two headings: (1) the Santa Cruz perjury case of 1529, an outgrowth of the litigation initiated by Martín López against Cortés in 1528, with the transcript followed immediately by the translation; and (2) translated extracts of the Nobiliario of Martín López Osorio (discussed more fully as "E" of the present bibliographical note), especially Martín López' 30-item interrogatory of 1540 and the related testimony of six witnesses.

The original documents from which these transcripts were made were in the possession of Conway in 1928. This volume of the Conway collection is available at the Library of Congress.

(C) DOCUMENTS RELATING TO VARIOUS SUITS

This material concerns two interrelated legal actions, in the first of which sawyer Diego Hernández was suing Cortés in 1529; in the second, a product of the adverse decision suffered in the Hernández case, Cortés sued the ex-judges, the Lics. Matienzo and Delgadillo.

The Conway volume was assembled in 1928, the original materials having been transcribed for him in Seville from a document running to 67 folios. At present both the transcript and translation are at Cambridge, while Aberdeen has the translation.

(D) FRANCISCO MALDONADO CONTRA MARTIN LOPEZ, 1533–1539

The above title for the material involved is deceptive, in that in the course of the trial proceedings many items reaching back to 1529 were reproduced completely and incorporated into the court records. Aside from illumining a little-known aspect of Cortés' career, his Tehuantepec shipbuilding project, and the careers of such lesser figures as Maldonado and López, this material excellently illustrates the seemingly interminable tendencies of colonial litigants.

The original of this material consisted of 268 folios. Although bound in one volume of the Conway collection, the Conway transcript of this item was divided into four parts (he called them volumes), each with separate pagination. This transcript—there is no translation—is presently found at both Cambridge and Aberdeen.

(E) NOBILIARIO OF MARTIN LOPEZ OSORIO

The original of this material, consisting of 205 folios, dates from 1624 and is the cumulative effort of grandchildren of Martín López the conquistador. Constructed as it was about fifty years after the conquistador's death, much of it is marginal to the study of his life. The most significant material regarding Martín López the hidalgo-shipwright-conquistador is found in folios 1–45, a translation of which is in item "B" above.

At present Aberdeen has a three-volume photostatic reproduction of the original manuscript. The Library of Congress has one volume of transcript, containing the materials pertinent to the life of Martín López.

(F) MISCELLANEOUS DOCUMENTS
RELATING TO MARTIN LOPEZ
AND OTHER PAPERS

This hodgepodge of six items, assembled by Conway in 1939, represented an effort on his part to marshal certain materials concerning Martín López. It includes the following:

(1) a translation of folios 1–45 from the Nobiliario of Martín López Osorio. (This document, a complete transcript, constitutes "E" above; and a better translation of this very same material is found in "B" above.)

(2) a transcript of extracts from "D" above.

(3) a translation of the extracts from "D."

(4) a partial translation of material published by Fernando Fernàndez del Castillo regarding Diego Hernández and Martín López in the *BSMGE*, XLIII (1931), 17–40. Neither the document concerning Diego Hernández, listed as Hospital de Jesús, 146/29, nor that concerning Martín López, listed as Hospital de Jesús, 147/39, can be found now in the Archivo General de la Nación in Mexico City.

(5) a photostatic copy of pages from *Biblioteca Histórica de la Iberia*, XX (1875), 13–29 and 113–122, giving Martín López' testimony of 1565 in behalf of Tlaxcalan services during the conquest.

(6) a translation of the *ENE*, I, 136–152.

Although the volume does demonstrate further the capacity of A. J. Baker as a translator, as well as someone's discriminating taste in the extraction of the heart of the lengthier material on the Maldonado-López suit, this Conway item offers no manuscript material that is not in better form elsewhere in his collection. This volume is at Cambridge and Aberdeen.

At his first meeting with G. R. G. Conway, the author was without knowledge of the wealth of the library's holdings. When Martín López' brigantines were mentioned, Conway's eyes twinkled—and the eyes of the present writer in turn shone with pleasure on learning what was behind Conway's interest in the ships and the shipwright of the conquest.

While the Conway materials and the manuscripts behind them, which to date have had little exploitation, enlarge the view of the conquest, the great collection of documents of Francisco del Paso y Troncoso offer countless tidbits on the careers of individual major and minor conquistadors. Housed in the Archivo Histórico del Instituto Nacional de Antropología e Historia, and more commonly referred to as being in the Museo Nacional, the transcripts produced by and for Paso y Troncoso include numerous statements of the merits and services of individual conquistadors. The total collection is described by Manuel Carrera Stampa in his *Misiones Mexicanas en Archivos Europeos;* the specific items employed in connection with the present study are listed in the bibliography.

A third and final historical source on which special comment is due is the *Crónica de la Nueva España* by Francisco Cervantes de Salazar. Unduly enthusiastic appraisals of this work have been succeeded by undeservedly derogatory judgment in recent years. A more detailed study of sixteenth-century historiography undoubtedly will indicate that the work merits neither critical extreme. The present writer states unequivocally that Cervantes de Salazar's *Crónica* is the best-balanced piece of sixteenth-century historical writing on the subject of the siege of Tenochtitlán. Drawing upon information afforded him by many conquistadors, Cervantes de Salazar produced a work that blends the heavy emphasis on the great commander, seen in Cortés' and López de Gómara's writings, with the heavy emphasis Bernal Díaz was destined to give the ordinary soldier.

The balance of Cervantes de Salazar, the detail of the Paso y Troncoso transcripts, and the unexploited wealth of the Conway materials have been particularly helpful to the present writer.

MANUSCRIPT MATERIALS

Great Britain

Documents Relating to Various Suits (Conway Collection), University of Cambridge.

Francisco Maldonado contra Martín López, 1533–1539 (Conway Collection), University of Cambridge.

Martín López, Conquistador—Documents, 1528–1574 (Conway Collection), Aberdeen University.

Miscellaneous Documents Relating to Martín López and Other Papers (Conway Collection), University of Cambridge.

Mexico

Archivo de la Catedral (Mexico City), Libro 1º de bautisimos de la cathedral, desde noviembre de 1536 hasta octubre de 1547.

Archivo General de la Nación (Mexico City), Hospital de Jesús, 146/29.

Museo Nacional (Mexico City), Francisco del Paso y Troncoso Collection:

Leg. 1, Núm. 49 bis.

Leg. 42, Núm. 13.

Leg. 93.
Leg. 94.
Leg. 95.
Leg. 96.
Leg. 97.

Spain

Archivo General de Indias (Seville)
Audienciá de México 98.
Escribanía de Cámara 178 B.
Patronato 54–3–1.
Patronato 57–1–1.
Patronato 63–1–15.

United States

Martín López, Conquistador—Documents, 1529–1550 (Conway Collection), Library of Congress.
Nobiliario of Martín López Osorio (Conway Collection), Library of Congress.

PUBLISHED MATERIALS

Aguilar, Francisco de (Alfonso Teja Zabre, ed.). *Historia de la Nueva España*. México, 1938.
Aiton, Arthur S. (tr. and ed.). *The Muster Roll and Equipment of the Expedition of Francisco Vázquez de Coronado*. Ann Arbor, 1939.
Alamán, Lucas, *et al*. (eds.). *Diccionario Universal de Historia y de Geografía*. 10 vols. México, 1853–1856.
———. *Disertaciones sobre la historia de la República Megicana desde la época de la conquista que los españoles hicieron a fines del siglo XV y principios del XVI de las islas y continente americano hasta la independencia*. 3 vols. México, 1942.
Alcalá, Manuel. *César y Cortés*. México, 1950.
Alcocer, Ignacio. *Apuntes sobre la antigua México-Tenochtitlán*. Tacubaya, 1935.
Alva Ixtlilxochitl, Fernando de. *Historia Chichimeca*, in Vol. II of Alfredo Chavero (ed.), *Obras históricas de Don Fernando de Alva Ixtlilxochitl*.
———. *Décima tercia relación de la venida de los españoles y principio de la ley evangélica*, in Vol. IV of Bernardino de Sahagún, *Historia general de las cosas de Nueva España*.
The Anonymous Conqueror (Marshall H. Saville, tr. and ed.). *Narra-*

tive of Some Things of New Spain and of the Great City of Temestitan, Mexico. New York, 1917.

Apenes, Ola. "The Pond in Our Backyard," *Mexican Life*, XIX, No. 3 (1943), 15–18, 60.

———. (comp. and ed.). *Mapas Antiguos del Valle de México*, México, 1947.

Aragón, Javier O. "Expansión territorial del Imperio Mexicano," *Anales del Museo Nacional de Arqueología, Historia y Etnografía*, 4ª época, VII (1931), 5–64.

Arteaga Garza, Beatriz, and Pérez San Vicente, Guadalupe. (comps.) *Cedulario Cortesiano*. México, 1949.

Ballesteros, Antonio. "Estudio histórico sobre Hernán Cortés," *Boletín de la Real Academia de la Historia*, CXXIII (Julio–Septiembre, 1948), 33–45.

Ballesteros Gaibrois, Manuel. "Heràn Cortés y los indígenas," in Instituto Gonzalo Fernández de Oviedo, *Estudios Cortesianos—recopilados con motivo del IV centenario de la muerte de Hernán Cortés (1547–1947)*, 25–36.

Bancroft, Hubert Howe. *The Native Races*. 5 vols. San Francisco, 1882–1883.

———. *History of Central America*. 3 vols. San Francisco, 1883–1887.

———. *History of Mexico*. 6 vols. San Francisco, 1883–1888.

Bandelier, Adolph F. "On the Art of War and the Mode of Warfare of the Ancient Mexicans," *Tenth Annual Report* of the Peabody Museum of American Archaeology and Ethnology, II (1877), 95–161.

Barlow, R. H. "Some Remarks on the Term 'Aztec Empire,'" *The Americas*, I (January, 1945), 345–349.

———. (ed.). "Relación de Zacatula, 1580," *Tlalocan*, II, No. 3 (1947), 258–268.

———. (ed.). "Resumen analítico de 'Unos Annales Históricos de la Nación Mexicana,'" in Vol. II of Salvador Toscano (ed.), *Fuentes para la historia de México*.

———. *The Extent of the Empire of the Culhua Mexica*. Berkeley, 1949.

Batres, Leopoldo. *Plano de la ciudad de Tenochtitlán en el año de 1519 —Ensayo de reconstrucción formado por Leopoldo Batres*. México, 1892.

Bayle, Constantino. "Cortés, Padre de los Indios," in Institución de Servicios Culturales, *Estudios Hispanoamericanos—homenaje a Hernán Cortés en el IV centenario de su muerte*, 7–27.

Benítez, Fernando. *La Ruta de Hernán Cortés*. México, 1950.

Berlin, Heinrich, and Barlow, R. H. (eds.). "Códice de Tlatelolco," in Vol. II of Salvador Toscano (ed.), *Fuentes para la historia de México.*

Bermúdez Plata, Cristóbal. *Catálogo de pasajeros a Indias durante los siglos XVI, XVII y XVIII.* 3 vols. Sevilla, 1940.

Campos, Jorge. "Hernán Cortés en la dramática española," in Instituto Gonzalo Fernández de Oviedo, *Estudios Cortesianos—recopilados con motivo del IV centenario de la muerte de Hernán Cortés (1547–1947),* 171–197.

Cañamaque, Francisco. "¿Por qué y cómo fué a Méjico Hernán Cortés?" *Revista de España,* CIV (1885), 229–232.

Carreño, Alberto María. "Cortés, hombre de estado," *Boletín de la Real Academia de la Historia,* CXXIII (Julio–Septiembre, 1948), 171–183.

Carrera Stampa, Manuel. *Misiones Mexicanas en Archivos Europeos.* México, 1949.

Castillo Ledon, Luis. *La Fundación de la Ciudad de México, 1325–1925.* México, 1925.

Cavo, Andrés (Carlos María de Bustamante, ed.). *Los tres siglos de Méjico durante el gobierno español hasta la entrada del ejército trigarante.* Jalapa, 1870.

Cervantes de Salazar, Francisco (Joaquín García Icazbalceta, tr. and notes; and Julio Jiménez Rueda, ed.). *México en 1554.* México, 1939.

———. *Crónica de la Nueva España.* Madrid, 1914.

Chamberlain, Robert S. (tr. and ed.) *The First Three Voyages to Yucatan and New Spain, According to the Residencia of Hernán Cortés.* Coral Gables, 1949.

Chauvet, Fidel de J. *Tlatelolco, interesante recopilación histórica.* México, 1945.

Chavero, Alfredo (ed.). *Obras históricas de Don Fernando de Alva Ixtlilxochitl.* 2 vols. México, 1891–1892.

———. (ed.). *Lienzo de Tlaxcala,* in Junta Colombina de México (ed.), *Homenaje á Cristóbal Colón: Antigüedades Mexicanas.*

———. *Explicación del Lienzo de Tlaxcala.* México, 1892.

———. *Apuntes viejos de bibliografía mexicana.* México, 1903.

Clavigero, Francisco Javier. *Historia antigua de México.* 4 vols. México, 1945.

Codex Florentino, in Vol. IV of Bernardino de Sahagún (Francisco del Paso y Troncoso, ed.), *Historia de las cosas de Nueva España.*

Codex Ramírez, in Manuel Orozco y Berra (ed.), *Relación del origen de los indios que habitan esta Nueva España.*

Codex Telleriano-Remensis, in E. T. Hamy (ed.), *Codex Telleriano-Remensis; manuscrit mexicain du cabinet de Ch. M. Le Tellier.*

Congreso Internacional de Americanistas, *Actas de la undécima reunión, México, 1895*. México, 1897.

El Conquistador Anónimo. *Relación de algunas cosas de la Nueva España y de la gran ciudad de Temestitan Mexico*, in Vol. I of Joaquín García Icazbalceta (ed.), *Colección de documentos para la historia de México*.

―――. (León Díaz Cárdenas, ed.). *Relación de algunas cosas de la Nueva España, y de la gran ciudad de Temestitlán, México*. México, 1941.

Conway, G. R. G. *An Englishman and the Mexican Inquisition, 1556–1560*. Mexico, 1927.

―――. "Hernando Alonso, a Jewish Conquistador with Cortés in Mexico," *Publications of the American Jewish Historical Society*, XXXI (1928), 9–31.

―――. (ed.). *The Last Will and Testament of Hernando Cortés, Marques del Valle*. Mexico, 1939.

―――. (ed.). *La Noche Triste: Documentos: Segura de la Frontera en Nueva España, año de MDXX*. México, 1943.

Cook, Sherburne F., and Simpson, Lesley Byrd. *The Population of Central Mexico in the Sixteenth Century*. Berkeley, 1948.

Corbett, Sir Julian S. (ed.). *Fighting Instructions, 1530–1816*. London, 1905.

―――. *Some Principles of Maritime Strategy*. New York, Bombay and Calcutta, 1911.

Cortés, Hernán. *Cartas de relación de la conquista de Méjico*. 2 vols. Madrid, 1942.

―――. (Francis Augustus MacNutt, tr. and ed.). *Fernando Cortés—His Five Letters of Relation to the Emperor Charles V*. 2 vols. New York and London, 1908.

Cuevas, Mariano (comp.). *Cartas y otros documentos de Hernán Cortés novísimamente descubiertos en el Archivo General de Indias*. Sevilla, 1915.

Custance, Sir Reginald Neville. *War at Sea, Modern Theory and Ancient Practice*. London, 1919.

Dávila Garibi, J. Ignacio. "Una heroina anónima. La indita de Tecpantzinco," *Boletín de la Sociedad Mexicana de Geografía y Estadística*, 5ª época, XVII (1931–1934), 99–124.

Delgado, Jaime. "Hernán Cortés en la poesía española de los siglos XVIII y XIX," in Instituto Gonzalo Fernández de Oviedo, *Estudios Cortesianos—recopilados con motivo del IV centenario de la muerte de Hernán Cortés (1547–1947)*, 393–469.

Denhardt, Robert M. "The Truth About Cortés's Horses," *Hispanic American Historical Review*, XVII (November, 1937), 525–532.

――――. "The Equine Strategy of Cortés," *Hispanic American Historical Review*, XVIII (November, 1938), 550–555.

De Rebus Gestis Ferdinandi Cortesii, in Vol. I of Joaquín García Icazbalceta (ed.), *Colección de documentos para la historia de México*.

Díaz del Castillo, Bernal (Alfred Percival Maudslay, tr. and ed.). *The True History of the Conquest of New Spain, in Vols*. XXIII, XXIV, XXV, XXX, and XL of the Hakluyt Society, series II. 5 vols. London, 1908–1916.

――――. (Joaquín Ramírez Cabañas, ed.). *Historia verdadera de la conquista de la Nueva España*. 3 vols. México, 1944.

Dibble, Charles E. (ed.). *Códice en Cruz*. 2 vols. México, 1942.

Dorantes de Carranza, Baltasar. *Sumaria relación de las cosas de la Nueva España, con noticia individual de los descendientes legítimos de los conquistadores, y primeros pobladores españoles*. México, 1902.

"The Drainage of the Valley of Mexico," *The Scottish Geographical Magazine*, XII (1896), 155–156.

Durán, Diego. (José F. Ramírez, ed.). *Historia de los Indios de Nueva España y islas de tierra firme*. 2 vols. México, 1867–1880.

Esteva, Adalberto A. (ed.). *México pintoresco: antología de artículos descriptivos del país*. México, 1905.

Excelsior (Mexico City). 1951.

Ezquerra, Ramón. "Los compañeros de Hernán Cortés" in Instituto Gonzalo Fernández de Oviedo, *Estudios Cortesianos—recopilados con motivo del IV centenario de la muerte de Hernán Cortés (1547–1947)*, 37–95.

Fernández de Navarrete, Martín *et al.* (eds.). *Colección de documentos inéditos para la historia de España*. 112 vols. Madrid, 1842–1895.

Fernández de Oviedo y Valdés, Gonzalo. *Historia general y natural de las Indias*. 4 vols. Madrid, 1851–1855.

Fernández del Castillo, Francisco. "Tres Conquistadores y Pobladores de la Nueva España," in Vol. XII of *Publicaciones del Archivo General de la Nación*. México, 1927.

――――. "Algunos documentos del Archivo del Marquesado del Valle (Hospital de Jesús)," *Boletín de la Sociedad Mexicana de Geografía y Estadística*, XLIII (1931), 17–40.

Fernández Duro, Cesáreo. *Disquisiciones náuticas*. 6 vols. Madrid, 1877–1881.

――――. *Las joyas de Isabel la Católica, las naves de Cortés y el salto de Alvarado*. Madrid, 1862.

————. *Tradiciones Infundadas.* Madrid, 1888.

————. *Armada española desde la unión de Castilla y Aragón.* 9 vols. Madrid, 1895–1903.

Franck, Harry A. *Trailing Cortez Through Mexico.* New York, 1935.

Friederici, Georg. *Die Schiffart der Indianer.* Stuttgart, 1907.

Gage, Thomas (A. P. Newton, ed.). *The English-American—A New Survey of the West Indies, 1648.* London, 1928.

Galindo y Villa, Jesús. *Reseña histórico-descriptiva de la ciudad de México.* México, 1901.

————. "México, la ciudad capital," *Boletín de la Sociedad Mexicana de Geografía y Estadística,* XLIII (Enero, 1934), 397–411.

————. *Geografía sumaria de la República Mexicana.* México, 1946.

García de Palacio, Diego. *Diálogos Militares.* (Vol. VII of *Colección de Incunables Americanos: Siglo XVI*). Madrid, 1944.

————. *Instrucción Nautica para Navegar.* (Vol. VIII of *Colección de Incunables Americanos: Siglo XVI*). Madrid, 1944.

García de Polavieja, General Camilo (ed.). *Hernán Cortés—Copias de documentos existentes en el Archivo de Indias y en su palacio de Castilleja de la Cuesta, sobre la conquista de Méjico.* Sevilla, 1889.

García Granados, Rafael (ed.). *Cortés Ante la Juventud.* México, 1949.

García Icazbalceta, Joaquín (ed.). *Colección de documentos para la historia de México.* 2 vols. México, 1858–1866.

————. (ed.). *Nueva colección de documentos para la historia de México.* 5 vols. México, 1886–1892.

————. "Conquista y colonización de Méjico. Estudio histórico," *Boletín de la Real Academia de Historia,* XXV (1894), 5–39.

García y Cubas, Antonio. *Atlas geográfico, estadístico é histórico de la República Mexicana.* México, 1858.

————. "Valle y Ciudad de México durante el siglo XVI," in Congreso Internacional de Americanistas, *Actas de la undécima reunión, México, 1895,* 208–214.

Gardiner, C. Harvey. "La Batalla Naval de Tenoxtitlán," *Hoy,* June 10, 1950, p. 27.

————. "The First Shipping Constructed in New Spain," *The Americas,* X (April, 1954), 409–419.

————. "Tempest in Tehuantepec, 1529: Local Events in Imperial Perspective," *Hispanic American Historical Review,* XXXV (February, 1955), 1–13.

Gibson, Charles. *Tlaxcala in the Sixteenth Century.* New Haven, 1952.

Gillmor, Frances. *Flute of the Smoking Mirror—A Portrait of Nezahual-coyotl Poet-King of the Aztecs.* Albuquerque, 1949.

Gómez de Orozco, Federico. "Las primeras comunicaciones entre México y Perú," *Anales del Instituto de Investigaciones Estéticas,* II, Núm. 7 (1941), 65–70.

González Obregón, Luis (Blanche Collet Wagner, tr.). *The Streets of Mexico.* San Francisco, 1937.

Graham, R. B. Cunninghame (Robert Moorman Denhardt, ed.). *The Horses of the Conquest.* Norman, 1949.

Green, Fitzhugh, and Frost, Holloway. *Some Famous Sea Fights.* New York, 1927.

Hamy, E. T. (ed.). *Codex Telleriano-Remensis; manuscrit mexicain du cabinet de Ch. M. Le Tellier.* Paris, 1899.

Hay, Guillermo. "Apuntes geográficos, estadísticos e históricos del distrito de Texcoco," *Boletín de la Sociedad Mexicana de Geografía y Estadística,* 2ª época, II (1870), 541–555.

Hayner, Norman S. "Mexico City: Its Growth and Configuration," *The American Journal of Sociology,* L, No. 4 (January, 1945), 295–304.

Helps, Sir Arthur. *The Life of Hernando Cortés.* 2 vols. in 1. London, 1871.

Henderson, Colonel G. F. R. *The Science of War—a Collection of Essays and Lectures, 1891–1903.* New York and Bombay, 1906.

Hernández, Francisco (Joaquín García Pimentel, tr. and ed.). *Antigüedades de la Nueva España.* México, 1945.

Hernández Varela, Alfonso. "Los peligros a que ha estado expuesto el Valle de México debido a su situación orohidrográfica y las diferentes obras de defensa construídas para salvaguardar las vidas y los intereses de sus inhabitantes," *Boletín de la Sociedad Mexicana de Geografía y Estadística,* LVII (Septiembre–Diciembre, 1942), 363–388.

Herrera, Antonio de. *Historia general de los hechos de los castellanos en las islas y tierra firme del mar océano.* 4 vols. Madrid, 1726–1730.

Hough, Walter. "The Venice of Mexico," *National Geographic Magazine,* XXX (July, 1916), 69–88.

Humboldt, Alexander von (John Black, tr.). *Political Essay on the Kingdom of New Spain.* 4 vols. London, 1814.

Icaza, Francisco A. de. *Diccionario autobiográfico de conquistadores y pobladores de Nueva España.* 2 vols. Madrid, 1923.

Iglesias, Ramón. *Cronistas e Historiadores de la Conquista de México: el ciclo de Hernán Cortés.* México, 1942.

Illescas, Gonzalo de. *Historia Pontifical,* in Joaquín Ramírez Cabañas (ed.), *Conquista de México.*

"Información recibida en México y Puebla el año de 1565, a solicitud del gobernador y cabildo de naturales de Tlaxcala, sobre los servicios que prestaron los tlaxcaltecas a Hernán Cortés en la conquista de México, siendo los testigos algunos de los mismos conquistadores," *Biblioteca Histórica de la Iberia,* XX (1875), 13–29; and 113–122.

Institución de Servicios Culturales. *Estudios Hispano-americanos—homenaje a Hernán Cortés en el IV centenario de su muerte.* Badajoz, 1948.

Instituto Gonzalo Fernández de Oviedo. *Estudios Cortesianos—recopilados con motivo del IV centenario de la muerte de Hernán Cortés (1547–1947).* Madrid, 1948.

Jal, Auguste. *Archéologie Navale.* 2 vols. Paris, 1840.

———. *Glossaire nautique. Répertoire polyglotte de termes de marine anciens et modernes.* Paris, 1848.

Jiménez de la Espada, Marcos. "No fué tea, fué barreno," *Boletín de la Real Academia de Historia,* XI (1887), 235–238.

Johnson, Willis Fletcher. *The History of Cuba.* 5 vols. New York, 1920.

Junta Colombina de México (ed.). *Homenaje á Cristóbal Colón: Antigüedades Mexicanas.* México, 1892.

Kingsborough, Lord Edward King. *Antiquities of Mexico.* 9 vols. London, 1831–1848.

Kirkpatrick, F. A. *The Spanish Conquistadores.* London, 1946.

Kubler, George. "The Name 'Tenochtitlán,'" *Tlalocan,* I, No. 4 (1944), 376–377.

Las Casas, Bartolomé de. *Historia de las Indias,* in Vols. LXII–LXVI of Martín Fernández de Navarrete *et al.* (eds.), *Colección de documentos inéditos para la historia de España.*

Leduc, Alberto; Lara y Pardo, Luis; and Roumagnac, Carlos (eds.). *Diccionario de geografía, historia y biografía mexicanas.* Paris and México, 1910.

León de la Barra, Ignacio. "Geografía histórica: Tenochtitlán y Tlaltelolco," *Boletín de la Sociedad Mexicana de Geografía y Estadística,* XLVII (Septiembre, 1937), 69–77.

Leonardo de Argensola, Bartolomé Juan. *Primera Parte de los Anales de Aragón que prosigue los del Secretario Gerónimo Çurita desde el año MDXVI, del Nacimiento de Nº. Redentor,* in Joaquín Ramírez Cabañas (ed.), *Conquista de México.*

Le Riverend, Julio (ed.). *Cartas de relación de la conquista de América.* 2 vols. México, 1946.

Linné, S. *El Valle y la Ciudad de México en 1550: Relación histórica fundada sobre un mapa geográfico, que se conserva en la biblioteca de la Universidad de Uppsala, Suecia.* Stockholm, 1948.

López de Gómara, Francisco (Joaquín Ramírez Cabañas, ed.). *Historia de la conquista de México*. 2 vols. México, 1943.

López-Portillo y Weber, José. *La Conquista de la Nueva Galicia*. México, 1935.

Lowery, Woodbury (Philip Lee Phillips, ed.). *A Descriptive List of Maps of the Spanish Possessions within the present limits of the United States, 1502–1820*. Washington, 1912.

Mackenzie, Compton. *Marathon and Salamis*. London, 1934.

MacNutt, Francis Augustus. *Fernando Cortes and the Conquest of Mexico*. New York and London, 1909.

Madariaga, Salvador de. *Hernán Cortés, Conqueror of Mexico*. New York, 1941.

Mahan, Captain A. T. *Naval Strategy Compared and Contrasted with the Principles and Practice of Military Operations on Land*. Boston, 1911.

Marden, Luis. "On the Cortes Trail," *National Geographic Magazine*, LXXVIII (September, 1940), 335–375.

Marroqui, José María. *La Ciudad de México*. 3 vols. México, 1900–1903.

Martyr D'Anghera, Peter (Francis Augustus MacNutt, tr. and ed.). *De Orbe Novo*. 2 vols. New York and London, 1912.

Mateos, Juan. *Apunte histórico y descriptivo sobre el Valle de México y breve descripción de la obra de su desagüe y del saneamiento de la capital*. México, 1923.

Mateos Higuera, Salvador. "Códice de la conquista," in "Colección de Estudios Sumarios de los Códices Pictóricos Indígenas," *Tlalocan*, III, Núm. 1 (1949), 22–24.

Maudslay, Alfred P. "The Valley of Mexico," *The Geographical Journal*, XLVIII, No. 1 (July, 1916), 11–26.

Mendieta Gerónimo de. *Historia eclesiástica indiana*. 4 vols. México, 1945.

Mendoza, Eufemio. "Anáhuac-México-Tenochtitlán," *Boletín de la Sociedad Mexicana de Geografía y Estadística*, 2ª época, IV (1872), 263–273.

Mexico [City]. Cabildo (Ignacio Bejarano et al., eds.). *Actas de cabildo de la ciudad de México*. 26 vols. México, 1889–1904.

Millares Carlo, A., and Mantecón, J. I. (eds.). *Indice y extractos de los Protocolos del Archivo de Notarías de México, D. F.* 2 vols. México, 1945–1946.

Mirabal Lausan, Joaquín. "Mapas, códices y planos existentes en el Departamento de Cartografía de la Sociedad Mexicana de Geografía y Estadística, hasta el 31 de agosto de 1937," *Boletín de la Sociedad*

Mexicana de Geografía y Estadística, XLVII (Diciembre, 1937), 129–231.

Montoto, Santiago, *et al.* (eds.). *Colección de documentos inéditos para la historia de Ibero-América.* 14 vols. Madrid, 1927–1935.

Moorhead, Max L. "Hernán Cortés and the Tehuantepec Passage," *Hispanic American Historical Review,* XXIX (August, 1949), 370–379.

Mora y Villamil, Ignacio de. "Elementos para la marina," *Boletín de la Sociedad Mexicana de Geografía y Estadística,* 1ª época, IX (1862), 300–336.

Morison, Samuel Eliot. *Admiral of the Ocean Sea—A Life of Christopher Columbus.* 2 vols. Boston, 1942.

Motolinía (Toribio de Benavente). *Historia de los indios de la Nueva España,* in Vol. I of Joaquín García Icazbalceta (ed.), *Colección de documentos para la historia de México.*

———. (Elizabeth Andros Foster, tr. and ed.). *Motolinía's History of the Indians of New Spain.* Berkeley, 1950.

Muñoz Camargo, Diego (Lauro Rosell, ed.). *Historia de Tlaxcala.* México, 1947.

New York Times. 1951.

"Noticias," *Boletín de la Real Academia de la Historia,* X (Mayo, 1887), 329–348.

Núñez Ortega, A. "Los navegantes indígenas en la época de la Conquista," *Boletín de la Sociedad Mexicana de Geografía y Estadística,* 3ª época, IV (1878), 47–57.

O'Gorman, Edmundo. "Catálogo de pobladores de Nueva España," *Boletín del Archivo General de la Nación,* XII (1941), 237–291, 455–506, 713–742; XIII (1942), 95–160, 267–332, 465–505, 611–687; XIV (1943), 317–351, 479–501, 657–713; and XV (1944), 169–195.

Oman, Sir Charles. *A History of the Art of War in the Sixteenth Century.* New York [1937].

Orozco y Berra, Manuel. "Memoria para la carta hidrográfica del Valle de México," *Boletín de la Sociedad Mexicana de Geografía y Estadística,* 1ª época, IX (1862), 337–509.

———. *Materiales para la cartografía mexicana.* México, 1871.

———. *Historia antigua y de la Conquista de México.* 4 vols. in 2. México, 1880.

———. "Los conquistadores de México," in Vol. IV of Bernardino de Sahagún, *Historia general de las cosas de Nueva España.*

———. (ed.). *Relación del origen de los indios que habitan esta Nueva España.* México, 1944.

Pacheco, J. F.; Cárdenas, F., *et al.* (eds). *Colección de documentos inéditos relativos al descubrimiento, conquista y organización de las antiguas posesiones de América y Oceanía.* 42 vols. Madrid, 1864–1884.

Pardo Riquelme, Antonio. "El ejército de Cortés," in Instituto Gonzalo Fernández de Oviedo, *Estudios Cortesianos—recopilados con motivo del IV centenario de la muerte de Hernán Cortés (1547–1947)*, 97–104.

Paso y Troncoso, Francisco del (comp.). *Epistolario de Nueva España 1505–1818.* 16 vols. México, 1939–1942.

Peñafiel, Antonio. *Nombres geográficos de México—Catálogo alfabético de los nombres de lugar pertenecientes al idioma 'nahuatl'—estudio jeroglífico de la matricula de los tributos del Códice Mendocino.* México, 1885.

———. *Nomenclatura geográfica de México—Etimologías de los nombres de lugar correspondientes a los principales idiomas que se hablan en la República.* 2 vols. México, 1895–1897.

———. (ed.) *Colección de documentos de la historia mexicana.* 6 vols. México, 1897–1903.

Pereyra, Carlos. *Hernán Cortés.* Buenos Aires, 1947.

Pérez de Oliva, Fernán. *Algunas cosas de Hernán Cortés y México,* in Joaquín Ramírez Cabañas (ed.), *Conquista de México.*

Pérez Martínez, Héctor. *Cuauhtémoc—Vida y Muerte de una Cultura.* Buenos Aires, 1948.

Phillips, George Brinton. "The Metal Industry of the Aztecs," *American Anthropologist,* New Series, XXVII (1925), 550–557.

Phillips, Philip Lee. *A List of Maps of America in the Library of Congress—preceded by a list of works relating to cartography.* Washington, 1901.

———. *A list of Geographical Atlases in the Library of Congress—with bibliographical notes.* 4 vols. Washington, 1909–1920.

Pomar, Juan Bautista. *Relación de Tezcoco, escrita en 1582,* in Vol. III of Joaquín García Icazbalceta (ed.), *Nueva colección de documentos para la historia de México.*

Porras Muñoz, Guillermo. "Martín López, carpintero de ribera," in Instituto Gonzalo Fernández de Oviedo, *Estudios Cortesianos—recopilados con motivo del IV centenario de la muerte de Hernán Cortés (1547–1947)*, 307–329.

Prescott, William H. *History of the Conquest of Mexico.* 3 vols. London, 1843.

Priestley, Herbert Ingram. *The Mexican Nation, A History.* New York, 1930.

Quintanar, Emilio. "Inventario del archivo del Hospital de Jesús," *Bole-*

tín del Archivo General de la Nación, VII (Abril–Mayo–Junio, 1936), 273–299; (Julio–Agosto–Septiembre, 1936), 437–459; (Octubre–Noviembre-Diciembre, 1936), 600–618; VIII (Abril–Mayo–Junio, 1937), 233–302; and (Julio–Agosto–Septiembre, 1937), 406–471.

Ramírez Cabañas, Joaquín (ed.). *Conquista de México.* México, 1940.

Rawson, Edward Kirk. *Twenty Famous Naval Battles; Salamis to Santiago.* New York and Boston, 1899.

La Real Academia de la Historia (ed.). *Colección de documentos inéditos relativos al descubrimiento, conquista y organización de las antiguas posesiones españoles de Ultramar.* 25 vols. Madrid, 1885–1932.

La Real Academia Española (ed.). *Diccionario de la lengua castellana.* Madrid, 1899.

Recopilación de leyes de los reynos de las Indias. 4 vols. Madrid, 1756.

Reyes, Vicente. "La ley de la periodicidad de la lluvia en el valle de México," *Boletín de la Sociedad Mexicana de Geografía y Estadística,* 3ª época, IV (1878), 314–319.

———. "El régimen de los vientos en la ciudad de México y sus relaciones con la higiene," *Boletín de la Sociedad Mexicana de Geografía y Estadística,* 3ª época, IV (1878), 553–561.

Rhode, Francisco José. "Hernán Cortés, el gran soldado (Problemas militares de la conquista)," in Rafael García Granados (ed.), *Cortés Ante la Juventud,* 187–205.

Riva Palacio, Vicente (ed.). *México a través de los siglos.* 5 vols. México, 1888–1889.

Robertson, William. *History of America.* 3 vols. London, 1825.

Rodgers, Vice-Admiral William Ledyard. *Greek and Roman Naval Warfare—a Study of Strategy, Tactics and Ship Design from Salamis (480 B.C.) to Actium (31 B.C.).* Annapolis, 1937.

———. *Naval Warfare under Oars, 4th to 16th Centuries: A Study of Strategy, Tactics, and Ship Design.* Annapolis, 1940.

Romero Solano, Luis. *Expedición Cortesiana a las Molucas, 1527.* México, 1950.

Rubio Mañé, Ignacio. "Panorama etnográfico del territorio conquistado por Hernán Cortés," *Boletín de la Real Academia de la Historia,* CXXIII (Julio–Septiembre, 1948), 47–56.

Sahagún, Bernardino de (Francisco del Paso y Troncoso, ed.), *Historia de las cosas de Nueva España.* 8 vols. Madrid, 1905–1907.

———. *Historia general de las cosas de Nueva España.* 5 vols. México, 1938.

Sánchez-Arjona, Eduardo. "Relación de las personas que pasaron a esta Nueva España, y se hallaron en el descubrimiento, toma e conquista della," *Revista de Archivos, Bibliotecas y Museos,* 3ª época, XXXVI (1917), 419–430; XXXVII (1917), 111–127; XXXIX (1918), 89–99.

Sandoval, Fernando B. (ed.) "El Astillero del Carbon en Tehuantepec, 1535–1566," *Boletín del Archivo General de la Nación,* XXI, Núm. 1 (Enero–Febrero–Marzo, 1950), 1–20.

Saville, Marshall H. *The Wood-Carver's Art in Ancient Mexico.* New York, 1925.

Schäfer, Ernesto. *Indice de la Colección de Documentos de Indias.* 2 vols. Madrid, 1946–1947.

Scholes, Walter V. "The Diego Ramírez Visita in Meztitlán," *Hispanic American Historical Review,* XXIV (February, 1944), 30–38.

———. *The Diego Ramírez Visita.* Columbia, 1946.

Segarra y Julea, José. *La Ruta de Hernán Cortés.* Madrid, 1910.

Shepard, Arthur MacCartney. *Sea Power in Ancient History—The Story of the Navies of Classic Greece and Rome.* Boston, 1924.

Silburn, Percy Arthur Baxter. *The Evolution of Sea Power.* London and New York, 1912.

La Sociedad de Bibliófilos Españoles. *Nobiliario de Conquistadores de Indias.* Madrid, 1892.

Soler Jardón, Fernando. "Notas sobre la leyenda del incendio de las naves," in Instituto Gonzalo Fernández de Oviedo, *Estudios Cortesianos—recopilados con motivo del IV centenario de la muerte de Hernán Cortés (1547–1947),* 537–559.

Solís y Rivadeneyra, Antonio de (Thomas Townsend, tr.). *The History of the Conquest of Mexico by the Spaniards.* London, 1753.

———. (José de la Revilla, ed.). *Historia de la Conquista de Méjico.* (Vol. IV of *Colección de los mejores autores españoles*). Paris, 1858.

Sosa, Antonio H. *Parque Nacional Xicoténcatl, Estado de Tlaxcala.* México, 1951.

Spinden, Herbert J. *Ancient Civilizations of Mexico and Central America.* New York, 1917.

Suárez de Peralta, Juan (Justo Zaragoza, ed.). *Noticias históricas de la Nueva España.* Madrid, 1878.

Subirá, José. "Hernán Cortés en la música teatral," in Instituto Gonzalo Fernández de Oviedo, *Estudios Cortesianos—recopilados con motivo del IV centenario de la muerte de Hernán Cortés (1547–1947),* 105–126.

Tamayo, Jorge L. *Geografía general de México.* 2 vols. México, 1949.

Tapia, Andrés de. *Relación sobre la conquista de México,* in Vol. II of Joaquín García Icazbalceta (ed.), *Colección de documentos para la historia de México.*

Teja Zabre, Alfonso. *Tragedia de Cuauhtémoc*. México, 1934.

Tezozomoc, Hernando Alvarado (Manuel Orozco y Berra, ed.), *Crónica mexicana*. México, 1944.

Thompson, J. Eric. *Mexico before Cortez: An Account of the daily Life, Religion, and Ritual of the Aztecs and Kindred Peoples*. New York, 1933.

Tiempo (Mexico), XIX Núm. 479 (July 6, 1951), 13.

"Tlatelolco a través de los tiempos," *Memorias de la Academia Mexicana de la Historia*, III–V (1944–1946).

Torquemada, Juan de. *Monarquía Indiana*. 3 vols. México, 1943–1944.

Torres Lanzas, Pedro. *Relación descriptiva de los mapas, planos, & de México y Floridas existentes en el Archivo General de las Indias*. 2 vols. Sevilla, 1900.

Toscano, Ricardo. "Descripción geográfica del Distrito Federal," *Revista Mexicana de Geografía*, I (Octubre–Diciembre, 1940), 141–181.

Toscano, Salvador (ed.). *Fuentes para la historia de México*. 2 vols. México, 1947–1948.

Toussaint, Manuel; Gómez de Orozco, Federico; and Fernández, Justino. *Planos de la Ciudad de México*, México, 1938.

Ulloa, Francisco de. "Memorial sobre el descubrimiento y expedición cortesiana a las Californias," in Vol. II of Julio Le Riverend (ed.), *Cartas de relación de la conquista de América*.

Uztarroz, Juan Francisco Andrés de. *Segunda parte de los Anales de la Corona, y Reyno de Aragón, Desde el Año MDXXI, hasta el XXVIII*, in Joaquín Ramírez Cabañas (ed.), *Conquista de México*.

Vaillant, George C. *Aztecs of Mexico*. New York, 1944.

Valle, Rafael Heliodoro. *Cristóbal de Olid—Conquistador de México y Honduras*. México, 1950.

———. *Bibliografía de Hernán Cortés*. México, 1953.

Valle-Arizpe, Artemio de. *Por la vieja calzada de Tlacopan*. México, 1937.

———. (ed.). *Historia de la ciudad de México según los relatos de sus cronistas*. México, 1939.

Valverde, Antonio L. "Leyenda de América: Las Naves de Hernán Cortés," in *Contribuciones para el estudio de la Historia de América: homenjae al Doctor Emilio Ravignani*. Buenos Aires, 1941.

Vasconcelos, José. *Hernán Cortés, creador de la nacionalidad*. México, 1944.

Vázquez de Tapia, Bernardino (Manuel Romero de Terreros, ed.). *Relación del conquistador Bernardino Vázquez de Tapia*. México, 1939.

Vázquez Santa Ana, Higinio. *Apuntes geográficos é históricos del estado de Tlaxcala.* Tlaxcala, 1928.

Velasco, Alfonso Luis. *Geografía y estadística de la República Mexicana.* 20 vols. México, 1889–1898.

Villar Villamil, Ignacio de (ed.). *Cedulario heráldico de conquistadores de Nueva España.* México, 1933.

Vivo, Jorge A. *Geografía de* México, 1949.

Wagner, Henry R. (tr. and ed.). *The Discovery of Yucatan by Francisco Hernández de Córdoba.* Berkeley, 1942.

———. (ed.). *The Discovery of New Spain in 1518, by Juan de Grijalva.* Berkeley, 1942.

———. *The Rise of Fernando Cortés.* Los Angeles, 1944.

West, Robert C., and Armillas, Pedro. "Las chinampas de México—poesía y realidad de los 'Jardines Flotantes,' " *Cuadernos Americanos,* L (1950), 165–182.

Wilgus, A. Curtis. *Maps Relating to Latin America in Books and Periodicals.* Washington, 1933.

———. *Histories and Historians of Hispanic America.* New York, 1942.

Wilson, Robert Anderson. *A New History of the Conquest of Mexico.* Philadelphia, 1859.

Winship, George Parker (tr. and ed.). *The Journey of Coronado: 1540–1542.* New York, 1922.

Winsor, Justin (ed.). *Narrative and Critical History of America,* 8 vols. Boston and New York, 1884–1889.

Wright, I. A. *The Early History of Cuba, 1492–1586.* New York, 1916.

Zamacois, Niceto de. *Historia de Méjico desde sus tiempos más remotos hasta nuestros dias.* 18 vols. in 20. Méjico, 1876–1882.

Zurita, Alonso de. *Breve y sumaria relación de los señores de la Nueva España.* México, 1942.

243

Index

245

www.ingramcontent.com/pod-product-compliance
Ingram Content Group UK Ltd.
Pitfield, Milton Keynes, MK11 3LW, UK
UKHW041911060225
454777UK00001B/226